T2 with coal empties climbing to Annfield Plain, early 1920s

UNIFORM WITH THIS BOOK

Graham S. Hudson *The Aberford Railway and the History of the Garforth Collieries*

John Thomas *The Callander & Oban Railway*

Rex Christiansen *The Cambrian Railways*

and R. W. Miller *Volume 1: 1852-1888, Volume 2: 1889-1968*

N. S. C. Macmillan *The Campbeltown & Machrihanish Light Railway*

Patrick J. Flanagan *The Cavan & Leitrim Railway*

H. A. Vallance *The Great North of Scotland Railway*

H. A. Vallance *The Highland Railway*

Edward M. Patterson *A History of the Narrow-gauge Railways of North East Ireland*
Part One: *The Ballycastle Railway*
Part Two: *The Ballymena Lines*

Edward M. Patterson *A History of the Narrow-gauge Railways of North-West Ireland*
Part One: *The County Donegal Railways* (second edition)
Part Two: *The Londonderry & Lough Swilly Railway*

H. W. Paar *A History of the Railways of the Forest of Dean*
Part One: *The Severn & Wye Railway*
Part Two: *The Great Western Railway in Dean*

John Marshall *The Lancashire & Yorkshire Railway* Volumes 1 & 2

David L. Smith *The Little Railways of South West Scotland*

R. A. Williams *The London & South Western Railway* Volume 1

G. A. Brown *The Lynton & Barnstaple Railway*

J. D. C. A. Prideaux
and H. G. Radcliffe

Colin G. Maggs *The Midland & South Western Junction Railway*

John Thomas *The North British Railway, Volume 1*

Rex Christiansen *The North Staffordshire Railway*
and R. W. Miller

W. J. K. Davies *The Ravenglass & Eskdale Railway*

A. D. Farr *The Royal Deeside Line*

Robin Atthill *The Somerset & Dorset Railway*
and O. S. Nock

John Thomas *The West Highland Railway*

THE RAILWAYS OF CONSETT
AND NORTH-WEST DURHAM

THE RAILWAYS OF CONSETT AND NORTH-WEST DURHAM

by
G. WHITTLE

DAVID & CHARLES : NEWTON ABBOT

ISBN 0 7153 5347 0

COPYRIGHT NOTICE

© G. WHITTLE 1971

All rights reserved. No part of this publication may be reproduced, stored in a retrieval system, or transmitted, in any form or by any means, electronic, mechanical, photocopying, recording or otherwise, without the prior permission of David & Charles (Publishers) Limited

Set in eleven point Pilgrim
and printed in Great Britain
by Bristol Typesetting Company Limited
for David & Charles (Publishers) Limited
South Devon House Newton Abbot Devon

Contents

	LIST OF ILLUSTRATIONS	9
	PREFACE	11
1	THE STANHOPE & TYNE RAILWAY	13

Wagonways of north-west Durham – from Weardale to Tyneside – many inclines – traffic and finances – Consett – the Durham Junction Railway – Pontop & South Shields Railway – Sacriston & South Shields Railway

2	RAILWAY DEVELOPMENT ON TYNESIDE	36

N & CR in north-west Durham – progress to the 1862 amalgamation – Tanfield wagonway changes – Pontop & Jarrow – other wagonways

3	ENTER THE STOCKTON & DARLINGTON	53

S & D expansion – Waskerley—Moorland railway centre – further W & DJ improvements – Crook—Tow Law deviation – passengers across the moors – traffic development and operations – passenger traffic contrasts – a veteran replaced

4	TO CONSETT VIA LANCHESTER	73

Cleveland iron ore to Consett – an early setback and no progress – progress to opening – opening – Consett terminus – traffic development and operations – growth of passenger traffic – NER bus services – Blackhill MPD – end of Knitsley viaduct

5 THE STRUGGLE FOR THE DERWENT VALLEY   92
   LNWR route to Newcastle? – 1861 confrontation – NER 'Blaydon & Conside' branch – rails in the Derwent valley – opening and early services – passenger traffic development – goods and mineral traffic – Swalwell—Rowlands Gill widening – other improvements

6 PONTOP BRANCH PROGRESS   118
   Some minor adjustments – local pressure for improvements – Annfield—East Castle – West Durham & Tyne project – the South Pelaw—Annfield Plain deviation line – improvements near Consett – engine sheds – Tyne Dock iron ore – passenger growth 1894-1920 – mainly coal

7 TYNESIDE CONSOLIDATION   144
   Dunston Extension Railway – the Derwenthaugh branch – Atlas curve and Blaydon loops – Newcastle & Carlisle line services – Blaydon MPD – station alterations

8 TRAINS AND TRAFFIC TO THE NINETEEN SEVENTIES   156
   Post-1923 pattern – forty years on the Lanchester Valley – run-down west of Consett – withdrawal in the Derwent valley – last railway to Consett – changes on Tyneside – end of the Tanfield branch – an inevitable decline

9 LOCOMOTIVES   179
   Locomotive survey – early years – NER standardisation – the NER 0-8-0s – Consett region – Tyneside region – NER rolling stock – LNER period: some new arrivals – the last LNER years: renumbering – steam climax – decline of steam – steam finale – diesels and industrial locomotives

10 ACCIDENTS AND INCIDENTS   199
   Derailment on Knitsley viaduct – accidents at

Ouston junction – South Pelaw derailment - Hell Hole wood landslip – Beamish runaway collision –two events at Blaydon – other accidents – the snow hazard – Oxhill crossing – the Lintz Green murder – 'Wor Nanny's a mazer'

APPENDIXES

1	Chronology	213
2	Mileages	217
3	Receipts, expenses and traffic	221
4	Miscellany	226
5	Recent times	236

BIBLIOGRAPHY   239

ACKNOWLEDGEMENTS   240

INDEX   241

List of Illustrations

T2 0–8–0 with coal empties climbing towards *frontispiece*
Annfield Plain in later NER days *(Victor Welch)*

PLATES

Waldridge incline bank foot, 1956 *(T. E. Rounthwaite)*	33
T2 at Weatherhill *(K. Hoole)*	33
Class O 0–4–4T at Blaydon, 1947 *(H. C. Casserley)*	34
Class Q 4–4–0 with Carlisle—Newcastle train, Ryton *(Photomatic Ltd)*	34
Class U 0–6–2T leaving Tanfield East *(T. E. Rounthwaite)*	51
Fugar incline *(T. E. Rounthwaite)*	51
Clearing the line at Waskerley, 1933 *(Mrs. G. Holden)*	52
Carr House West signal box in the snow *(Author)*	52
Tow Law station *(T. E. Rounthwaite)*	69
Tow Law—Darlington train at Crook *(T. E. Rounthwaite)*	69
Knitsley station *(R. Goad)*	70
K1 2–6–0 with special train at Lanchester *(K. Hoole)*	70
Train to Blackhill at High Westwood, 1909 *(D. Graham)*	87
Train to Newcastle crossing Ebchester embankment *(F. Chaplin)*	87
NER steam autocar at High Westwood *(W. Charlton)*	88
Blackhill signal box *(T. E. Rounthwaite)*	88
Hownes Gill viaduct *(Author)*	121
Fogoes viaduct, near Lintz Green *(Author)*	121
O1 2–8–0 with iron ore train, West Stanley *(S. E. Teasdale)*	122
9F 2–10–0 heading ore train, South Pelaw *(K. Hoole)*	122
Coal trains passing at South Pelaw, 1955 *(T. E. Rounthwaite)*	139
3MT 2–6–0 at Tow Law *(F. Tweddle)*	139
No 63371 at Gateshead, 1964 *(P. H. Groom)*	140
Another T2 leaves Burnhill junction with goods for Consett *(K. Hoole)*	140

View east at Blaydon station *(Author)*	157
P3 0–6–0 crossing Derwenthaugh bridge *(Author)*	157
Waskerley Shed, 1935 *(H. C. Casserley)*	158
No 63400 simmering at Blaydon Shed *(P. H. Groom)*	158
J39 waiting with Newcastle train at Blackhill *(J. House)*	175
Special train at Consett station, 1963 *(H. C. Casserley)*	175
Type 2s with ore train near Beamish *(Author)*	176
Coal train at Oxhill crossing, 1969 *(Author)*	176

IN THE TEXT

Stanhope & Tyne Railway and other lines, 1840	19
The railways of north-west Durham	24 & 25
Tow Law	62
Consett—Crook	64
Burnhill station and junction	65
Lines at Stanhope Kilns (Crawley)	67
Witton Gilbert station	81
Lanchester station	84
Knitsley station	85
Relly Mill junction area	90
Gradient profile of Blaydon & Consett branch railway	100
Rowlands Gill station	106
Swalwell station, 1922	112
NER excursion-working timetable, 11 August 1873	114
Blackhill station	115
Junctions east of Blaydon	116
South Pelaw connections	129
Annfield Plain 1894 station	130
Ouston junction—Annfield Plain deviation and other lines	131
Junctions at Consett (simplified)	133
Consett 1896 station	135
Shield Row station	143
Tyneside	145
Norwood Junction	147
Blaydon station	154
Ryton station	155
First BR timetable: Consett area, 1948	165

Preface

North-west Durham as defined in this book is that area of the county lying to the west of the Newcastle—Gateshead—Chester-le-street—Durham main railway line, and west and north-west of Durham city excluding the Deerness Valley—Brandon region. The Weardale area forms the southern fringe of this region, and the railways running from the edge of that dale, from Crawley (Stanhope) and Crook to Consett, will be described. The Tow Law—Crook district and especially Crook itself are usually considered as being part of south-west Durham, Crook being only six miles from Bishop Auckland – hence the title of this book.

The region is fringed by Northumberland on the north (across the Tyne) and on the west, and the valley of the river Derwent cuts into it from Derwenthaugh on the Tyne southwestwards to Shotley Bridge (near Consett) and beyond. This river in fact forms the county boundary from near Chopwell southwards. Another valley, that of the Browney and its tributaries, breaks up the rolling Durham plateau between Consett and Durham city, and the river flows into the river Wear just west of Durham. The Wear itself flows north to Chester-le-Street and then east to the sea at Sunderland and is separated from the broad Team Valley by a low watershed north of Chester-le-Street. The river Team flows from near Stanley into the Tyne at Dunston on the Gateshead boundary.

Apart from the Derwent and Browney river systems, north-west Durham is a high rolling plateau which extends to the very edge of the Tyne, Team and Wear valleys. The high land forms a pronounced transition from the valleys as evidenced by the hilly land south of the Tyne such as Lobley Hill, south west of Gateshead, and west of Chester-le-Street, and north of Crook. The district south-west of Consett is part of the Durham moors, actually the fringe of the Pennine chain, and in places rises to over 1,700ft above sea level.

The railways of this predominantly hilly area tend, not surprisingly, to have steep gradients. Inclined planes with ropes pulling wagons up very steeply graded lines were common, as will be shown in Chapter 1. The coal mining industry was the major influence on the nineteenth century development of the region, and this especially encouraged early railway building in the form of wagonways. This industry is now a shadow of its former self and there is much truth in the correlation of the decline of coal and railways. It was primarily coal mining that gave what was largely an agricultural area an industrial basis, and increased the population considerably over a century or more, creating many villages and towns, notably Stanley. Some other industries did play an important role, none more so than the iron industry, which gave rise to the town of Consett.

This book describes the growth of the railway network in the region, its subsequent operations and fortunes, and the decline and abandonment of much of the system. Since the decline has mainly been in fairly recent years, it seems opportune to record this history before memories fade, and evidence of the existence of the extensive network disappears.

The whole of north-east England was, of course, the cradle of railways, but not a great deal will be said about pre-1830 railway (wagonway) growth. There is an excellent study of this by C. E. Lee entitled *The wagonways of Tyneside*.

CHAPTER ONE

The Stanhope & Tyne Railway

WAGONWAYS OF NORTH-WEST DURHAM

At about 1830 the area of north-west Durham between the River Tyne and the Pontop—Tanfield—Beamish region some eight miles to the south was traversed by a number of wagonways engaged in moving coal from mines to riverside staiths. Some focused on the Tyne but the Beamish wagonway connected the mines in that district with staiths on the River Wear. There were two major lines running to the Tyne. One of these was the Main Way from the Pontop—Dipton district to Derwenthaugh staiths via Bryan's Leap, Rowlands Gill and the valley of the River Derwent. The other was the Tanfield wagonway, or Old Way, from the Tanfield Moor region to Dunston staiths via Tanfield Lea, Marley Hill and Lobley Hill. Both were over a century old for much of their routes, and in the middle of the eighteenth century they had been linked together by a branch from Tanfield Moor colliery running north-westwards to join the Main Way. The Main Way itself, north of Bryan's Leap, dated from about 1710, while most of the Tanfield line dated from 1725–7. The latter had originally extended across the Beckley Burn near Causey by means of the 103ft span Causey Arch, or Dawson's Bridge, to reach Dawson's Drift colliery. The arch was of stone, carried two lines of rails and was built in 1727; it was often referred to as the world's oldest railway bridge. A diversion of the line some thirty to forty years later made the bridge redundant, but it still stands today. Nearby, the line also included some notable cuttings and an embankment 100ft high and 300ft broad at its base. By the early years of the nineteenth century the Main Way south of Rowlands Gill had fallen into disuse but it had extended its Thornley branch from Winlaton Mill eastwards to Spen (Garesfield). Garesfield colliery developed here after about 1837 and the mining village of High Spen grew up. The Tanfield line reached to South Moor and Pontop and had a short branch to Marley Hill colliery, with the Tanfield Moor colliery probably the most productive over a long period of the collieries served by the line.

The Beamish wagonway, running approximately east to west from Fatfield staiths, reached Beamish South Moor, and had long branches to Pelton Moor and to Deaney Moor near Sacriston. This latter branch was known as the Waldridge wagonway. By 1830 most of the coal from the Pontop, Tanfield and surrounding districts went to Dunston, while the Beamish, Pelton and Waldridge areas sent most of their coal to the Fatfield staiths. The former Main Way had become the Garesfield wagonway, serving a limited area near Rowlands Gill.

FROM WEARDALE TO TYNESIDE

In 1831 the idea evolved for a wagonway from Stanhope to the River Tyne. The plan is attributed to William Wallis of Westoe (South Shields), who secured the leases of the Medomsley and Pontop collieries in that year, and made a tentative arrangement with Cuthbert Rippon of Stanhope for working limestone near that small town. By building a wagonway linking Stanhope with the Medomsley and Pontop collieries and continuing this to the Tyne, it was considered that such a line could have a large mineral traffic and would allow industries to develop satisfactorily. Traffic might also be acquired from other collieries on the route and the prosperous lead mines in the Weardale region would also be able to use the line. There were lead smelters at Stanhope and at Rookhope five miles to the north-west.

The promoters of the plan included William Harrison, an energetic north-eastern wagonway promoter, and financial backing from London was assured. The route of the line to the Tyne from the Pontop district was not finally settled but there was every prospect of a line to the Derwenthaugh staiths. This course would utilise part of the Main Way as well as certain disused sections of the line from the Pontop district to near Burnopfield, and these would have to be relaid. However, William Harrison suggested with great foresight that the proposed line should run to the Tyne near its mouth where larger vessels than keel boats (which served Derwenthaugh, for instance, carrying coal to vessels near the river mouth) would be able to dock. This would require over thirty miles of railway and would cost more than by running it to Derwenthaugh. Also a number of inclined planes would be required to take the line from the Durham plateau down to the lower land of the Team valley and north-east Durham. This was no great problem as the westerly parts of the line also required a series of such inclines. Inclines were common on existing wagonways, and there were several on the Tanfield line. They were quite efficient and avoided the great expense of heavy engineering works in order to secure easier gradients suitable for locomotive or horse haulage. The promoters therefore agreed to the plan to reach South Shields at the mouth of the Tyne, and decided not to seek parliamentary powers for their scheme in order to mask its magnitude and thus obtain reasonable wayleave rights (rental for traversing the various landowners' properties). The scheme was therefore most ambitious, involving a railway of about thirty-four miles length from the valley side of the Wear at Stanhope to the mouth of the Tyne, passing over the Durham moors, the Durham plateau, north of the market town of Chester-le-Street, and then over the comparatively flat lands of north-east Durham.

In December 1831 wayleave negotiations began, by which date the promoters of the 'Stanhope and Tyne Railroad' had reached agreements on leasing Pontop colliery and the Stanhope limestone quarries. Early wayleaves were obtained for the western part of the line on reasonable terms, for example, £25 per annum over one and three quarter miles of Stanhope Fell from the Bishop of Durham, and £160 per annum over Waskerley Park, Muggleswick Common and White Hall Farm from the Dean and Chapter of Durham (average £26 per mile). The route of the line from Stanhope as far as Medomsley was surveyed by T. E. Harrison (the son of William), but because of the deeply cut valleys of the Pont Burn and its tributaries east of Medomsley, the line was to run to the south of this district, and a branch line projected to serve Medomsley. During 1832 a Deed of Partnership was drawn up and the share capital of the company was fixed at £150,000. During the year the intentions of the promoters became more widely known and as a result the landowners towards the eastern end of the line sought high, often extortionate wayleaves. £300 per mile was reached for some sections near South Shields, but in places even this figure was exceeded. Thus the company had to pay £30 per annum for passing over some 66yd of one farm at Boldon and £50 for passing over 110yd of another – rents equivalent to £800 per mile. Even the Dean and Chapter of Durham obtained £200 per mile (£510 per annum) for the line passing for two and a half miles through their leaseholds in South Shields, Westoe and Harton townships. These high wayleave rents contributed greatly to later financial difficulties.

Construction work began in July 1832 with T. E. Harrison as engineer and was at first concentrated on the west end of the line. Besides the thirty-four miles of main line, the branch to Medomsley was to be one and a half miles long, and there was planned a two mile long link line to reach the Tanfield wagonway at Harelaw (named the Tanfield Moor, or Harelaw branch) near Annfield, as well as a two furlong line at Carr House to reach a colliery named the Stuart pit. A passenger service on the line was not considered; it was to be essentially a long wagonway. Later, however, when the line opened, a passenger service on part of the line was considered. The Newcastle & Carlisle Railway, which was also in the course of construction, had every intention at this time of having a passenger service, but it must be remembered that this line was not to have recourse to inclined planes on its main line, inclines not being particularly well adapted to handling passenger carriages. Another feature of the S & T was the absence of large towns on its route, except for South Shields itself, although even this settlement had only 9,000 inhabitants at this time. Washington, a mining village, was perhaps the main settlement (over 2,000 inhabitants), although Chester-le-Street was only one and a half miles from the course of the line (almost 2,000 inhabitants).

Robert Stephenson, son of the great George, was employed by the S & T as consulting engineer, and it is often considered surprising that this champion of the locomotive was, with Harrison, responsible for the number of inclined planes on the line. However it was the physical nature of the north-west of Durham that largely determined this feature rather than the wishes of Stephenson.

Rapid progress was made at the western end of the route. Earthworks were kept to a minimum, the rails being laid on the prepared formation almost regardless of gradients. From the Stanhope terminus (actually Crawley, on the valley side above the town) the line was raised to its summit of 1,445ft above sea level by two steep inclines, Crawley and Weatherhill banks. A deep cutting and a short tunnel (Hog Hill tunnel) occurred near Crawley. The tunnel was wide enough for a double line, but most of the S & T was planned as single track (gauge 4ft 8in).

By October 1832 work had progressed to the edge of the moors at Healeyfield, eight miles from Crawley and the section to Hownes Gill was ready to be started. The directors called for tenders for 3,000 tons of rails and a suitable quantity of chairs for the new work. Adequate supplies of iron rails were available from Tyneside area ironworks. Hownes Gill was a major problem for the S & T. It was a glacial spillway forming a 150ft deep gorge 800ft wide, aligned across the course of the railway and unavoidable without an expensive and difficult detour. A bridge was the obvious solution, but the S & T was unwilling to meet such expense. There was also the fact that it would take an appreciable amount of time to erect a bridge across this formidable obstacle. The only solution was to have inclined planes down each side of the gorge. As a result, serious traffic delays were experienced at Hownes Gill for many years, and more about this will be mentioned shortly. East of the ravine there were two more inclines of moderate steepness, at Carr House, and by the beginning of 1833 the construction work had reached the section beyond the Carr House east incline at Leadgate. At the foot of this incline, the branch line to Medomsley colliery ran off northwards on moderate gradients.

Throughout 1833 work went on remarkably rapidly all the way to South Shields, and the directors were obviously determined to have traffic operating at the earliest possible opportunity. In May 1834 the railway was opened west of Carr

House, by which time the rest of the line was reaching completion, except for the Tanfield Moor branch, where little had yet been done. In the meantime three collieries had agreed to send their coal on the new line, these being Waldridge, Washington and Tanfield Moor collieries. Waldridge had been using the Beamish wagonway system to transport its coal. The S & T directors had at one stage considered using part of this wagonway's route for their own line in the Pelton region, but this plan had come to nought, and as a result the S & T competed with the wagonway for the coal from the Pelton district. To allow Waldridge coal to join the S & T line, a junction was made between the lines near Pelton.

Then, in September 1834, the whole railway was officially opened, including the coal drops erected by the riverside at South Shields. At Stanhope, lime kilns had been set up to serve the local limestone deposits, and lime depots had been established along the line. On 10 September the first coal arrived to be shipped at the S & T drops, appropriately from the company's own Medomsley colliery. The last one and a half miles into South Shields saw the hundred coal wagons joined by some of the directors in a special coach drawn by a locomotive accompanying the wagons to the riverside. The wagons were drawn by horses to the drops and the coals were loaded on to the vessel, or the *Salley*. Coal later arrived from Waldridge and Washington collieries, but Tanfield Moor colliery was unconnected with the S & T until 1835, when the branch line to Harelaw, joining the Tanfield wagonway, was completed. Then the coal from Tanfield Moor which had for so long been sent northwards to Dunston, went southwards to reach the new railway and then eastwards to the mouth of the Tyne.

MANY INCLINES

The features of the Stanhope & Tyne, in particular its numerous inclined planes, deserve more detailed mention. The initial incline out of Stanhope—Crawley incline reached 1 in $7\frac{1}{4}$ at its steepest and was worked by a 50hp George Stephenson design stationary engine. This incline took two wagons – sometimes three – at a run, so that in a fourteen-hour day some 120 to 140 wagons could be worked up or down. Then came

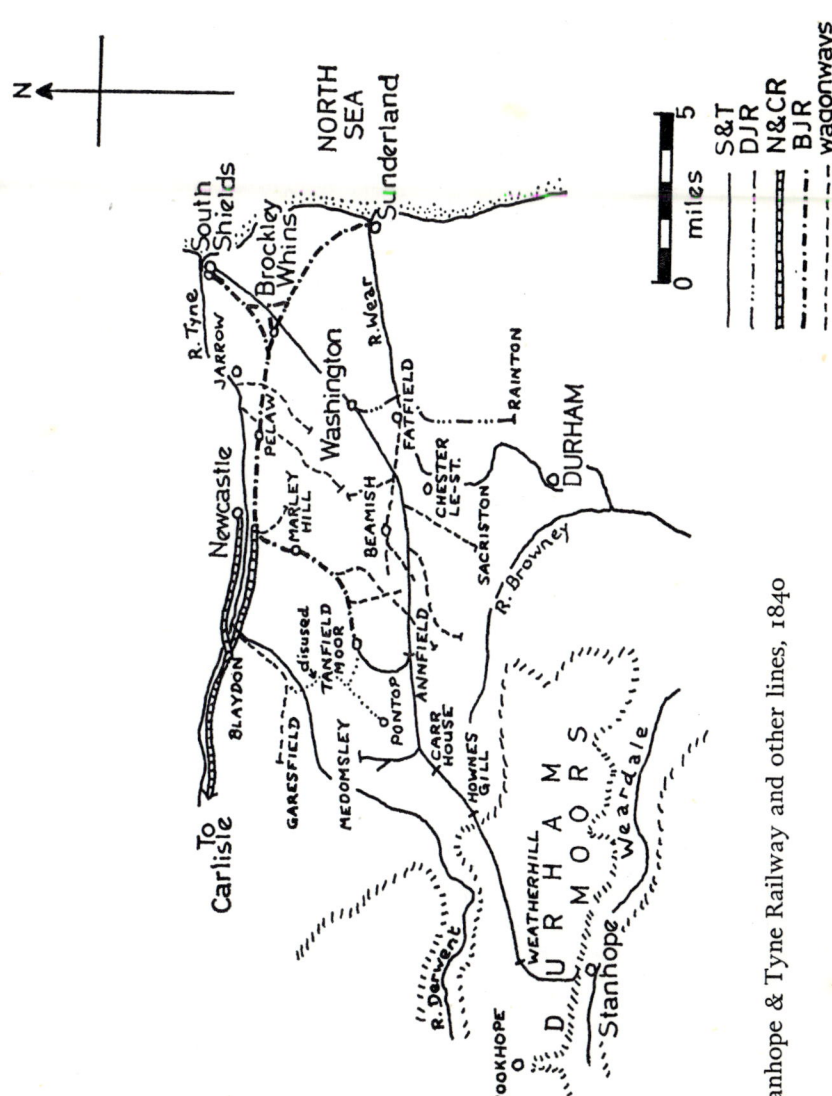

Stanhope & Tyne Railway and other lines, 1840

Weatherhill incline, which was 1 mile and 128yd long, with gradients of 1 in 12, 1 in 21 and 1 in 32, and a short length of 1 in 10¼. The average gradient on the bank was 1 in 13. At its moorland summit the line was the highest of any public railway line in England at any time. Here was situated the first of the lime depots out of Stanhope which could be used by the inhabitants of villages, such as Blanchland, on the edge of the moors. There was a passing loop on this incline, and the 50hp stationary engine could run four or six wagons at a time.

For the 3 miles and 352yd eastwards from Weatherhill engine, the railway fell by only 134ft, and there were gradients of 1 in 80 and 1 in 88, while certain stretches were almost level. This section, which crossed 'the wild tract of Waskerley Park', was worked by a wheel house at Parkhead, where wagons were attached to a tail rope and let down the slope to the next section, Meeting Slacks incline. The whole section from Weatherhill to Meeting Slacks usually had trains of twelve wagons, and a speed of nine miles per hour was attained. Also, this high moorland stretch of railway was largely unfenced from the moors, and another feature was the often severe deep snow drifts that interfered with railway traffic. In 1844 the operation of the Parkhead section was altered by attaching the ropes directly to the Weatherhill engine as well as to that at Meeting Slacks, and this imposed a strain on the engine's capacity, and necessitated using first-grade coal to fulfil its increased obligations.

Meeting Slacks engine was of 40hp and built by R & W Hawthorn. The incline was 1 mile 453yd long and had gradients of 1 in 33 to 1 in 58, with 100yd at 1 in 26½. The engine worked eight wagons at a run but could exceed this number. In later years the railway village of Waskerley developed at the foot of this incline. Next in this succession of inclines was Nanny Mayor's bank, a self-acting incline some 1,122yd in length with gradients of 1 in 10 and 1 in 13. Trains of eight wagons each way worked over it, the descending loaded wagons raising the ascending empties. This incline brought the line to the fringe of the moors west of Healeyfield and signs of settlement and agricultural activity were more in evidence. Of the 3 miles 385yd eastwards to Hownes Gill, about 2 miles 699yd were almost level, with much of the remainder at 1 in 132. Horses hauled the wagons for $1\frac{1}{4}$ miles from Nanny Mayors to Healeyfield bridge, and the horses then rode in 'dandy' carts the rest of the way to the ravine. At the ravine the railway had reached 800ft above sea level, a descent of 350ft from the top of Nanny Mayors bank.

The operation of traffic across Hownes Gill gorge was, according to Tomlinson, 'one of the most original features of the railway'. On the floor of the gorge was a 35hp stationary engine manufactured by Robert Stephenson, which worked both precipitous slopes. The wagons were lowered down the slopes in cradles, one on each incline, the wagons being held horizontally, and only one was taken across the ravine at a time. Turntables at the top of each incline and at each foot manoeuvred the wagons. The sides of the gorge were about 150ft high and the span at this point was 266yd. Only twelve wagons on average could be taken across the gorge in an hour, and it soon became a bottleneck. By 1844, for instance, it was remarked by William Bouch in a report upon the railway that traffic was 'nearly equal to the powers of the Howen's Gill apparatus', and he recommended that a bridge should be constructed. This suggestion was not acted upon at that time and the gorge remained a hindrance to traffic for a number of years longer.

To the east of the ravine there was the 1 mile 779yd long Carr House west incline at 1 in 71, leading to Carr House stationary engine. This was the first long section of line from Crawley itself that had its gradient falling westwards. Carr House engine was a 50hp structure which worked also the Carr House east incline, 812yd long and with a 1 in 108 gradient. Carr House was itself for some years a bleak, upland, thinly populated district, and after 1840 it was transformed by the development of the town of Consett. The Medomsley branch had its junction facing east towards South Shields and was reasonably level. The main line continued eastwards with another nine inclined planes before reaching the levels of north-east Durham. A few level sections were interspersed between the inclines, however, and such sections were worked by horses.

The fairly level section from Carr House east to East Castles (or East Castle) two and a quarter miles long, was operated by horses. There then came the two inclines over Annfield hill, which reached 1 in 27 at their steepest. A stationary engine on top of the hill (which was really a ridge running from Pontop Pike, 1,035ft high) worked both Annfield west and east banks, the former 662yd long and the latter, also known as Loud Bank, 1,056yd long. There was then another level stretch to West Stanley worked by horses, bringing the railway to the fringe of the Tanfield district coalfield. The branch to Harelaw had cut off near the foot of the Loud Bank incline. Four self-acting inclines followed to lower the line to the Chester-le-Street district. These were the Stanley, Twizell, Eden Hill and Waldridge inclines, the steepest slope on any being 1 in 17. On Waldridge bank the gradient was mainly 1 in 24. Between Eden Hill and Waldridge banks was the Pelton level (1,131yd), again with horse haulage. From some 800ft above sea level near Annfield, the line reached 250ft at Pelton Fell in just over four miles. Another short level followed Waldridge incline and then there was a short incline worked by a stationary engine near High Flatts. This engine also worked the preceding three quarter mile Stella Gill level by a tail rope. The S & T was now at the Durham turnpike road north of Chester-le-Street, east of which there were no steep gradients and few engineering works except for a half-mile cutting through an undulating area near Fatfield. Despite the easy gradients the line from the turnpike to near Fatfield – almost two miles – was worked by a double engine at Vigo, west of Fatfield, and two inclined planes. This last part of the line from Fatfield to South Shields was almost level, with a very short section of 1 in 166, and steam locomotives operated on this part. The S & T had seven locomotives by 1837 and these also operated the passenger trains, shortly to be mentioned.

The S & T incline-ropes were tarred hemp and rarely lasted over ten months. There were sixty great ropes on the inclines with a total length of sixty-eight miles. The speed of the ropes was from seven to eleven mph and they pulled loads of between twenty-four to ninety-six tons. In 1839 it was estimated that the cost of working the principal self-acting inclines was £415 per mile and by the stationary engines £485 per mile. In January of each year the whole railway was closed for a week to enable the works to be overhauled and the inclines inspected and ropes replaced. The closure coincided with closure of the local collieries at the same time so that much traffic was unaffected.

TRAFFIC AND FINANCES

Early traffic on the S & T was chiefly lime from Stanhope to the nine depots along the line, coal to South Shields, and other minerals such as lead and stone. The passenger service on the line began on 16 April 1835 between South Shields and the Durham turnpike, about a mile north of Chester-le-Street. It seems to have been operated simply to supplement the company's income; which was a good reason but unfortunately was not a financial success. In 1835 a total of 2,814 passengers was carried at a loss of £220. By 1838, 17,490 passengers were carried but the profit came to no more than £117 15s 0d (£117.75). The S & T traffic manager himself recommended discontinuation of the passenger service but the directors regarded it as a 'great public convenience'. Passenger mileage in 1838 was only two per cent of the traffic mileage altogether.

Stanhope lime kilns produced 50–60 chaldrons of lime daily and as demand exceeded output new kilns were erected at Annfield. Both sets of kilns sent 9-10,000 chaldrons of lime to the depots annually and used 10,000 tons of coal per annum. Coal from private collieries, such as Waldridge, used railway wagons on hire from the S & T company. The S & T itself extended its Medomsley branch for over a mile in 1839 to serve a new colliery on the fringe of the Derwent valley, and in the same year an extension was made of the Waldridge wagonway to Sacriston to serve expanding colliery activities there. All the coal from this three mile long branch passed on to the S & T. At approximately the same date another wagonway was built nearby to reach the William pit at Craghead, which was sunk in 1839. This line joined with the S & T at the top of the Waldridge incline on Pelton level. Later it was extended southwards to reach Burnhope to serve a new colliery there, and later still, a short branch was made to serve mines at Holmside. As time passed, new collieries which were sunk in the whole district around the S & T line used the line to reach the Tyne, but in its early period the S & T served only a handful of pits. However,

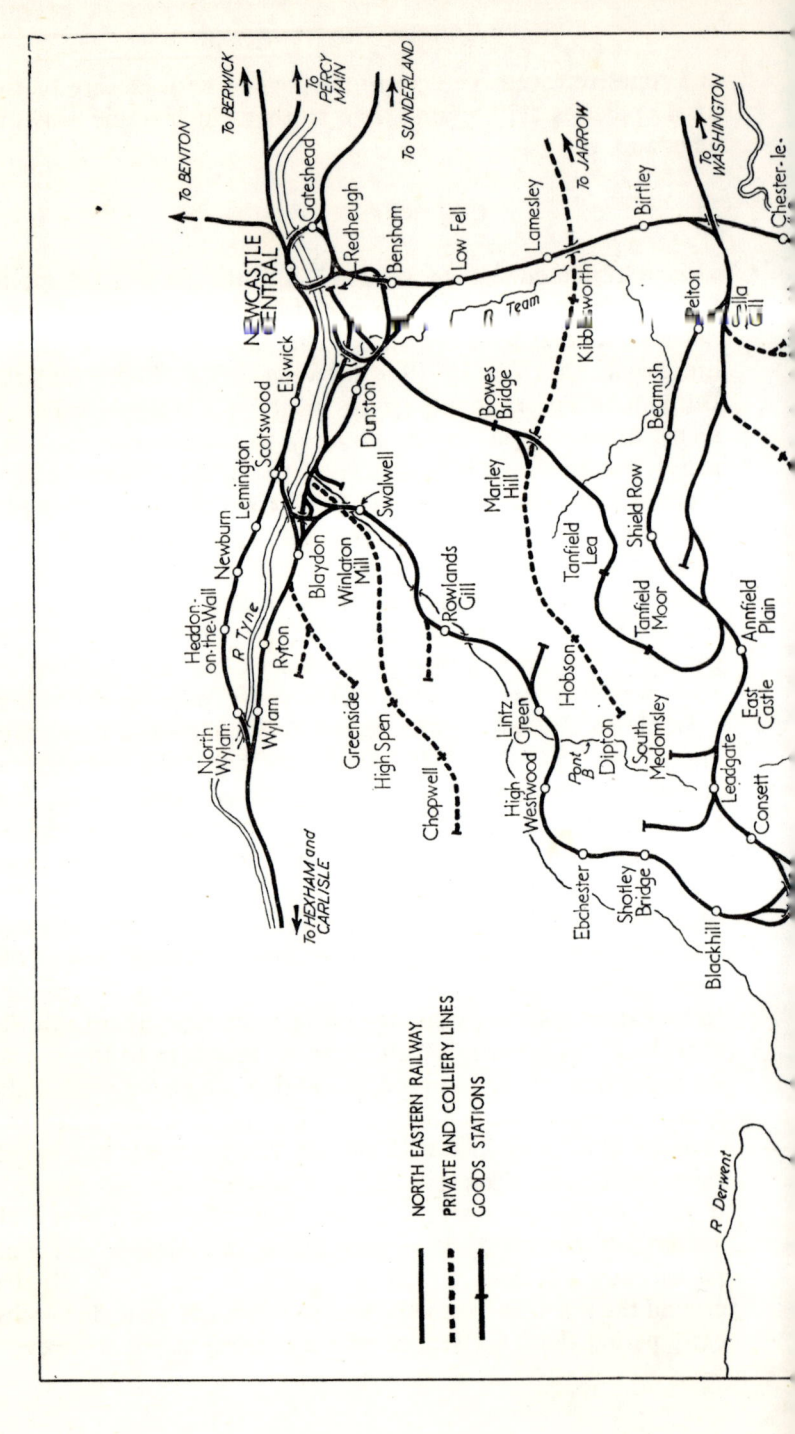

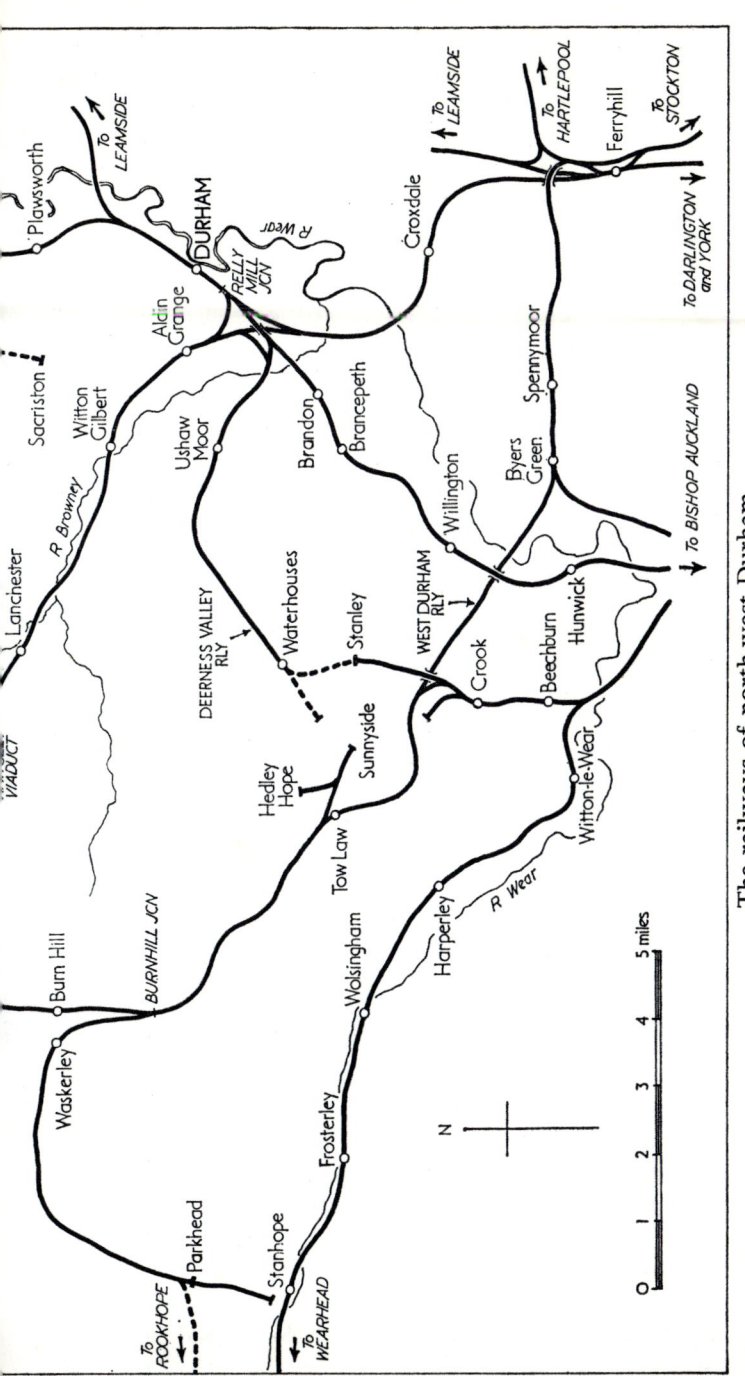

The railways of north-west Durham

the company made a profit of £9,839 on the sale of coal from its own collieries during 1838 and from all coal traffic a profit of £2,393 0s 3d (£2,393.01) was made in 1840. The three South Shields coal drops of 1834 had expanded into a total of eight by 1839.

In both 1835 and 1836 the company paid a five per cent dividend, borrowing the money to pay it. No further dividends were paid, for even with coal profits, the wayleaves bill was causing a heavy annual deficit, a fact not disclosed by the directors for some time. The annual wayleave bill was about £6,300, and in 1838 the total expenses of working traffic was over £5,998. In 1835 the company considered constructing a dock at a point west of South Shields but nothing was done. This is of interest because the site was that of the much later Tyne Dock. In 1839 the company again considered a dock at South Shields, and this time the matter was pursued and an Act was obtained on 1 July 1839 to build a dock under the title of the Tyne Dock Company, with a capital of £150,000. The area of the dock was twenty acres and the promoters were mainly shareholders of the S & T. Although tenders were invited nothing was to be done, as the true state of the S & T finances was made known soon afterwards.

In 1839 the directors decided to cease producing lime, as surprisingly, it was not making a profit. The early demand which had led to the building of Annfield kilns had fallen off despite the high hopes of having an export trade to Scotland. Much more serious and probably one might say 'the last straw' was the loss of the Tanfield Moor colliery traffic in 1840. The Brandling Junction Railway had acquired the Tanfield wagonway some years earlier, and from May 1837 had begun relaying it with heavier and better rails. This process was shortly interrupted for various reasons, but by late 1839 the wagonway had been relaid for much of its course, as far as Tanfield Lea. In 1840 Tanfield Moor was reached and the coal from the mine was once more sent to Dunston. The loss of this traffic to the S & T meant a loss of £5,000 a year, which the company simply could not afford. The Tanfield Moor branch then became disused.

At the end of 1840, the true financial state of the company was at last fully revealed to the shareholders, and an Extraordinary General Meeting was held on 29 December at which the hopelessness of the situation was discussed. It was proposed to dissolve the company and vest its property in a new company with a capital of £400,000. The S & T owed some £440,852 and on a 'liberal computation its assets were worth £307,883.'

On 2 January 1841 the company adopted its shareholders' proposal and in ten days £250,000 had been subscribed towards the proposed capital. The railway itself was now closed pending a settlement of the financial problem. On 5 February the S & T company was dissolved and twenty-five of the forty-nine proprietors of the old company were shareholders in the new company, named The Pontop & South Shields Railway. The new company was to operate the line only east of the Pontop district, actually from Carr House east, and the west end of the line was to be sold to the new Derwent Iron Co, which had set up an ironworks at Carr House, later known as Consett.

CONSETT

In the vicinity of Carr House were deposits of iron ore, and with coal supplies nearby and a railway able to bring limestone from Stanhope, Mr Jonathan Richardson realised that an iron industry in the neighbourhood of Carr House was an economic possibility. In 1840 he established the Derwent ironworks at Carr House beside the S & T, run by the Derwent Iron Co. Houses were built for the workers, many of whom were Irishmen, and a village and later a township grew up on this rather inhospitable fringe of the Pennines. Later a second, somewhat smaller ironworks was built at Blackhill – the Shotley Bridge Iron Co – at the 'tin works' not far from the Derwent ironworks. Within ten years Consett had a population of about 2,500 and it was to continue to grow even as the iron industry continued to prosper during the century. The presence of the ironworks at Consett was in no small measure a reason for further railway development in the region at a later date.

The Derwent Iron Co quickly stepped in when it saw its establishment threatened by the difficulties of the S & T company. It negotiated with the latter and its P & SS successor to continue a steady supply of limestone traffic from Stanhope.

However, the ending of the traffic on the S & T in late 1840 made the matter urgent, as limited limestone stocks were held at the ironworks, and the railway was the means of outlet for the iron products. The P & SS agreed to sell the line west of Carr House to the Derwent Co, and this was effected in the early part of 1841. The iron company's section was named the Derwent Railway. The P & SS retained the Medomsley branch, but the colliery and all other former S & T colliery interests were later sold, this being stipulated by the dissolution Act of 1842, which gave a time limit of two years to effect the sales.

THE DURHAM JUNCTION RAILWAY

Before going on to consider the early years of the P & SS, mention must be made of the Durham Junction Railway, virtually a branch of the S & T. In 1833 there was a plan to link the S & T with the Hartlepool Railway and to have a branch line to Monkwearmouth. This scheme was greatly modified in 1834 into the Durham Junction Railway, incorporated by an Act of 16 June 1834 (4 Will IV c 57) with powers to raise £80,000 by shares and £34,000 by loans. The S & T invested £40,000 in the scheme by purchasing half of the shares. The DJR was intended to run from the S & T at Washington to Durham, crossing the river Wear by a notable viaduct. The work on the line was supervised by T. E. Harrison of the S & T, and the costs of the Wear viaduct near Fatfield appear to have greatly increased the total costs of the line, which otherwise had few engineering difficulties. The line was truncated to end at Rainton Meadows, several miles to the north-east of Durham, although it was still hoped to build the remainder to Gilesgate, Durham, at some date.

The line was opened for mineral traffic in August 1838, serving coal mines on its course. Traffic on the five mile line was operated by S & T locomotives and stock. In 1840 a passenger service started on the line in conjunction with the S & T and Brandling Junction lines. The S & T service itself between Washington and the Durham turnpike was discontinued as a result. The DJR service was from Rainton to Gateshead, using the Brandling Junction lines from Brockley Whins to Gateshead. On 9 March 1840 a connection was made between S & T and Brandling Junction at Brockley Whins in the South Shields direction, but it was only on 19 August 1844 that a south to west curve was opened to allow through running from the DJR to the Brandling line.

The S & T difficulties did not help the DJR, which was itself in financial straits, and it struggled on until it sold out in 1843 for only £88,500 to the 'railway king' George Hudson, whose newly completed Newcastle and Darlington Junction Railway was to use much of the DJR metals. An Act of 1844 confirmed the sale. Although the DJR itself never reached Durham, the N & DJ built its City of Durham Branch from Belmont (near Rainton) to Gilesgate, opened in 1844.

PONTOP & SOUTH SHIELDS RAILWAY

The P & SS was incorporated by an Act of 13 May 1842 (5 Vic c 27) and had an authorised capital of £339,800 with powers to borrow a further £60,200. Coal was the line's staple traffic, but receipts were still overshadowed by the annual wayleaves bill of almost £6,000. In 1842 a profit from collieries of over £590 had altered by 1844 to a deficit of some £1,152. Clearly the P & SS was not heading for immediate success, but the 'railway mania' of the 1840s, and George Hudson in particular, affected its fortunes. The N & DJ line already mentioned was opened with great ceremony on 18 June 1844, establishing a continuous line of rails between London and the river Tyne at Gateshead. The N & DJ from Darlington joined the Durham Junction line near Rainton, and the company used the DJR, P & SS and Brandling Junction lines to reach Gateshead. A part of the P & SS was thus part of the 'east coast route'. Hudson, on behalf of the N & DJ, soon acquired the three companies (whose metals were used by the N &DJ) – the DJR and Brandling lines in 1844, and in 1845 the P & SS. The latter kept its nominal independence until 1 January 1847, and was absorbed by the York and Newcastle Railway (as the N & DJ had become). Thus in 1847 the P & SS and its rival, the Tanfield branch were owned by the same company. Earlier, in 1843, the Brandling Junction had delivered another pin-prick to the P & SS by re-establishing the disused Tanfield Moor branch in conjunction with the Derwent Iron Co. From 26 December 1843 therefore, the Derwent Iron Co traffic had ben diverted from the P & SS via Harelaw. After 1847 this situation was no longer necessary and most of the traffic was returned to the Pontop branch (as the P & SS will now be called), which had an easier outlet to the south at Washington.

On 1 October 1850 the York Newcastle & Berwick Railway opened a new line between Washington and Pelaw to shorten the distance for east coast main-line trains. By this time the Tyne had been bridged, and there was a continuous line of rails from London to Edinburgh and beyond. The new cut-off line was about five miles in length, and left only a short section of the old S & T through Washington as the Pontop branch's contribution to the main line. However it left the Washington—Brockley Whins—South Shields line more open for an increasing coal traffic. In 1849 the plan for a dock west of South Shields had been revived and work had actually begun but was suspended in 1850. The YNB directors stated on 1 March 1850 that they were not sufficiently convinced of the necessity for these docks and said that additional staiths at South Shields were enough to meet the needs of the coal trade. This was in spite of an increasing number of mines using the Pontop branch in the Pelton, Beamish, Stanley and Annfield districts. In fact the fall of George Hudson and the associated financial problems caused the new attitude. When the NER was formed in 1854 it was soon decided that the South Shields coal shipping facilities were insufficient for the needs of the traffic, and the Tyne Dock project was again brought to light. Work on it began in late 1855 (contractors: Jackson Bean & Gow; NER resident engineer Mr Hodgson) and the dock was opened on 3 March 1859. It covered fifty acres and accommodated 400 to 500 vessels. It had four jetties, two of which were intended exclusively to handle coal, and new spur railways were built to reach the dock from the nearby Brockley Whins—South Shields lines. The NER directors reported to their shareholders on 18 February 1859 'their decided opinion that when sufficient time has elapsed fully to develop the capabilities and advantages of this Dock, it will not only yield a good return on the capital expended but will give a stability and completeness to the Company's trade in the Tyne, which could not have been obtained by any less comprehensive scheme'. The dock had 'capabilities for the shipment of coal unequalled in any other dock in the United Kingdom'.

A major improvement was made to the Stella Gill—Fatfield section of railway in 1856-7. On 5 May 1856 a contract was awarded to G. Forster and W. Lawton of Sunderland for nearly £18,161 to convert this line into double track, using 82lb per yard rails. The work was to be done within sixteen months. A penalty of £100 per day was to be paid to the NER 'for every day traffic should be stopped or interfered with during construction'. Materials for the work were delivered at Washington station, Durham turnpike, and Stella Gill, and stone came from 'Pensher, Usworth, Mr Cail's quarry (Gateshead), Benton, or Long Bank, or other white standstone to be approved by the Engineer'. The work was completed and opened on 8 June 1857, locomotive haulage replacing the stationary engines. The Durham turnpike crossing was replaced by a bridge – 'to be built on a Memel timber platform 3 inches in thickness supported by larch or beech piles not less than 10 inches diameter having wrought iron shoes 18lbs in weight each; the arch to be brickwork set in cement; a layer of well tempered clay puddle, 12 inches in depth to be laid over the arch and backing'. The line was embanked on each side of this new bridge for some distance. (Much later, in 1893, the turnpike bridge was reconstructed using wrought iron girders by the Darlington Wagon & Engineering Co for £1,558 9s [£1,558.45].) The 1857 works included new reception sidings at Stella Gill for traffic from the inclines west of this point, which replaced the Fatfield sidings. Henceforth locomotives worked traffic all the way between Stella Gill and South Shields. A small engine shed was also built at Stella Gill (see Chapter 6) and cost about £3,000. Of more lasting importance was the shed sanctioned at Tyne Dock in 1858, and built in 1861-2 at a cost of approximately £15,000. It was later enlarged, but Stella Gill shed remained comparatively small.

In 1860 the Board of Trade allowed the NER to run passenger trains between the main line at Washington, and Stella Gill and a regular service commenced in March 1862. Before this began the line was occasionally used by special trains for various events, as in September 1861 when the Durham County Rifle Association had a meeting at Pelton. For a certain period in this month in connection with the meeting, a special train left Washington at 9.45am for Stella Gill returning from the latter at 4.34pm. The regular passenger service had intermediate stations at Vigo and Chester-le-Street, and the station at Stella Gill was actually named 'Pelton'. During 1864 another intermediate station was opened at Biddick Lane, which served Fatfield. The trains provided connections with the east coast main-line trains. The service was withdrawn, never to re-appear when the NER opened its Team Valley branch for passenger traffic on 1 December 1868, and this new line had a station in the centre of Chester-le-Street. The Pelton service ceased from January 1869. The Team Valley line, incidentally, passed beneath the old Stanhope & Tyne line (on its 1857 embankment) just west of the Durham turnpike bridge, with no connection between the lines. A girder bridge carried the S & T over the newer line.

SACRISTON & SOUTH SHIELDS RAILWAY

Soon after the Tyne Dock was opened in 1859 the NER was faced by a project for a new railway virtually paralleling the Pontop branch between the Stella Gill area and South Shields. This was the Sacriston & South Shields Railway scheme fostered by coal owners in the Sacriston—Pelton districts, who felt that the NER rates on their coal conveyed to Tyne Dock were too high. The proposed railway followed the course of the Pontop branch very closely from the Tyne to Pelton, cutting off to follow the line of the Waldridge—Sacriston wagonway equally closely.

Typical rates charged by the NER in May 1860 on chaldrons of coal to Tyne Dock were:

Beamish Colliery	3s	8d ($18\frac{1}{2}$p)	per chaldron
Waldridge Colliery	4s	$1\frac{1}{2}$d ($20\frac{1}{2}$p)	,, ,,
Craghead Colliery	4s	$3\frac{1}{4}$d (21p)	,, ,,
Byron Colliery, Sacriston	4s	$1\frac{1}{2}$d ($20\frac{1}{2}$p)	,, ,,

The rate for a chaldron (53cwt) was actually fixed at the rate for 54cwt of screened coal or 56 cwt of unscreened and small

Page 33: *ON THE STANHOPE & TYNE RAILWAY*
(above) *Waldridge incline bank foot, 1956;* (below) *T2 0–8–0 shunting at Weatherhill*

Page 34: *NEWCASTLE & CARLISLE RAILWAY*
(above) *Class O 0–4–4T No 7329 at Blaydon with Newcastle—Hexham train, 11 October 1947;* (below) *in March 1921, Class Q 4–4–0 No 1929 passes Ryton with a Carlisle—Newcastle train*

coal. The rate increased the greater the distance from Tyne Dock – thus Medomsley colliery was charged at 5s 10d (29p), being twenty one and a half miles distant. Beamish colliery was nine and a half miles and Byron and Waldridge eleven and a quarter miles from the dock (excluding wagonway distance).

The NER discussed the matter with the Sacriston promoters and common sense prevailed. Significant rate concessions were made and an agreement on dues was made to last for fifteen years. In fact the Tyne Dock rates were not disturbed for much longer than fifteen years, even in times of mining expansion and prosperity, which reflects highly on the NER.

As a last point on Pontop coal traffic in this period, it is of interest to note the growth in the traffic by 1859. In 1854 a total of 299,337 chaldrons of coal were handled at the South Shields staiths from the Pontop branch. In 1859 the amount at South Shields from the line was 334,309 chaldrons. No less than about twenty-five collieries east of Consett used the Pontop branch, ranging from mines at Usworth and Washington to Medomsley and West Derwent collieries, on the Medomsley branch. The great era of coal prosperity for the former Stanhope & Tyne was under way.

CHAPTER TWO

Railway Development on Tyneside

N & CR IN NORTH-WEST DURHAM

A description of all the details of the early history of the Newcastle & Carlisle Railway is not intended, but as the N & CR passed through part of north-west Durham, some points cannot be omitted.

The N & CR was promoted in 1825, a canal having been previously projected. The company sought a capital of £300,000, which was subscribed for within a fortnight of the prospectus being issued in March 1825. In December of that year the directors proposed various branch lines to the main Newcastle—Carlisle line to obtain more traffic, and one of these branches was within Durham, from the south end of the Scotswood bridge projected to carry the main line across the river Tyne, to Swalwell 'to receive coals coming down the vale of Derwent and for the convenience of the manufacturing and populous town of Swalwell'. However, the N & CR scheme languished until 1829, largely because of the difficulties in fixing the course of the line and because of protracted negotiations with landowners, some of whom were most reluctant to see a railway on their doorsteps. By 1829 there still remained one recalcitrant landowner at Riding Mill, who refused at any price to sell land to the N & CR, and apparently this land covered the whole valley floor at this point and the line could not be satisfactorily deviated except at great expense and inconvenience. Public opinion came to the rescue and forced this gentleman to sell the necessary land, but he and several other landowners refused to countenance steam locomotive haulage on the line near their houses, insisting on horse haulage or other alternatives. The Bill drawn up in 1829 contained a clause prohibiting the use of steam locomotives at certain points, including one within Durham – 'within the distance of 1,000yd to the east of Stella Hall, nor nearer on the west than the point where the line of the said railways or tramroads shall be constructed by a certain common highway called the Water Lane.' Stella Hall was situated just to the west of Blaydon and close to the Tyne, the projected railway route being between the Hall and the river. Indeed the projected railway closely followed the course of the Tyne as far as Hexham, and the river South Tyne, beyond that town, to Haltwhistle, before leaving the Tyne system and entering Cumberland. The actual route was not fully determined at some points, particularly the section west of Scotswood. There was an alternative route to the crossing of the Tyne to Blaydon, and this was simply to continue the line along the north bank of the river through Lemington and Newburn, and to cross the river at Newburn or Wylam. As the Tyne was somewhat narrower here than at Scotswood, less expense would be incurred with a bridge. However this would mean missing Blaydon, the largest town between Newcastle and Carlisle (with some 4,000 inhabitants) and the site of several industries, notably a lead smelter. A disadvantage of the Blaydon route was the low-lying land beside the river between Stella and Ryton which was subject to periodic flooding. Also the north bank had coal mining activities around Lemington, with riverside staiths and a wagonway to several pits, with a notable colliery further to the west at Wylam. The N & CR engineer, Francis Giles, considered the question and declared 'Upon the whole I cannot but express my decided opinion that the Lemington line in point of expense and in the excellence of its planes and general eligibility is without question the best.' He proposed a bridge from west of Newburn to Crawcrook mill on the south bank west of Ryton, or even at Wylam depending upon the attitude of coal owners there. At first the Crawcrook bridge was planned as a wooden structure with five spans of fifty-four feet; later it was decided that the bridge should have twelve spans of thirty feet. Whether this line would indeed have better gradients is doubtful, as there was a rather high area between Scotswood and Lemington which fell away suddenly on the west side, which created a reasonable slope. On the south bank there was no such obstacles and the gradients would in fact be easy. Very much later a railway was made west of Scotswood which required an expensive tunnel through the ridge of high land. In any event the N & CR directors overruled Giles, and determined to have the line through Blaydon, with a bridge at Scotswood.

A road bridge was also planned to be built at Scotswood at this time to carry the Hexham turnpike into Newcastle, and this fact was mentioned in the N & CR Act of 22 May 1829 (10 Geo IV c 72) which sanctioned the sixty-three miles of the N & CR line, as well as a single branch line of half a mile within Newcastle. The 1825 Swalwell branch was not mentioned. The Scotswood Bridge clause empowered the N & CR to carry road and pedestrian traffic over their railway bridge and charge tolls should the nearby road bridge (just to the east) not be ready. Existing ferry boat services here were to be compensated and no ferries allowed within 600yd of the railway bridge. Also 'no locomotive or moveable steam engine shall be used on the said railways or tramroads for drawing wagons or other carriages or for any purpose whatsoever within view of . . .' and here followed the list of residences where this applied, including Stella Hall and the Hall of a certain gentleman near Riding Mill. The list of houses was such that any use of locomotives on the whole line would have been virtually impossible, and how the N & CR overcame this difficulty will be mentioned shortly. The company was allowed to raise £300,000 by shares (of £100 each), which had already been subscribed for, and to borrow another £100,000 – not a great deal of capital for such a large scheme. Several large engineering works would be necessary, especially in the Cumberland section, such as the Wetheral and Corby viaducts, and the embankments and cuttings near Brampton. This fact was soon to be obvious to the directors when work was under way, and lack of ready capital was to dog the company persistently.

The line was of 4ft 8½in guage, and construction began in March 1830 at both ends of the line, but not to the east of Blaydon. Blaydon had a quayside on the Tyne, and the Scotswood road bridge was being built, so that the directors decided that the first priority was to have the railway open from Carlisle to Blaydon, which was only three miles from Newcastle and would have easy access to the larger town for goods and passengers. The railway was easily graded between Blaydon and the county boundary just east of Wylam. Stations were placed within Durham at Blaydon and Ryton, while Wylam was only just in Northumberland. A station was also planned at Scotswood, and the Newcastle terminus was planned to be at the Shot Tower, but this section was being left until later, as stated.

Meanwhile during 1831 a new scheme, the Blaydon Gateshead & Hebburn Railway came into being, planning its line from the N & CR at Blaydon along the south side of the Tyne to Hebburn through Gateshead, a distance altogether of nine miles. The two companies held discussions and an important outcome was that they decided to build a bridge across the Tyne from Redheugh. During 1832 work went on on the N & CR, although it was interrupted for a short period early in the year by lack of funds. A Bill for more capital had hastily to be prepared, and it was passed on 23 June 1832, allowing the raising of £100,000. Quickly £25,000 was borrowed from the Exchequer Loan Board to allow work to resume.

The N & CR was planned as a double line of rails, although at first some sections were only to have a single line in the interests of opening for traffic as soon as possible. Between Blaydon and Stocksfield there was a double line from the outset and the steepest gradient was only 1 in 317 between Prudhoe and Stocksfield. On 17 March 1834 the directors reported that the final works were being done from Blaydon to Stocksfield and work was progressing to Hexham. From 1 July a new engineer was in control – John Blackmore, although he actually superintended the work before this date. Francis Giles remained as consultant. Blackmore appears to have been an able engineer and he designed several of the N & CR works. At the end of the year goods traffic had begun on the line east of Stocksfield, mainly of coal traffic from collieries at Prudhoe and Wylam, and lead traffic, and steam locomotives were working the traffic. The company had acquired three locomotives and rolling stock, and these were running past Stella Hall without regard to the condition in the 1829 Act. There was no protest, however; this was to come later from elsewhere. During the year the Blaydon Gateshead & Hebburn Railway had been incorporated by an Act of 22 May (4 Will IV c 26) and work on this line soon commenced. However, by the early part of 1835 the Hebburn company's capital ran out and no more could be obtained. Only about a mile of the line was completed and the N & CR stepped in and offered to help the company out of some of its difficulties by taking over the route as far east as Redheugh. The Hebburn company agreed, hoping to build the Redheugh—Hebburn line when they raised more capital, something which did not happen.

On 3 March 1835 the eighteen mile Blaydon—Hexham line was opened officially for traffic, and two special trains were run from Blaydon to Hexham and back carrying 600 people, with many more watching the event. The next day the regular passenger service began with two trains daily each way on week-days. Stage-coaches linked with trains at Blaydon to carry passengers to Newcastle over the Scotswood road bridge, which had opened a few years earlier. Both Blaydon and Ryton stations had two platforms mainly of wooden construction, as with others on the line. Trains drove on the right hand line on double sections (Stocksfield—Hexham was single), and the locomotives were painted red. First class coaches had roofs and were painted yellow, lined black, while the second class coaches were open and were white, lined green. Later composite carriages with roofs entered service on the N & CR, and all the coaches were painted mainly claret after 1843.

Early N & CR receipts were:

1835	Passengers	Goods & Parcels
June	£143 12s 6d (£143.62)	£53 15s 8d (£53.78)
July	£162 11s 0d (£162.55)	£53 10s 1d (£53.50)

Up to 18 July 1835 some £346,731 had been spent on the N & CR construction and expenditure was £95 per week.

Soon after this opening came trouble. A landowner near Riding Mill (the same family that had delayed progress in 1829) obtained an injunction to prevent the use of locomotives near his house as stipulated by law. All passenger trains ceased, and goods services were stopped east of Riding Mill, cutting off Hexham, which had a heavy lead traffic to Blaydon smelter. There was a massive local outcry, and after some days the landowner was forced to relent, despite the justice of his case by law. The services were duly restored after a month as the N & CR negotiated with all of the landowners mentioned in the 1829 Act regarding their views. Apparently all were favourable and a Bill was prepared to legalise the situation, but the locomotives were only to burn coke to prevent too much smoke. This Act was passed on 17 June 1835 (5 Will IV c 26) and the opportunity was taken to insert clauses permitting more capital to be raised – £90,000 by shares; and £60,000 by loans.

In 1835 the Brandling Junction Railway was formed to build a line from Gateshead to Sunderland with a branch to South Shields paralleling the Stanhope & Tyne from Brockley Whins. The Blaydon Gateshead & Hebburn Railway had lost all support, and the Brandling Junction paid £9,000 to the N & CR in an agreement that the latter should not seek to advance east of Redheugh. The Blaydon—Redheugh branch was almost level for its four miles, closely following the Tyne. It crossed the river Derwent at Derwenthaugh and the river Team at Dunston by wooden bridges, and also crossed the Tanfield wagonway initially with no connection. The Blaydon to Derwenthaugh section ($1\frac{1}{4}$ miles) was opened to goods in June 1836, the same month as the main line was pushed further westwards from Hexham to Haydon Bridge. Passenger services were extended between Blaydon and Haydon Bridge, and the latter became the railhead for the heavy lead traffic from the Northern Pennines (Alston and Allendale districts).

1 March 1837 saw the opening of the Derwenthaugh—Redheugh line to a temporary station at Redheugh quay opposite Newcastle. Here passengers and goods were ferried across the Tyne to a building on the northern side, a temporary station at The Close. The directors had meanwhile decided not to go ahead with the expensive bridge at Redheugh, and reverted to the original plan. The route into Newcastle was now 'fully settled', and John Blackmore designed a bridge at Scotswood. A regular passenger service began between Blaydon and Redheugh with an intermediate station at Derwenthaugh to serve the 1,500 inhabitants of nearby Swalwell. This service was from the first regarded as a branch service, the trains connecting at Blaydon with the Haydon Bridge trains, but with road coaches still providing a quicker access from Blaydon to Newcastle.

During 1836 the company had also opened the twenty miles of its line from Carlisle to a colliery near Greenhead, leaving only a middle section unfinished, and road services linked trains on the two sections in operation. In 1838 work progressed on the Blaydon—Newcastle line, while on 18 June the Haydon Bridge—Blenkinsopp colliery link was opened, establishing a completed line between Carlisle and Blaydon, connecting the navigable river Tyne with the Carlisle Canal to the Solway Firth. Five special trains left Carlisle on the opening day travelling to Redheugh during the morning. Celebrations were held in Newcastle at the expense of the N & CR directors, and in the afternoon the cavalcade returned to Carlisle bearing the Newcastle dignitaries and others. There were further rejoicings in Carlisle and in the evening the trains returned to Tyneside in pouring rain, undoubtedly ending the festive spirit among those in open carriages. Matters worsened when one train became derailed at Milton, so that it was only at 6am the next day that the last of the travellers reached Redheugh station. A regular passenger train service began between Blaydon and Carlisle, by which time there were nine locomotives in service. The Redheugh branch continued to have a connecting service. For goods the Redheugh station was better than Blaydon, as larger vessels could reach the quay there.

The N & CR had locomotive sheds at Blaydon and Redheugh, as well as at Hexham, Haydon Bridge and Carlisle. It was later to have a depot at Newcastle, while its locomotive fuel came from its coke ovens at Derwenthaugh. Surplus coke was sold. In September 1838 new coal staiths were opened at Dunston, and the first use of them was by a train from Prudhoe colliery.

The Blaydon to Newcastle (Shot Tower) section of line was officially opened on 21 May 1839. The line closely followed the north side of the Tyne with easy gradients except for a short section of about 1 in 120 at the terminus. As the stations were not ready, the regular passenger service was not started until 21 October 1839, but goods traffic used the line. Landslips caused temporary closure of the line from about 22 October—2 November 1839. The Close station remained for goods also until closed on 3 January 1842. Scotswood Bridge was an eleven span timber skew bridge with 35ft headroom over the river at low tide. It was designed by Blackmore and 'built wholly of timber with the exception of the abutments' and 'it consisted of a series of trussed ribs resting upon ten piers which were composed of piles braced together, the span of each opening being 60ft measured on the skew line.' Just east of the bridge was Scotswood station.

Passenger services in 1839 consisted of five trains on weekdays daily each way between Newcastle and Carlisle, and two trains each way on Sundays. Redheugh branch trains continued to connect with the main service at Blaydon. Times of departure of trains westbound from Blaydon and Redheugh were:

Redheugh	dep	5.30am	9.00	12.30	2.30	5.00	6.30
Blaydon	dep	5.45	9.12	12.45	2.45	5.12	6.45
Carlisle	arr	9.30	12.00	4.30	7.00	8.00 Haydon Bridge	

Sundays

Redheugh	dep	9.00am	5.00pm
Blaydon	dep	9.15	5.15
Carlisle	arr	12.15	8.15

Trains from Carlisle left Blaydon for Newcastle and Redheugh at 9.15am, 11.45, 4.45, 7.00 and 7.45 on weekdays, and at midday and 8.00pm on Sundays. Departure and arrival times at Newcastle were the same as those at Redheugh.

PROGRESS TO THE 1862 AMALGAMATION

An addition to the N & CR lines in county Durham came during 1847 with the opening of the half mile long Swalwell branch on 24 May. This served a colliery and several industries in the town of Swalwell and ran from the Redheugh branch at Derwenthaugh. The N & CR terminus in Newcastle had been extended eastwards to a temporary station at Forth Banks on 1 March 1847, but the company planned to use the new central station a further quarter of a mile to the east, when it was built. Central station was to be opened on 29 August 1850, and the N & CR was linked with the lines of the York Newcastle & Berwick Railway there, this company being joint owner of the station with the N & CR. Forth station became the Newcastle goods station of the N & CR. The N & CR was also linked with the YNB at Redheugh. On 15 January 1839 the Redheugh incline, of 1 in 23 gradient and worked by a 60hp stationary engine, had been opened between Redheugh quay station and the Brandling Junction Railway at Gateshead. The Tanfield line was also connected with the N & CR and the incline (at Redheugh bank foot junction).

In August 1850 the Redheugh branch passenger service was withdrawn, but, probably because of local demand it was restarted in November 1852 and included a service on the Swalwell branch. The Redheugh line service was ended east of Derwenthaugh in May 1853 and the Swalwell service ceased from December of the same year. The Blaydon—Derwenthaugh service continued until February 1868, when the opening of Swalwell station on the new Blaydon & Consett branch allowed its withdrawal.

In 1858 there was a basic N & CR main line service of four trains each way between Newcastle and Carlisle and a Newcastle—Hexham train each way, with two Sunday Newcastle—Carlisle trains each way. On Saturdays, however, there were no fewer than ten additional trains each way between Newcastle and Blaydon, and three of these in each direction continued (by reversing) to Derwenthaugh, to serve Swalwell. At Derwenthaugh the battery of coke ovens operated by the N & CR was doubled in 1852.

An interesting event which may be alluded to in passing was the leasing of the N & CR by George Hudson on behalf of the York Newcastle & Berwick Railway company from 1 August 1848 to 31 December 1849. This was the result of the Caledonian Railway offering a lease, in March 1848, which prompted Hudson's counter-offer. As the YNB had paid a nine per cent dividend in 1847 (and the N & CR five and a half per cent), the N & CR directors accepted this offer, but it was never ratified, as the YNB shareholders themselves were not widely in favour of it. Thus the N & CR resumed its independence from 1 January 1850.

On 9 May 1860 Scotswood railway bridge was burnt down by a fire while it was being tested by the Board of Trade. This bizarre event caused all trains to be diverted to Newcastle along the Redheugh branch and up the incline to reach Newcastle over the High Level Bridge. On 5 May the Tyne Improvement Commission had published a report upon the bridge stating it 'presents great obstructions to the waterway and is the cause of inconvenience and damage to passing craft . . . is in a state of great dilapidation . . . cannot be efficiently repaired'. Thus four days later Col Yolland of the Board of Trade examined the bridge and locomotives were run over it for his benefit. Hot ashes lodged in the ballast went unnoticed and in the afternoon fire broke out and the whole bridge was destroyed in about two and a half hours. This effectively solved the Board of Trade's problem in the matter! Early in 1861 a single track temporary wooden bridge was opened. A permanent structure was opened in 1868 at a cost of £20,000. This was a double track iron girder bridge, supported on iron piers and having six spans. Before this was built the Tyne Improvement Commission, mindful of the hazards to navigation of the late bridge, requested the NER to build an 'opening' bridge. This met with a reply from the railway company that it 'cannot entertain the question of reconstructing the above bridge as an opening bridge'. One effect of the heavy traffic using the Redheugh branch in 1860–1 was the replacement of the two wooden bridges over the rivers Derwent and Team, the latter during 1860, both as iron girder structures.

The N & CR was amalgamated with the NER on 17 July 1862. This followed five years of persistent effort by the smaller company to achieve this aim, dogged by opposition from other railways, notably the North British. The NBR had opened its Border Counties Railway from Hexham to Riccarton Junction on 1 July 1862 and in the preceding years had been considering means of making an entry into Newcastle when this event occurred. It had regarded the independence of the N & CR as vital to its plans, as it did not want the NER blocking it at Hexham as it did at Berwick. More of this background is mentioned later in Chapter 5. It is enough to say here that the NER and the NBR came to an agreement over the N & CR whereby the amalgamation with the NER was not to be opposed by the Scottish company provided it was granted running powers over the N & CR into Newcastle. This was laid down in the Amalgamation Act, and thus NBR trains ran between Hexham and

Newcastle Central station and also to Redheugh goods station. Then it was possible for a passenger to board a NBR train at Blaydon or Ryton, and go to Edinburgh, Galashiels, Hawick etc via Hexham and the North Tyne valley. In this way the N & CR line between Hexham and Newcastle acquired a unique status lasting until the 1923 grouping. Another effect of the amalgamation was that the NER obtained the use of the Citadel station (joint LNWR–Caledonian) at Carlisle, the London Road station becoming the goods station.

TANFIELD WAGONWAY CHANGES

It is now necessary to note some of the changes on the Tanfield wagonway from the 1830s. Mention has been made of its acquisition by the Brandling Junction Company who began relaying it southwards from Dunston in 1837, reaching Tanfield Moor Colliery in 1840. The line had a 1 in 40 ruling gradient, and there were several inclined planes on it. Lobley Hill self-acting incline just south of Dunston was fifty chains long, and at 1 in 16 to 1 in 18. There was a relatively level section before the Fugar incline (also called Sunnyside incline), which was one mile four chains in length, and reaching 1 in 11 in gradient, with sections at 1 in 21 to 1 in 46. This also was a self-acting incline. At the southern extremity of the line was the Tanfield Moor incline, reaching 1 in 9 and 1 in 15 between Tanfield Lea and Tanfield Moor. In 1843 the southern section to the Stanhope & Tyne via Harelaw was reopened, while in 1854 a line was opened from Tanfield Moor, north westwards to Lintz colliery. There were also three inclines worked by stationary engines on the Tanfield branch. One engine was at Bowes Bridge near Marley Hill, which hauled sets of wagons up and down the 1 in 40 to 1 in 51 northwards to Fugar bank top, and also worked the section southwards, named Causey east bank, which reached 1 in 57. Another engine worked the moderate Causey west bank which extended northwards from Tanfield East. Horses worked the traffic on the intermediate sections until July 1881, when the stationary engines were closed, and the inclines worked by them, and the horse haulage sections changed over to locomotives. Bowes Bridge locomotive depot was erected on the site of the stationary engine there.

Near here was also the branch to Marley Hill colliery, which linked there with the Pontop & Jarrow Railway, shortly to be mentioned. Bowes Bridge shed housed two locomotives, and operated all the traffic between Tanfield Lea and Fugar bank top. The branch rose from about fifty feet above sea level at Dunston beside the Tyne to 500ft at Tanfield Lea in six and a half miles, then to almost 800ft at Tanfield Moor (one and a half miles).

On 16 June 1842 the Brandling Junction Railway began to operate a passenger service on the Tanfield branch. This was between Tanfield Lea and Gateshead, and there were four recognised stations at Tanfield Lea, Bowes Bridge, Fugar Bar and Redheugh, and an unofficial stopping place by the Whickham turnpike at Lobley Hill. It operated only on Saturdays and the journey took an hour. At first a passenger coach was used, but later coal wagons were provided; all in all not a good service for the 2,600 inhabitants of Tanfield chapelry. This service did not last long, and disappeared when the Brandling Junction disappeared into George Hudson's empire.

There were several branches of the Tanfield line besides those mentioned. A short branch came to serve Watergate colliery not far from Lobley Hill, while the wagonway branches from the Tanfield Lea district southwards to Shield Row and Stanley appear to have closed by the end of the nineteenth century, this area being well served by the Stanhope & Tyne line and the improved route of the 1890s.

PONTOP & JARROW

In 1844 the owner of the newly sunk Burnopfield colliery negotiated with John Bowes, owner of the Marley Hill colliery, to build a wagonway and link the two mines. This was agreed and the two and a half mile line was built and opened during 1845, linking with the branch from the Tanfield line at Marley Hill. Horses worked the traffic except on an inclined plane from the colliery down to Crookgate (Hobson incline). In June 1847 two locomotives were introduced to shunt at Marley Hill, and by 1850 it seems that more engines had arrived and were working all traffic. Marley Hill colliery at this time was very productive and had a large battery of coke ovens. In 1853

Bowes became dissatisfied with the rates on the Tanfield branch which he felt were too high, and planned his own railway to the Tyne. The obvious outlet was westwards from the Burnopfield line to Derwenthaugh, utilising the disused course of the Main Way, and joining the Garesfield wagonway at Winlaton Mill. Instead of this he decided to build a line eastwards to join the Jarrow—Kibblesworth wagonway at Kibblesworth colliery a distance of two and a half miles. At the same time he decided to extend the Burnopfield line southwards for one and a half miles to serve the new Dipton Delight pit, and also to offer an outlet to his Pontop south colliery and Pontop coke ovens further south. The Dipton extension was built in 1853–4 and opened at the same time as the Delight pit began production in April 1855. Meanwhile the Marley Hill—Kibblesworth line had been opened on 20 September 1854 after fourteen months' work. The coal and coke from Marley Hill, Burnopfield, Dipton and other installations now went to staiths at Jarrow instead of Dunston, and the NER lost £20,000 a year in receipts as a result. The whole fifteen miles of line from Jarrow to Dipton was named the Pontop & Jarrow Railway, and always remained independent of the NER. In 1932 it was to be renamed the Bowes Railway. In 1860–1 an important new colliery opened at Byermoor, one and a quarter miles east of Marley Hill, and new coke ovens were opened nearby on the site of the closed Crookbank colliery. In 1863 there was a proposed one mile extension of the line from Dipton to Pontop, including a 1 in 8 incline, but this was not done. This line would have climbed Pontop Pike 1,025ft above sea level, the highest area of land in the district.

At Pickering Nook, just south of Hobson, the Pontop & Jarrow crossed the one and a half mile long Tanfield Moor—Lintz wagonway of 1854 without a connection. In fact the latter had a short tunnel beneath the Dipton line. The Pontop & Jarrow had its own short branch to Lintz colliery, competing with the other line. Both lines suffered when the Blaydon & Consett branch opened in 1867, the Lintz traffic thence largely passing on to the new line by a branch from Lintz Green station, which also served South Garesfield colliery nearby. The Tanfield Moor—Lintz wagonway had closed by 1896. A feature of the P & J at Marley Hill was its level crossing with the

Tanfield branch, and the NER built a signal box there at one corner. Just after 1900 locomotives took over the traffic on Hobson incline, simplifying operations on the Pontop & Jarrow.

OTHER WAGONWAYS

At Blaydon in 1853 the Blaydon Main colliery opened and a wagonway was built for the short journey to Derwenthaugh staiths, as well as a junction with the Redheugh branch (Blaydon Main junction). The Derwent valley branch later crossed this line by an overbridge, just as it did the Garesfield wagonway just to the east. From the N & CR line further west arose two colliery branches. One of these was the one and a quarter mile line from west of Blaydon station to Blaydon Burn colliery and brickworks. Then came a line from Stella to Towneley (Emma) colliery, Ryton, which went past Stargate colliery. There were staiths on the Tyne at Stella. Beyond Stella there was a third branch, the Stella Coal Company's line from Addison to Stargate colliery; this included the $\frac{3}{4}$ mile long Addison incline up the Tyne valley side. There were large coke ovens as well as a colliery at Addison itself. Sidings linked these to the N & CR line.

68,770 tons of coal and coke were carried from Addison by the NER in 1870. For many years large quantities of coke went from Addison to West Cumberland by the N & CR for the iron industry.

The Stella Coal Co bought the Blaydon Main colliery in 1884 to add to their others west of Blaydon. The Stella—Emma line was two miles long, and it and all the other wagonways mentioned, including the Tanfield line, were mainly single track.

Perhaps more significant was the Garesfield wagonway, a remnant of the historic Main Way. It served sporadic mining activities at Garesfield and Thornley, near Winlaton Mill, until the opening of Lord Bute's Garesfield colliery at High Spen in 1837. The line was extended for about $1\frac{1}{2}$ miles westwards to reach the pit. The route of the line up the side of the Derwent valley from Winlaton Mill was steeply graded.* At Derwenthaugh the line ran to the staiths, but was in time linked to the Redheugh branch facing eastwards.

* a $1\frac{1}{2}$ mile long inclined plane.

In 1889 the Consett Iron Co entered the picture and paid £140,000 for the Garesfield colliery, railway and the staiths. It also began expanding mining activities at Chopwell, two miles south west of High Spen, and during 1891-4 the wagonway was extended to Chopwell where the main event was the opening of Chopwell colliery in 1897. Coke ovens were also opened here, and the increasing traffic on the Garesfield line led to the remodelling in 1899 of Derwenthaugh quay to meet the extra traffic. In 1911 the company reported that the Derwenthaugh staiths 'have for some time been working at or near their full capacity [and] it has been considered necessary to provide for an extension'. This was done in 1912-13. During 1907 the Consett Co acquired the coal royalty at Whittonstall in Northumberland, two miles west of Chopwell, and in 1908 the railway was extended to the Whittonstall 'saw mill drift'.*
The Chopwell—Whittonstall line additionally was electrified, unlike the rest of the Garesfield line, and lasted until 1966, latterly under NCB auspices. The Consett Iron Co opened a cokeworks near Winlaton Mill in 1929, two miles south of Derwenthaugh, and this is still in operation under NCB control. The cokeworks, known officially as Derwenthaugh cokeworks, has ensured the survival of the Main Way line north of this point although it has now lost its section south of this point altogether.

On the fringe of the region was the Team colliery wagonway from the Tyne at Dunston to Team colliery, five miles to the south east, a line dating from the late eighteenth century. The Pelaw Main wagonway was eventually linked to it at Team colliery. The Team line is now closed between Norwood and Lamesley, and the Team Valley trading estate covers this area, but the southern part of the line is still in use and is operated by the NCB. The section includes an incline up the east slope of the valley which crosses the NER main line (once the Team Valley branch) on a girder overbridge spanning the four tracks.

---

* The Whittonstall line was at 2ft 2in gauge.

Page 51: *TANFIELD BRANCH*
(above) *Class U 0–6–2T No 69090 leaves Tanfield East for Bowes Bridge 21 September 1956;* (below) *Fugar incline, showing passing loop*

Page 52: *SNOW SCENES*
(above) *Clearing the line at Waskerley, 1933;* (below) *Carr House West, looking to bank top, with the Consett steelworks on the right*

CHAPTER THREE

Enter the Stockton & Darlington

S & D EXPANSION

From Tyneside we now return to the Consett district in the early 1840s and consider the entry of the Stockton & Darlington Railway from its stronghold in S W Durham. The S & D had for some years been pushing its rails north westwards by means of subsidiary companies. An Act of 15 July 1837 had incorporated the Bishop Auckland and Weardale Railway which was meant to run from the S & D near Bishop Auckland to Frosterley in Weardale, with a branch to Crook, but for various reasons limited itself to connecting Crook with South Church near Bishop Auckland. It opened on 8 November 1843 and was the first railway to serve both Bishop Auckland and Crook. The line was worked by the S & D, and the terminus at Crook was beside the road to Wolsingham.

It then seems that the Derwent Iron Co approached the S & D regarding a possible extension of the new railway to link with the Stanhope & Tyne and so provide the ironworks with a southern outlet. The iron company also offered to sell their railway to the S & D if the latter constructed the extension from Crook. The S & D quickly surveyed the country between Crook and Carr House, which was basically part of the eastern Pennines and by no means likely to lend itself to an easily graded line. Nevertheless negotiations were held with landowners on wayleaves and the most practicable route selected. The major difficulty for a railway lay in the steep slopes which surrounded Crook on the west, north and east, the township lying at the head of the Beechburn valley. Crook lay at about 550ft above sea level while just two miles to the north the land was over 1,000ft above sea level. A inclined plane was the obvious means of surmounting this obstacle to reach the higher land to the north. The route chosen connected with the Derwent Railway at a point on Muggleswick Common at the head of Nanny Mayor's incline, and the new line was to be some eleven miles long, largely crossing a thinly populated upland area. The line was known as the Weardale Extension Railway, and work on its construction was pursued rapidly during 1844. There were numerous cuttings of small length but often of great depth, and the initial incline out of Crook—Sunnyside incline – was $1\frac{3}{4}$ miles long and reached a gradient of 1 in 13. It was, however, the only incline on the line. At Crook the line was built from a point south of the existing station northwards, as it was not easy to extend the line directly from its roadside terminus.

The contractor was James Bray for the mainly single track line and so rapid was construction, using Derwent Iron Co rails, that the line was ready by early 1845. Just north of Crook it connected with the West Durham Railway, which had opened in 1841 and extended eastwards to join the Clarence Railway at Byers Green. A new station was planned at Crook on the extension line, and another station was projected at Tow Law, where an ironworks was planned and colliery development had begun. The junction with the S & T at Nanny Mayor's bank top was named Waskerley Park and it was planned to have sidings and other facilities there. The Derwent Iron Co had agreed to sell its own line to the S & D and the latter merged this with the new railway to form the Wear & Derwent Junction Railway. The headquarters of this subsidiary company of the S & D was to be at Waskerley Park which was the hub of the new system, although a very inhospitable moorland location. Later of course, Waskerley became a well-known railway village, and its railwaymen were renowned for their toughness, a feature bred by the bleak and desolate local environment.

In April 1845 the W & DJ engineer reported on the state of the works as 'not being considered altogether satisfactory on account of the few hands that are now employed', but the railway was opened on 14 May 1845. During this month £1,558 3s 1d (£1,558.15$\frac{1}{2}$) was paid to the Derwent Iron Co for perfect rails to replace faulty ones, while in June it was reported that lime depots, fence walling, gates and a few other items were still not complete. The company apparently restarted the lime production at Stanhope Kilns which the s & t had abandoned in 1839. Both lead and iron ore were to come on to the Weardale Extension Line from Stanhope as well as lime and limestone, while coal and coke from south-west Durham could be sent to Stanhope and the Derwent ironworks. In 1843 the construction costs of the Weardale Extension had been estimated at £60,000 and the cost of land £6,000. At the end of 1845 no less than £125,433 6s 2d (£125,433.31) had been spent on the line and on improvements to the former Derwent Railway. w & dj finances in 1845–6 were not reassuring:

	Receipts	Expenses
1845	£9,723 17s 8d (9,723.88)	£13,406 2s 0d (13,406.10)
1846	£17,167 18s 11d (17,167.94)	£19,405 8s 6d (19,405.43)

By the end of 1846, however, traffic was growing satisfactorily and the future was hopeful and in October 1846 a profit of £187 was made.

Mr Charles Attwood formed the Weardale Iron Co in 1845 to exploit Weardale iron ore resources following the opening of the Weardale Extension Line. Attwood wanted a railway from the w & dj line to Rookhope, centre of the iron activities (and also lead mining). The Weardale Iron Co thus built a five and a half mile line from Parkhead to Rookhope, which reached nearly 1,700ft above sea level and included a steep incline into the Rookhope valley. This opened in 1846. It is interesting to note that the w & dj considered building a branch of its own to Rookhope, and was finally abandoned when the other line was under way. The w & dj directors noted on 19 August 1846 their engineer's 'unfavourable report on Rookhope Branch' owing to 'the nature of the country, inclined planes 1 in 6 and 1 in 8 besides other very considerable works'; they therefore abandoned the 'idea of prosecuting said branch'. The iron company worked their branch with their own rolling stock and the line was of great benefit to the iron, lead and limestone mining around Rookhope. The lead mining industry was at its peak of prosperity; in 1847 the W & DJ had 200 lead wagons. On 21 July 1847 the directors' minutes include the sentence: 'Letters from the proprietors of Rookhope Lead Mines read'.

About one and a half miles north of Sunnyside incline (which was worked by a 50hp stationary engine), Mr Attwood planned his major ironworks, to use Weardale ore, limestone and local coal. His company, the Weardale Iron Co, had an existing works at Stanhopeburn near Stanhope, but the proposed works at Tow Law had the benefits of local coal and greater proximity to the outside world. On 7 January 1846, Attwood attended on a W & DJ committee and 'explained that he expects to have six furnaces ready, and which will be capable of working 300 tons of ironstone per week each in the early part of April next'. A firebrick company also set up at Tow Law, where as a result of these developments and of coal mining a town was to grow up in a hilly area, where population had been very sparse; indeed the only habitation nearby before the railway came was Tow Law farm. Thus the situation here was in some ways similar to that at Carr House (Consett). Tow Law ironworks was thus to give the railway more traffic and the growth of the township gave a greater passenger traffic than would otherwise have occurred.

The W & DJ passenger service commenced on 1 September 1845 from a station on the west side of Hownes Gill (for Consett) to Waskerley Park and thence to Crook. At Waskerley Park the trains connected with a Stanhope—Waskerley service, the trains combining for the journey south. There was as yet no permanent station at Waskerley for it was only on 19 November that the directors agreed 'that two rooms be erected in a plain and substantial manner at Waskerley Park, the one for the purposes of an office, and the other for that of a passenger station'. The trains had of course to negotiate the inclines of Nanny Mayor's and Sunnyside, which did not make for speed. Likewise the Stanhope—Waskerley trains had to negotiate the very steep Crawley and Weatherhill inclines in particular, and traverse a single line that was very busy with mineral traffic. The fortunes of the passenger service will be followed further after a consideration of developments at Waskerley.

WASKERLEY—MOORLAND RAILWAY CENTRE

Waskerley's development as a railway centre from 1845 was rapid. A locomotive depot was established, the shed opening in 1846 and housing four engines – and sidings were laid down as well as various stores and the railway offices. A village grew up to house the workers and eventually had a church and a school. A wagon repair shop was also set up, and in 1847 the importance of the depot was increased when the W & DJ opened a deviation route between Meeting Slacks and Weatherhill to allow locomotives to operate all the way from Sunnyside bank top to Weatherhill. In 1854 the traffic requirements had necessitated the erection of an additional engine shed. Waskerley's status as headquarters of the railway was brief, however, as in 1847 the W & DJ became part of the Wear Valley Railway (which included the Bishop Auckland & Weardale line) and a few months later the S & D leased the Wear Valley Railway for 999 years. In fact it was to absorb its subsidiary fully on 23 July 1858. For the purpose of this narrative, the term Wear & Derwent Junction will be retained for geographical convenience.

FURTHER W & DJ IMPROVEMENTS

In the 1850s various important improvements were made on the W & DJ line. The most important of these were the bridging of Hownes Gill and the replacement of Nanny Mayor's incline by a locomotive-worked deviation. Traffic was increasing during this decade, notably with iron ore traffic from Cleveland to Consett (and Tow Law). Near Crook in 1858 the S & D opened a branch from the Weardale Extension line to serve Stanley Colliery (and later also Wooley Colliery nearby), a line three and a half miles in length. It included a 1 in 16 incline, and came to have a further extension northwards into the Deerness valley, linking with the NER Deerness valley branch. At this same time the S & D considered replacing Sunnyside incline by a locomotive-operated line because the incline was a hindrance to traffic. A route was projected in 1857 and it was intended to obtain parliamentary sanction in 1858, but the Tow Law ironworks objected on the grounds that the new line would pass over ground upon which an extension of the ironworks was planned. The ironworks had not been entirely happy with the railway service in the past – several complaints of delays to traffic had been made at various times – and perhaps this was partly responsible for Attwood's attitude. In any event, the scheme was dropped. In 1857 Sunnyside incline was handling a million tons of traffic annually; it could handle 440 chaldron wagons in twelve hours. Obviously, however, the use of locomotives would speed up the traffic flow and particularly help the passenger train service operation. In 1859 a new S & D engine the *Gazelle* was tried on the incline and managed to take a carriage containing twelve persons up the 1 in 13 and 1 in 16 grades at 5–6mph. A new 0–6–0 engine managed to rush up the bank with four chaldron wagons, but a normal loaded coal train would obviously have great difficulty in climbing the bank. The deviation scheme was later to be revived.

It was in 1856 that the S & D decided to bridge Hownes Gill a few years after considering and rejecting such a course. However some improvement was effected in 1853 when the use of the cradles was dispensed with and three wagons at a time could be worked across the gorge, allowing 550 to 650 wagons daily to cross. By this period the Consett ironworks was taking an increasing traffic of limestone from Stanhope, and traffic was being decidedly hampered by the Hownes Gill operations. William Bouch in 1844 had advocated a 'tension iron viaduct . . . . upon four stone pillars of strong rubble, directing the whole space into five spans of fifty-three yards each, a structure of this kind could not be done for less than £10,000'. The 1856 design was by Thomas Bouch and approved by the S & D in December of that year. It was to be mainly of firebrick, and had twelve semi-circular arches 'supported on piers of light proportions carrying the railway at a height of 150ft above the surface of the ground'. The cost came to £14,000 and about two and a half million white firebricks made at Crook were used. The contractor was John Anderson and the bridge was wide enough only for a single line of rails. It had stone abutments and iron railings along each parapet. The 730ft long structure, of handsome appearance, was completed in seventeen months and opened on 1 July 1858. The S & D directors noted on 11 June 1858 that Mr Anderson had applied for 'a number of wagons laden with iron ore to be passed over the Hownes Gill bridge', and resolved 'that Mr Anderson be referred to the haulage contractors who may arrange the same incurring as little danger as possible'. The old inclines were dismantled and the station nearby closed, a new station opening at Carr House. The two Carr House inclines were closed at the same time to allow locomotives to reach the new station and the ironworks.

Nanny Mayor's incline continued to prevent the use of locomotives from Waskerley eastwards to Cold Rowley. At the latter place a small engine shed was opened in 1845 to work that section of line instead of horses. But the S & D had determined a route for a locomotive worked line to replace Nanny Mayor's by 1856, running from Burn Hill to near Healeyfield. The land for this, the two mile 'Waskerley deviation', was bought early in 1857 and on 28 August 1857 the tender of J. & T. Ridley of Hexham for £13,389 19s 0d (£13,389.95) was accepted for constructing the line. 65lb rails were laid.

Several notable engineering works occurred on the line including a half mile embankment over 60ft high north of Burn Hill and a deep cutting just south of this point, with another cutting partly through rock near Healeyfield. The line was double track, which was extended to Cold Rowley. It was of necessity very steeply graded, reaching 1 in 39, 42, and 47. The date of opening was 4 July 1859, when Nanny Mayor's incline was closed. Waskerley's importance as a locomotive depot was increased, but as a traffic centre the opening had a different result, for now Waskerley was not even on the Crook—Carr House line at all, and traffic from Stanhope to Carr House had to be reversed at the new junction south of Waskerley—Burnhill (originally Burn Hill) junction. Also the passenger service from Crook to Carr House no longer went through Waskerley, and to serve the village a new station was opened just north of Burnhill junction, named Burn Hill (later Burnhill). This was a mile from Waskerley, and besides the village served only a few isolated farms. The new station had two platforms, and the older station at Cold Rowley was given a second platform. Passenger accommodation at Burnhill was rather primitive, but the stone station buildings at Rowley with church-like arched main windows, were very handsome indeed.

A scheme promoted by the Derwent Iron Co, which very nearly succeeded, was the Stockton & Darlington and Newcastle & Carlisle Union Railway plan of 1856. The Derwent ironworks was beginning to use some haematite ore from Cumberland as well as Cleveland ore, the local sources no longer being used, and the Cumbrian ore had to reach Consett via the Newcastle & Carlisle Railway and Gateshead, reaching the Pontop branch at Washington, a most circuitous route. The new scheme was an eight mile cut-off line from the N & CR at Stocksfield to the S & D at Cold Rowley, passing by the fringe of the ironworks en route, and reaching ironworks installations by short branches. It was a heavily-graded line with several large engineering requirements (such as a bridge and embankment across the river Derwent at Ebchester), but it would shorten the journey from Carlisle to Consett by perhaps twenty miles. Apparently neither the N & CR nor the S & D opposed the line, and an act was passed to sanction the scheme on 14 July 1856 (19-20 Vic c 94). A total of £133,000 was authorised to build the line, and work was begun early in 1857. Since it was supported by the Derwent ironworks to a great extent, there seemed to be no likelihood of the plan failing but in November 1857 the collapse of the Northumberland & Durham District Bank, to whom the iron company owed about £1 million, caused cessation of all work. About one mile of railway near the ironworks was completed, but the work was never resumed. By 1859 there was the plan for a Derwent valley railway which overshadowed the Stocksfield project. The scheme was eventually buried by the NER Act of 23 June 1864 (27-8 Vic c 67) which relinquished the powers granted in the 1856 Act. The completed section of line was used by the ironworks.

CROOK—TOW LAW DEVIATION

By 1860 a new station had been erected on the W & DJ line in Crook. This was a squat single-storey brick structure with one through platform for trains in each direction. Soon afterwards the S & D again concluded that the removal of Sunnyside incline would greatly assist traffic between Crook and the north, and again a route for a locomotive worked line was surveyed. An Act was obtained on 3 June 1862 (25-6 Vic c 54) for a four and a half mile line, curving in a spiral fashion north of Crook to surmount the steep valley side. It was, like the incline, basically a single line and it diverged from Crook at the south end of the Stanley branch, swinging from north to north-west, and passing below the old route near Roddymoor before veering south westwards, westwards and back to north westwards. A new station was planned on the new line in Tow Law near the junction with the old. Also at Tow Law a deep cutting was needed to pass through Tow Law Hill itself. The whole line required almost continuous 1 in 51/52 gradients.

The amalgamation of the S & D with the NER in 1863 delayed progress with the line, but in 1865 work went ahead. A junction with the West Durham line was to be put in just north of Crook (West Durham junction), although the former retained its link with the old route to serve Peases West Colliery and coke ovens. Double track was laid to this junction, and there was to be a section of double line at Tow Law, but the line was basically built as single and the prospect of doubling was left 'till the line being built is opened throughout' (directors). There was a large iron traffic between Tow Law ironworks and Tudhoe ironworks near Spennymoor, and also iron ore from the Stanhope area to Tudhoe, using the West Durham Railway.

By the early part of 1867 work had progressed satisfactorily and the station at Tow Law was being built with a temporary single platform and booking office 'so there may be no obstacle in the way of its opening.' The new line was opened for goods traffic on 10 April, and on 17 June Col Rich of the Board of Trade inspected the line regarding passenger traffic, but was not completely satisfied. The S & D secretary, T. MacNay, wrote to the Board on 12 July that 'I will give your Lordships a fresh ten days notice when the Line is ready for re-inspection'. As Col Rich was on the continent, his colleague Col Hutchinson RE, made an inspection on 19 July. MacNay stated that it was pointed out to Hutchinson 'the difficulty of having a double platform at Crook'. He was also informed of the company's intention to have a new station at Tow Law and its belief that this 'seemed to render it unnecessary to double any part of the Line past the present old station'. However the inspector did not like single platforms on busy lines. Nevertheless MacNay commented: 'I would recommend that the new platform at Tow Law be immediately commenced and that a temporary provision be made for booking &c before the Government Inspector is invited to come down again. I see no need of a double platform at this place and I think the Government Inspector concurs in this view.' In October Col Rich agreed 'to waive the carrying out of certain of the said works but insists upon others being adopted in accordance with his recommendations to the Board of Trade'. The end result was

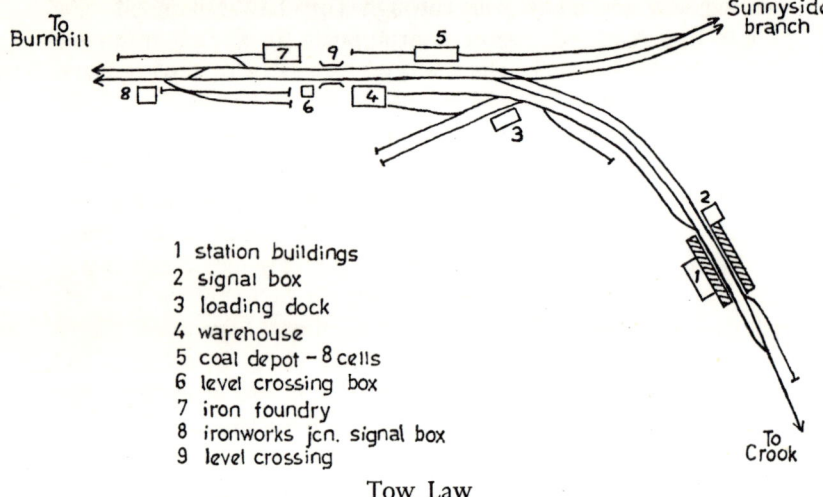

1 station buildings
2 signal box
3 loading dock
4 warehouse
5 coal depot – 8 cells
6 level crossing box
7 iron foundry
8 ironworks jcn. signal box
9 level crossing

Tow Law

that two platforms were made at Tow Law but Crook retained one. MacNay wrote to Col Hutchinson on 31 January 1868 'that Capt Tyler was passing Tow Law this morning and our Manager was in the same train, and pointed out to him what we were seeking to do to arrange for accommodating the passenger traffic upon the new line. He fully concurred in what I suggested in my last communication, and will be quite prepared to give either you or the Board of Trade any information that you may require for your guidance.' At last things were smoothed out and on 27 February 1868 Col Rich returned and approved the line for passenger traffic, the line to be worked by 'train staff'.

It was opened on 2 March and the Sunnyside incline was

closed, although the old route was otherwise retained to serve collieries at Sunnyside bank top and bank foot (Peases West—Roddymoor district). The passenger service using the new line in 1868 consisted of two trains each way daily on weekdays between Crook and 'Carrhouse'. The timetable was:

	am	pm		am	pm
Carrhouse	6.35	3.40	Crook	8.35	4.35
C. Rowley	6.45	3.50	Tow Law	8.50	4.50
Burn Hill	6.55	4.00	Burn Hill	9.05	5.05
Tow Law	7.10	4.10	C. Rowley	9.15	5.15
Crook	7.25	4.25	Carrhouse	9.25	5.25

PASSENGERS ACROSS THE MOORS

A few facts on the changes in the Crook—Consett service are necessary between 1845 and 1868, in view of the number of alterations in this period.

The original service of September 1845 was quickly amended for the winter, with the service from 31 October being curtailed to a Waskerley Park—Crook service only. From 1 April 1846 the full service was restored but later in the year the Stanhope—Waskerley service was cancelled. However passengers from Stanhope had the benefit of a service on the new line from Frosterley, two and a half miles east of the town, to Wear Valley Junction south of Crook, and thence to Bishop Auckland. A horse-bus service was run between Frosterley and Stanhope. This Wear Valley Railway service commenced on 3 August 1847. In April 1846 work on Waskerley Park passenger station was suspended and a new station ordered for Cold Rowley instead. The latter place was on the Darlington—Riding Mill—Corbridge turnpike road and it was proposed to alter the train times from Darlington (there were only two daily each way) if 'some parties' were willing to run an omnibus from Cold Rowley to Riding Mill to connect with Newcastle & Carlisle trains at Riding Mill station – the distance from Cold Rowley to Riding Mill being over twelve miles. Nobody offered to run an omnibus so nothing came of this. Cold Rowley station was in use by 1847, replacing the Hownes Gill terminus about a mile away. Fares on the Crook—Cold Rowley

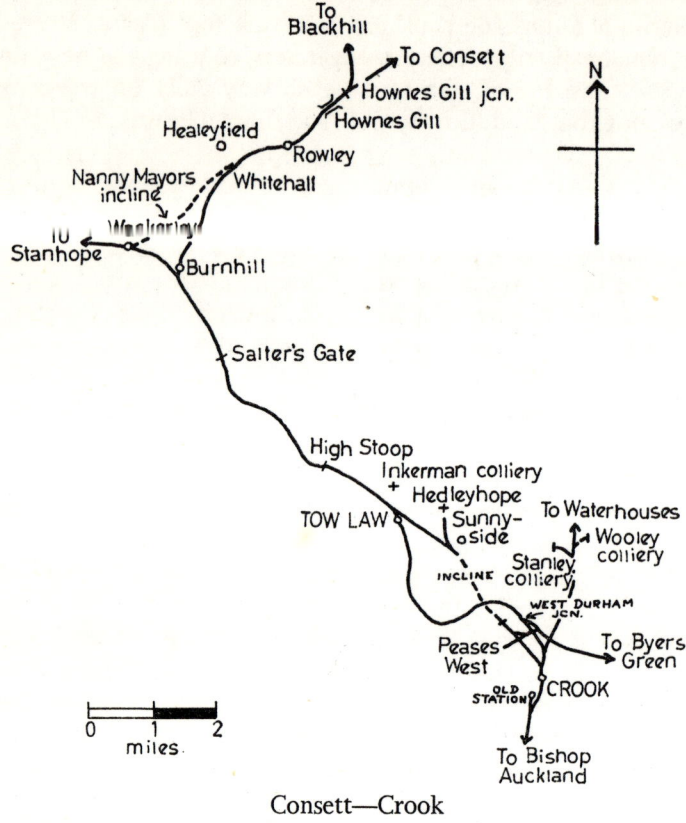

Consett—Crook

trains were two shillings (10p) first class single and one shilling and fourpence (6½p) second class. Before withdrawal the Waskerley—Stanhope fares had been ninepence (4p) and sixpence (2½p) for the two classes. In 1850 a Crook—Cold Rowley train took one and a quarter hours at the quickest in each direction. By 1869, with an altered route, no inclines, a terminus at Benfieldside and three intermediate stations, the time was down to forty-five minutes. In January 1857 the service was again extended to Hownes Gill to a temporary station, and in the following year after the Hownes Gill and Carr House alterations already mentioned, the new terminus was a station at Carr House, much more convenient than ever before for the inhabitants of Consett. In 1859 Burn Hill station opened to

ENTER THE STOCKTON AND DARLINGTON

replace Waskerley for passengers, but it had no goods traffic, this being concentrated at Waskerley.

On 1 October 1868 the short loop line from Hownes Gill to Consett (Lanchester Valley line) was opened, and passenger trains were diverted to Benfieldside, the Carr House station being closed. At the same time Cold Rowley was renamed Rowley.

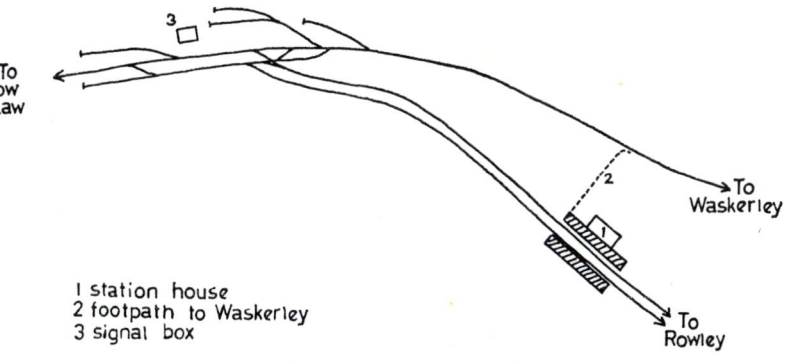

1 station house
2 footpath to Waskerley
3 signal box

Burnhill station and junction

An interesting account of passenger travel between Crook and Cold Rowley in about 1854 is described graphically by W. W. Tomlinson. He mentions the absence of signals and pointsmen on the line. The service consisted of two composite carriages with outside handbrakes attached to a number of mineral wagons. Down Nanny Mayor's bank the carriages ran loose behind a few loaded wagons; similarly down Sunnyside incline the coaches ran loose behind the train. There was a 15mph limitation for locomotives between Waskerley and Sunnyside. Up the Nanny Mayor's incline the regulations allowed for no more than two wagons accompanying the carriages. There was no van for the guard 'who not infrequently at weekends when the carriages happened to be very full, rode outside on the buffer'.

TRAFFIC DEVELOPMENT AND OPERATIONS

There was relatively little change upon the W & DJ line from the 1870s. Traffic in lead declined, as it had in the Weardale area, and the same was true of Weardale iron ore. Limestone traffic remained heavy and grew to a climax during the First World War, due to the increased production at Consett Ironworks. In the early 1880s the Tow Law ironworks was closed down, the Weardale Iron Co concentrating on its Tudhoe plant. This caused some loss of traffic to the W & DJ, but it had a much more serious effect on the West Durham Railway, part of which, near Crook, was actually closed as the line was rather superfluous for other traffic. Some other local mineral traffic developed, such as fluorspar from Stanhope and Rookhope and ganister from quarries between Rowley and Tow Law. These were served by sidings, as at Whitehall (near Healeyfield) and Burnhill. The main use made of the line by the Consett ironworks continued to be the Stanhope limestone traffic; for other traffic, such as iron exported from the works, the line was little used as other routes were orientated towards the main markets, such as Tyneside. The collieries around Tow Law and Crook were served by sidings, and some of the mines produced vast amounts of coal each year. Coke ovens beside some of the mines, such as at Peases West, also gave huge amounts of coke traffic to the railways. Near Tow Law the major pits were the 'Inkerman', 'Black Prince', 'West Thornley', 'Hedleyhope'* and 'Sunnyside' collieries, while Peases West colliery dominated the centre of Crook, and the Stanley and Wooley mines the area to the north. A great deal of coal and coke from these mines and ovens went from West Auckland across the Pennines to Tebay and Penrith by the South Durham & Lancashire Union Railway. Some statistics relating to this traffic may be given. During 1886 the traffic over the NER from some of these mines included 132,619 tons of coal from Sunnyside Colliery, 110,348 tons of coal and coke from Black Prince Colliery and 161,469 tons of coke from Peases West ovens. The latter traffic alone gave receipts of no less than £38,295, and of this particular traffic, about 80,000 tons was sent to Tebay or Penrith for the west coast iron industry. Similarly the West Thornley Colliery at Tow Law owned by the Weardale Iron & Coal Co sent 32,436 tons of coal and coke on to the railway in 1886, and a third of this (coke) went to Tebay. It is hardly surprising

* Reached by the ½mile Hedleyhope colliery branch (1866) – including an incline – from Sunnyside.

ENTER THE STOCKTON AND DARLINGTON 67

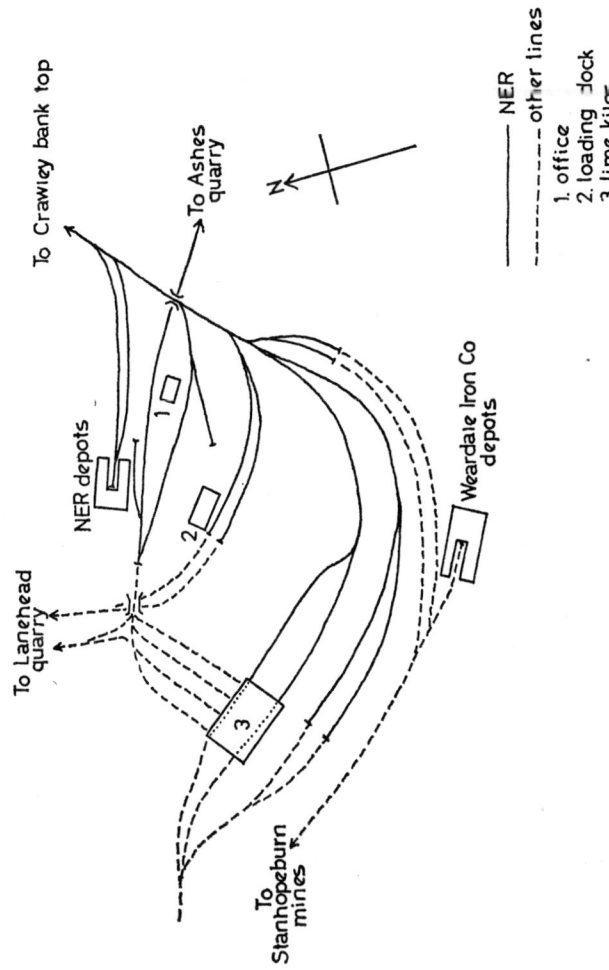

Lines at Stanhope Kilns (Crawley)

that Durham coal and coke trains blasting over Stainmore were a common feature of the period.

Turning to limestone traffic, in 1870 the total lime and limestone traffic from Stanhope was 3,590 tons from the railway owned properties. Near Crawley was the Ashes limestone quarry which received a new lease of life when acquired by the Consett Iron Co in 1901. Previously it had only been worked in a small way. By 1911 limestone traffic from the quarry on the S & T was 105,118 tons, all bound for Consett, and a further 9,470 tons came from Rookhope to Parkhead junction. In addition there was 15,791 tons of gravel traffic at Stanhope Kilns station. Traffic from Crawley continued at this high level up to and after World War I. Other local mineral traffic at this period included 12,212 tons of fluorspar from Stanhope Kilns, and 3,698 tons of lead traffic at Parkhead station (from Rookhope) in 1913. Limestone traffic from Rookhope was 18,013 tons in the same year.

From 1 January 1887 the NER renewed its lease of the Rippon property at Stanhope (now owned by Mrs V. Rippon) for twenty-one years on the old terms (the lease had expired on 1 January 1885): ½d per ton for all limestone worked out of her land (minimum £125 per annum); and 1/8th d per ton for all limestone carried over her land from other places. The NER had powers to terminate this lease at any time after seven years. On 4 August 1887 the NER stated that 'in order to enable the Company to fulfil their obligation to supply the Consett Iron Company with limestone it is necessary that a lease should be taken of the limestone in the copyhold land of Mr Henry Maddison at Stanhope and that he is willing to grant such lease on the following terms: Twenty-one years from 1 January 1887; Rent – ½d per ton for all limestone worked from this land (minimum £20 per annum); 1/8th d per ton for all other limestone carried over.'

Up to 1900 further leasings took place, including six acres from the Rectory of Stanhope in 1896, and the Bishop of Richmond's quarries and the Lanehead quarry (Ecclesiastical Commissioners) in 1898. The latter leases were actually made by Sir David Dale, Bart and Mr Henry Tennant 'on behalf of the NER'. Messrs Ord & Maddison also worked quarries around Stanhope, including the Ashes quarry between 1891 and 1901

Page 69: *WEARDALE EXTENSION*
(above) *Tow Law station from the south, with Sunnyside branch to the right;* (below) *Great Central Railway-designed A5 4-6-2T No 69842 with Tow Law—Darlington train, Crook, 2 April 1954*

Page 70: *LANCHESTER VALLEY BRANCH*
(above) *Knitsley station, looking south east;* (below) *K1 2-6-0 with a special train pauses at Lanchester en route to Consett, 1958*

and the Lanehead quarry, which was exhausted by about 1890. In 1898 the NER sold them rails for their quarries for £701 6s 9d (£701.34). Ord & Maddison also operated the Stanhope lime kilns (which ceased to function at the turn of the century for a long period) and when in 1886–7 the NER replaced the Crawley winding engine and all traffic up the incline ceased for several months, this firm had to rely on their other kilns at Bishopley, Weardale, where production was increased. In fact the NER compensated the firm to some degree by donating £102 10s 0d (£102.50) towards building a new line from Bishopley kilns to the Wear Valley branch to assist meeting the increased activity there.

Ganister (stone) traffic was of some importance between Rowley and Tow Law, and there was a considerable traffic for many years at Rowley in particular. In 1889 the Derwent Ganister Co had a siding laid down at Whitehall near Rowley to their quarry for some £80, and in 1916 the Cross Ganister Co had a siding and loading dock established near Parkhead for £295 and a £10 annual rental. In 1921 the High Houselip Ganister Colliery operated by the Tow Law Ganister & Coal Co obtained permission to work ganister beneath the Weardale Extension Railway, leaving pillars of stone to support the line south of Burnhill. During 1906 Rowley station handled 13,434 tons of ganister, and Tow Law 4,800 tons.

Livestock was always an important traffic at Tow Law due mainly to its local auction mart. In 1898 the number of head of livestock handled by the stations was 130 at Rowley, 9,632 at Tow Law and 7,249 at Crook. Rowley had only a livestock traffic from 1896, while there was no such traffic west of Burnhill. General goods traffic during 1898 was 13,249 tons at Rowley, 15,396 tons at Tow Law and 110,968 tons at Crook. Crook was always pre-eminent in goods totals. Its traffic included bricks, clay and scrap metals, excluding coal. In 1907 the brick traffic was 53,865 bricks at Crook station. At Tow Law there was an iron and steel foundry near the station reached by a siding, possibly a legacy of the former ironworks.

PASSENGER TRAFFIC CONTRASTS

By about 1900 Crook had over 11,000 inhabitants and since

1851 Tow Law had grown from a settlement of 2,000 people to one of 4,000. Rowley was a very small village, while Burnhill was merely a station serving a few farms and Waskerley village. This broad division between the populous and the sparse is reflected in the traffic for 1900:

	Passengers	Receipts (£)
Rowley	9,350	356
Burnhill	5,641	222
Tow Law	41,991	2,707
Crook	103,876	4,684

In 1907 the Crook—Consett (Blackhill) service consisted of basically five trains from Crook northwards and four in the opposite direction, only a small increase in service over the preceding 30 years. All these trains ran to and from Darlington. In addition there was a regular afternoon departure from Tow Law to Darlington. Additional trains consisted of a Wednesday and Saturday Bishop Auckland—Tow Law train each way, a Monday, Thursday and Saturday Crook—Tow Law morning extra, and a Saturday only Blackhill—Tow Law afternoon train. The timetable advertised connections with the service to and from Newcastle at Blackhill, and most trains offered good connections in this respect. Up to 1923 there was little change in the service, when there were basically four trains each way between Crook and Blackhill, and a number of extras serving only the populous Tow Law—Crook section.

A VETERAN REPLACED

In 1916 it was decided to replace the old S & T winding engine at Weatherhill, which had given over eighty years of service. At the same time some improvement to the siding accommodation was to be made, at a total estimated cost of £3,250. Nothing was done during the war period, but in 1919 the changes were finally made, a new engine house being erected on a new site. The work was completed by November at a cost of £4,046 5s 10d (£4,046.29). No doubt the very heavy mineral traffic, especially of limestone, had imposed a strain on the veteran engine which had performed eighty-five years of service by the time it was replaced.

CHAPTER FOUR

To Consett via Lanchester

CLEVELAND IRON ORE TO CONSETT

By about 1855 the expanding Derwent Iron Co at Consett was beginning to use increasing amounts of iron ore from west Cumberland and north Yorkshire (Cleveland) instead of the local ore, which had become increasingly uneconomic to work. The Cleveland ore reached Consett over the Stockton & Darlington line via Crook and Waskerley. As this traffic was increasing the NER wished to take a share in it. It therefore planned its own railway from Consett to the south, choosing the obvious and most practicable route south eastwards along the river Browney valley (including a tributary valley) to Durham. At Durham the NER was already constructing its branch from the main line at Leamside to Bishop Auckland through Durham and Brancepeth, a line which was opened to traffic during 1857. The projected route to Consett could most conveniently join the Bishop Auckland branch at a point west of Durham where the river Browney was bridged by the wooden Relly Mill viaduct. A junction could be made at the west end of this bridge and the line to Consett could turn off in a west north westerly direction and follow the river through Lanchester.

The NER surveyed a route for the line – named the Lanchester Valley branch – and drew up a Bill which was presented to Parliament during the 1857 session. It received the Royal Assent on 13 July 1857 (20 – 1 Vic c 46). The line was about twelve and a quarter miles in length, running from Relly Mill viaduct (one mile west of Durham) to the Derwent ironworks, through the Browney valley, the village of Lanchester, and north westwards along a tributary valley past Knitsley, and so on to Consett. The population of this whole region was not great but since the main consideration was to supply the ironworks with iron ore this was not important. The Act sanctioned a capital of £120,000 and the powers extended over five years.

AN EARLY SETBACK AND NO PROGRESS

The whole plan was soon jeopardised by the collapse of the Northumberland & Durham District Bank on 27 November 1857. Just as this event ended the Cold Rowley—Stocksfield railway scheme (as mentioned in Chapter 3), so all progress with regard to the Lanchester Valley branch ceased. With the future of the ironworks in doubt the NER cautiously decided to shelve its plan for the new railway. The Consett Ironworks was kept in operation in the next few years by means of financial help both from the NER and S & D, who obviously considered that it was in their interests that the iron industry should continue at Consett rather than for dereliction and depopulation to occur. At this time the ironworks had eighteen blast furnaces, and there were three separate sections of ironworks at Consett, Crookhall and Bradley; a foundry at Leadgate; collieries at Bradley, Iveston, Crookhall, Delves and Consett collieries; and a brickworks and several miles of company connecting railways and sidings.

The situation was unresolved by the end of 1859 and the NER decided to abandon the scheme as it had many other commitments. It discussed its abandonment proposal with its rival, the S & D in November, and decided to prepare notices of abandonment. But then the situation changed. On 15 December the Court of Chancery sanctioned an arrangement by which the Derwent ironworks could be carried on, and immediately, on 16 December, the NER made a decision to build the railway. This decision was made so swiftly that it seems likely that the railway rivalry (see Chapter 5) developing in north-west Durham at this time influenced the NER Board. An abandonment Bill in the process of being drawn up was therefore dropped.

PROGRESS TO OPENING

In February 1860 the directors ordered the branch to be staked out as soon as practicable, and decided to withdraw a Bill which had been prepared to extend the time limit for completing the line. Soon afterwards, however, it was resolved to let this Bill go forward and it was presented during the year. The Bill was passed by the House of Commons but failed in the Lords, owing to hostility to the NER by rival railway interests. In July a supply of 1,500 tons of rails weighing 66lb per yard was ordered for the line, and in September tenders were invited for the construction. The NER estimate of the costs of the railway was:

Works	£69,227
Land	18,360
Rails etc.	20,342
	£107,929

In October, nine tenders for the work were received, ranging from £66,169 16s 2d (£66,169.81) up to £89,934. The lowest tender, that of Messrs B. C. Lawton of Newcastle, was accepted. The line was to be basically a single track for its whole length. The gradient was steady from Relly Mill to Lanchester, being for the most part no steeper than 1 in 132 (with a length of 1 in 66 just south east of Lanchester) and having several miles of 1 in 220, 240, 264, 660 and level. From Lanchester to Consett, however, it stiffened to almost a continuous 1 in 80 ($1\frac{1}{4}$ miles) and 1 in 60 ($3\frac{1}{4}$ miles). The seven miles south east of Lanchester constituted the section where the line followed the broad Browney valley for most of the distance. North west of Lanchester the line had to climb steeply to reach the ironworks on its upland site, Lanchester being at about 400ft above sea level and Consett at nearly 800ft.

Most of the engineering was not of very great scale, but a notable exception was the very large viaduct planned at Hurbuck, one and a half miles north west of Lanchester. This was necessary at the point where the railway had to cross from one side of the Knitsley burn valley to the other on its climb to Consett.

Work on the line started in February 1861 and advanced rapidly during that year. The contractor brought stone from Benton quarry north of Newcastle by rail to Relly Mill. The earthworks were greatest on the Lanchester—Consett section, and included several cuttings through rock. There was also a short embankment fringing the deep valley south of Hownes Gill and another to the south east across a shallow valley. Several fairly large bridges were needed, including three across the Browney south east of Lanchester, and two road bridges in Lanchester itself. Wood, stone, or iron girders were used in the construction. The 700ft long Knitsley viaduct was mainly of wood, and had thirty-six spans of 20ft each and was a timber trestle structure of fragile appearance. It reached 70ft above the valley floor of the Knitsley burn beside the small hamlet of Hurbuck, and had sharp curves at both ends. There is an illustration of the viaduct in Tomlinson's *North Eastern Railway* (p. 608).

By the beginning of 1862 the line was almost complete. The stations erected over a mile from the village of Witton Gilbert and at Lanchester, Knitsley and Consett were rather Scottish in appearance by virtue of their station houses. These were built of faced stone blocks with stepped gable roofs of handsome appearance, a design not used on any other Durham line. The actual station buildings were constructed mainly of wood. The stations had one platform befitting a single line. Near Consett the new railway had a short tunnel perhaps thirty feet long through the embankment of the S & D – formerly the Stanhope & Tyne line – which carried the latter from Hownes Gill to Carr House bank top. There was no connection between the two lines.

In August 1862 the Board of Trade sanctioned opening of the line 'but required points and signals at the junction to be connected and indications to be fixed at all facing points'. The line was to be worked by 'train staff'.

OPENING

The Lanchester Valley branch was officially opened for traffic on 1 September 1862, which was after the time allowed by the Act of 1857. The first passenger train on the opening day was the 6.20am from Durham, which left with six passengers and proceeded to Consett, stopping at all stations. It returned to Durham with forty passengers. At 12.20pm a special opening train departed from Durham and among the passengers were the contractor Mr Lawton, the local NER passenger superintendent Mr Eglinton, and various local dignitaries. The *Durham Chronicle* described the progress of the train graphically, its reporter writing of scenes from the train, such as the 'numerous fields rich with golden grain', and 'in many places labourers busy in the harvest field suspended their operations for a moment and gazed with evident interest and curiosity at the passing train'. The report continued: 'The cattle and sheep browsing in the pastures did not exhibit the serene indifference generally manifested by animals which have become accustomed to the noise and rattle of the locomotive.'

At Lanchester the train was greeted by a crowd of onlookers and then departed on its climb to Consett. 'The train passed through a picturesque valley studded with plantations of fir trees and at length arrived by a sharp curve upon a magnificent timber bridge which crosses over a deep glen. This structure is of vast strength but it has an extremely light and graceful appearance.' After crossing the viaduct 'a change came o'er the spirit of the scene and the green pastures and waving fields of grain became intermixed with furze clad hills and heathery slopes. The train next passed through a cutting of solid rock and in a short time arrived at Knitsley station. Here there was nothing to do in the way of rejoicing, the station apparently being situated at some distance from any population. Beyond Knitsley there was a wide expanse of scenery of which plantations formed the predominating feature.'

When the train reached Consett the celebration party 'partook of champagne and co' at the house of Mr Priestman, one of the managers of the ironworks. At a luncheon on the same day at Lanchester the health was drunk of T. E. Harrison, the NER engineer, who had also been instrumental in the construction of the Stanhope & Tyne railway some thirty years previously. Speeches were made hoping that the new line would have the same effect in opening out industry in its area as the S & T had done. When the latter opened, there had been four coal mines working near it whereas now there were forty-five. Mr Charlton of the Consett ironworks said that 'the new line of railway would be a great relief to the Pontop line of railway, but he was not so sure that it would very materially benefit the Consett Ironworks unless the North Eastern directors should consent to a reduction in their present rates'. (Hear! hear! and laughter).

The railway had cost nearly £70,000 to construct and the government inspector who had examined it had expressed 'unqualified admiration of the substantial manner in which the works had been carried out'.

CONSETT TERMINUS

The Lanchester Valley terminus at Consett was about half a mile north of the tunnel through Carr House west embankment. The station was unfinished when the line opened because the NER had been in two minds as to whether it should be a permanent or a temporary structure in view of a proposal to have a station at Blackhill to the north. The sanctioning of the Blaydon & Conside (later Blaydon & Consett) branch strengthened support for a Consett station sited at Blackhill, as it was better placed to serve the growing urban sprawl of Consett and Blackhill.

However the NER decided in 1862 to build the Lanchester Valley terminus as a permanent station but in the event it was to be permanent for only five years, and it was replaced by a station at Blackhill in 1867. It was also decided in 1862 to construct the one and a half miles of line from Consett northwards to the Durham road at Blackhill, which would serve the Shotley Bridge ironworks at Blackhill and a colliery nearby. Both the 'permanent' terminus (which cost over £500) and the extension line were built by B. C. Lawton. The extension line was single track and included a deep cutting

TO CONSETT VIA LANCHESTER

partly through rock for over half a mile. The gradients were 1 in 63/66.

TRAFFIC DEVELOPMENT AND OPERATIONS

The initial passenger service on the line consisted of three trains daily each way with none on Sundays. In 1863 departures were at 6.20am, 12.20pm and 5.40pm from Durham, and at 8.0am, 1.45pm and 7.55pm from Consett, and the journey time was forty-five minutes. The timetable advertised connections at Durham for trains to Newcastle and Sunderland. It was, of course, a circuitous route from Consett to reach Newcastle via Durham, Leamside and Pelaw, but the line from Consett to Blaydon and Newcastle via the Derwent valley was already sanctioned.

In October 1862 the NER decided to build an engine shed for four locomotives beside Durham station, and obviously the presence of the new railway to Consett was a factor in this decision. The shed opened in 1864 and provided goods and passenger engines for all the lines around Durham, including the Lanchester Valley branch.

Cleveland iron ore reached Consett by journeying up the main line to Leamside and reversing there to reach Durham. Relly Mill junction faced towards Durham and it was some years before the Consett line had junctions in other directions at this location. The products of Consett ironworks went along the line as the most convenient route southwards. The period of control by the NER (and S & D up to 1863) ended in April 1864 when a new company, the Consett Iron Co Ltd, took over operation of the ironworks (effective from 15 August 1864). The output of the works at this period was about 80,000 tons of pig iron and 45,000 tons of finished iron per annum, and the most important commodities were iron plates and rails, the NER buying a lot of the latter. A certain proportion of this traffic used the Lanchester line.

Coal mining activities soon followed the opening of the railway, particularly around Lanchester, Witton Gilbert, and areas to the south east, and increased in importance during the 1870s. The iron ore traffic from Cleveland declined after the 1870s but imported ore from Sunderland was a substitute.

In 1874 the Consett Iron Co began to open out its coal royalty at Langley Park beside the railway near Witton Gilbert station. A coke works was also established. The Consett directors reported on 2 September 1876 that the coalfield 'now appears likely to prove of excellent coking quality. Before the end of 1876 the works will be sufficiently completed to allow of a considerable quantity of coke being suitable for sale.' Another important colliery was that at Bearpark, $2\frac{1}{2}$ miles south east of Witton Gilbert station, and there were two mines near Lanchester, that is, Lanchester and Malton collieries. The mining villages on the high land to the north east of the Browney valley, including Burnhope, Holmside, Sacriston and Edmondsley, were of course connected by wagonways to the S & T line, but for passenger trains used Lanchester or Witton Gilbert stations. The Edmondsley district also had the choice of the Team Valley branch passenger service from 1868, at Plawsworth station, this line offering a direct link to Newcastle. (The Team Valley line ran from Gateshead to Newton Hall junction, north of Durham, where it joined the Bishop Auckland branch; in 1872 it became a section of the 'new main line' from Gateshead to Ferryhill.)

Traffic had grown to such an extent by the early 1870s that the NER decided to double part of the Lanchester line. On 8 March 1872 doubling of the line between Rilly Mill [sic] and Aldin Grange was agreed upon, at an estimated cost of £4,000. Hardly had this been done when the development of Langley Park made it advisable to continue double track as far as that place. On 29 May 1874 this was decided upon, the estimated cost being £18,000. Ten tenders for this work were received on 8 October 1874 and that of J. C. Tone of Sunderland for £8,455 was accepted. On 3 December it was reported that the Consett Iron Co had applied for a connecting line between Langley Park colliery and the NER branch, and this was assented to, the cost to be borne by the NER and not to exceed £700. The length of this double track section was 3 miles 25 chains, and it established $4\frac{1}{4}$ miles of double track on the branch. The work necessitated new double track bridges, such as the two across the river Browney just south east of Witton Gilbert. Iron girders were prominent features of the new bridges. (In 1909–11 the superstructure of nine bridges between Aldin

Grange and Lanchester was renewed, steel girders replacing cast iron chiefly; many were thus rebuilt by the Cleveland Bridge & Engineering Co of Darlington.) As a result of the widening of the line, Witton Gilbert station received a second platform that was staggered and not opposite the original.

It was resolved on 26 June 1874 to 'rearrange' the sidings at Witton Gilbert at an estimated cost of £262.

In 1875 it was decided to lengthen Lanchester station platform and the cattle dock there was removed and resited, while at Knitsley the platform was lengthened in 1876 by thirty-one yards and an extra siding laid down for goods for some £125.

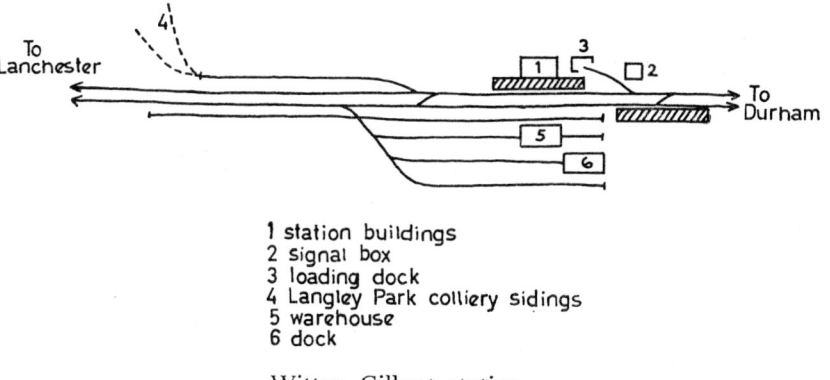

1 station buildings
2 signal box
3 loading dock
4 Langley Park colliery sidings
5 warehouse
6 dock

Witton Gilbert station

Again during 1875 it was resolved to improve the access from the Lanchester Valley branch southwards, mainly to allow traffic from Consett to run on to the 1872 line from Relly Mill to Hoggersgate (later Tursdale) junction, Ferryhill. Junctions were also made with the Bishop Auckland branch facing south, and the Deerness Valley branch. On 18 November 1875 tenders were received and that of W. Scott of South Shields was accepted for £22,355 (NER estimate £22,996 2s 8d: £22,996.13½). The new spurs and junctions were completed and opened in November 1877, thereby greatly improving the accessibility of the branch from the south. On the branch near Relly Mill, Baxter Wood No 1 signal box controlled movements towards Durham (Relly Mill jcn,) and the Ferryhill line (Bridge House jcn). Baxter Wood No 2 signal box was beside the new connecting spur to the Bishop Auckland branch facing south and the Deerness Valley line (Deerness Valley junction signal box). The panorama of lines thus created was spread out on each side of a road bridge known as Stone Bridge which was about half a mile south of Relly Mill junction.

The Lanchester branch was doubled as far as a point just north west of Lanchester station by 1883, thus completing double track over the busiest section. There was little colliery activity between Lanchester and Consett, and the Knitsley district remained the least populous or industrial of any beside the railway. Lanchester received a second platform while Knitsley was always to have only one. Needless to add, if the line from Lanchester to Consett south junction had been considered for doubling, there would have been the problem of widening Knitsley viaduct in particular. Thus this section always remained single, and trains exchanged tokens at the signal boxes at Consett South and Lanchester.

A new passenger station was opened on the line in 1883 to serve the colliery village of Bearpark. The station was named Aldin Grange until 19 June 1884, after which it was renamed 'Aldin Grange for Bearpark'. It cost about £500 and was built by W. C. Atkinson of Stockton, whose tender was accepted in November 1882. As the station was only a mile from Baxter Wood it was considered close enough to Durham not to require goods facilities, and nothing was done in this respect until 1900, when a coal depot was opened. An interesting fact is that as far back as August 1861, while the railway was under construction, the NER had received a memorial from the local 'land owners, mill owners, farmers, tradesmen and others' which stated 'the necessity and ultimate advantage of having a Depot for coal, stones, lime, manure, and merchandize near the crossing at Alden Grange'; such would be 'a great boon to the neighbourhood, there being no Depot nearer than at Gilligate [sic] Station in Durham'.

There had long been a local movement to obtain the station, led by the Rev A. W. B. Granville. For example on 27 February 1879 the NER had considered 'letters from Rev. A. W. B. Granville transmitting resolutions asking for a passenger station at Aldin Grange Bridge', and resolved 'that the former decision declining to grant this application be adhered to'.

Soon after opening the new station was improved and in

July 1883 the NER resolved to extend the waiting room accommodation and provide a new booking office for over £100.

In the 1880s goods traffic on the line was greatest at Lanchester and Witton Gilbert, the main centres of population, and much smaller at Knitsley. Livestock traffic was significant at Lanchester, the village having a livestock mart. Goods traffic in 1886 and 1896 was as follows:

	1886		1896	
	tons	head	tons	head
Knitsley:				
Goods & Minerals	1,043		678	
Livestock		221		114
Lanchester:				
Goods & Minerals	6,577		54,988	
Livestock		3,964		1,919
Witton Gilbert:				
Goods & Minerals	15,258		19,265	
Livestock		755		1,539

The very high traffic in 1896 at Lanchester is accounted for by an abnormally heavy coal traffic at the station in that year. In 1897 its goods and mineral traffic there was only 17,723 tons.

In the 1900s the most important items of goods traffic handled at the stations were bricks, manure and creosote tarpitch at Lanchester, creosote etc at Witton Gilbert, and a small stone traffic at Knitsley. There was a small timber traffic at all stations (except Aldin Grange) in the period up to World War I. At Knitsley this traffic in 1913 was 423 tons and the timber yard was reached by a siding from the station.

There was a continually large coal and coke traffic, especially from Bearpark and Langley Park. In 1886 the Bearpark colliery traffic was 53,437 tons of coal and coke, providing revenue to the NER of £8,277, while coke from Langley Park reached 91,742 tons with a revenue of £9,772. Malton colliery, south east of Lanchester, gave 9,232 tons of coal traffic in the first half of 1886 (NER receipts £1,146), the coal being used for industrial uses, whereas the bulk of the Bearpark and Langley Park traffic was for iron-making purposes. S. A. Sadler's Malton colliery had its siding link with the Lanchester line, facing

Durham, and Malton colliery junction signal box controlled the junction. There was initially one 'cross-over' on the Lanchester line for Malton traffic, but in 1897 another was laid for £135.

In 1929 the railway authorities suddenly became aware of the fact that there were no safety points for $1\frac{1}{2}$ miles on the 1 in 80 section between Knitsley and Lanchester to derail runaways. A pair of safety points and sand-drag were therefore installed 370yd north of Lanchester station, worked from the station signal box (cost £409).

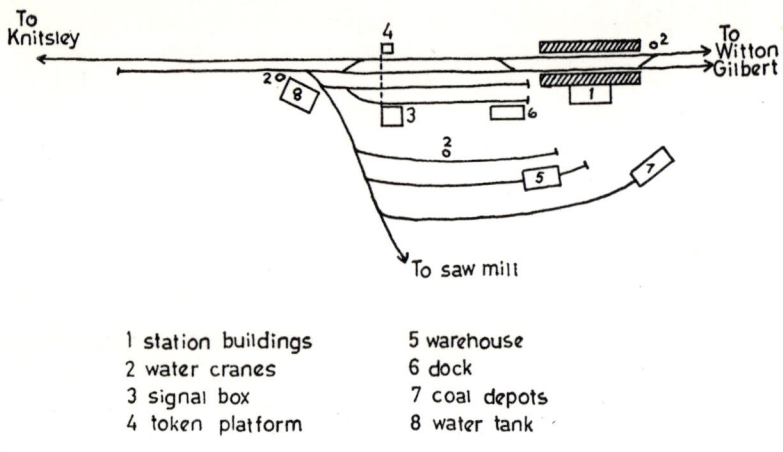

1 station buildings
2 water cranes
3 signal box
4 token platform
5 warehouse
6 dock
7 coal depots
8 water tank

Lanchester station

GROWTH OF PASSENGER TRAFFIC

When the Blaydon & Consett branch opened for passenger traffic on 2 December 1867, the passenger services on this line were amalgamated with the Lanchester Valley service as the 'Consett branch' passenger service. The station at Blackhill, named Benfieldside after the parish in which it lay, became the station for Consett, and the Lanchester Valley station was closed 'much to the disappointment of the inhabitants of that neighbourhood' according to the *Newcastle Courant*. This was not surprising as it meant that passengers in that vicinity now had a walk of over one and a half miles to reach the station. There remained three trains each way (Newcastle—Benfieldside—Durham) with none on Sundays, and there were only

TO CONSETT VIA LANCHESTER

first and second class coaches. Two of the trains each way were government trains. Benfieldside station had several later changes of name: It was renamed Consett on 1 November 1882 and in April 1885 became Consett & Blackhill. On 1 May 1896 it was renamed Blackhill in anticipation of the opening of a new station at Consett itself (Carr House) on the S & T line. Benfieldside had a number of sidings and handled much traffic for the Consett ironworks. A diagram of the station is included in Chapter 5. Blackhill drift colliery was not far from the station, while paper traffic came from the Shotley Grove paper mill and there was flour traffic from Shotley flour mill. The latter rented a grain store at the station from 1883 at £10 pa. Benfieldside was the interchange point for trains to Crook and beyond from 1868, while in 1896 the Newcastle—Annfield Plain—Blackhill service began.

Passenger traffic and receipts at Lanchester Valley stations in 1885 and 1900 were as follows:

	Passengers		Receipts (£)	
	1885	1900	1885	1900
Knitsley	3,935	5,130	211	237
Lanchester	27,464	38,615	1,528	2,167
Witton Gilbert	25,073	47,096	946	1,862
Aldin Grange	17,810	36,405	325	699

Much of the traffic at Aldin Grange was of people travelling into Durham, a fact indicated by the receipts.

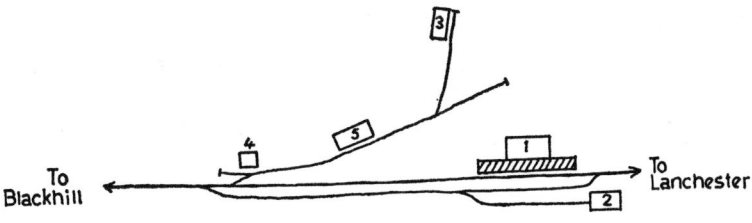

1 station buildings
2 coal depots
3 saw mill dock
4 signal box
5 loading dock

Knitsley station

The service on the branch was slowly improved but the line had fewer trains than its northern extension to Newcastle from the 1870s. It was nearly forty years before a regular Sunday service was introduced in 1899, but there were Sunday trains north of Benfieldside in the 1870s. In 1886 there were five trains each way between Durham and Benfieldside on weekdays and an extra train each way on Saturdays. By 1907 there were seven trains on weekdays from Blackhill to Durham and six in the opposite direction, as well as two trains each way on Sundays. The only change by 1914 was that there was an extra train on weekdays each way between Durham and Lanchester, serving the busiest part of the line. This left Lanchester at 7.35pm and returned from Durham at 10.40pm but the return journey was on Wednesdays and Saturdays only (and from 8 July 1914 only on Saturdays). The Blackhill and Newcastle trains left Durham at evenly spread intervals—at 7.22am, 10.02, 12.00, 2.34, 5.18 and 8.38pm, and trains to Durham left Blackhill at 7.13am, 8.58, 10.02, 12.59, 3.29, 6.11 and 8.24pm. The Sunday trains left Durham at 7.35am and 7.27pm, and from Blackhill to Durham at 8.29am and 8.18pm. The journey time for passenger trains on the branch was about forty minutes.

Coal mining had led to an increase in the population in the Browney valley at certain places quite considerably by the 1900s. Lanchester township's population had risen from 2,398 in 1861 to 4,640 by 1901, and Witton Gilbert had increased from 2,098 to 5,300 in the same period. Bearpark had 1,609 inhabitants in 1901. Certain districts remained mainly rural, and Langley parish covering 2,378 acres north of the Browney between Lanchester and Witton Gilbert had only 291 inhabitants in 1901. The largely rural area of Greencroft covering 3,050 acres north west of Lanchester had a mere 398 inhabitants. The colliery activities were thus rather localised within mainly rural areas.

During World War 1 Knitsley station was closed as an economy measure from 1 February 1916 for passengers and 1 December 1916 for goods, and was not to be reopened until 1925. It had always had a small traffic, as may be judged from a comparison of total traffic receipts and expenses in 1906:

Page 87: *IN THE DERWENT VALLEY* (*1*)
(above) *Class O No 1788 with Blackhill train at the newly opened High Westwood station, July 1909;* (below) *a Class VI 2–6–2T heads a train to Newcastle on Ebchester embankment, with Chopwell on the other side of the valley*

Page 88: *IN THE DERWENT VALLEY* (2)
(above) *NER steam auto car bound for Newcastle, arriving at High Westwood;* (below) *Blackhill signal box; token exchange point*

	Receipts (£)	Expenses (£)
Knitsley	502	216
Lanchester	3,817	535
Witton Gilbert	4,301	594
Aldin Grange	800	239

Minor alterations at stations included the construction of a station master's house at Aldin Grange for an estimated £390 in 1902–3 (a two-storey red-brick structure with slate roof); and alterations and additions to the stationhouse and buildings at Knitsley in 1911 for £450.

Not strictly on the branch but used by its passenger trains, was the Relly Mill viaduct across the river Browney. This was a wooden bridge like others on the original Bishop Auckland branch, and on 1 October 1896 it was decided to replace it by a brick structure for some £9,000. The tender of D. Shanks of Glasgow was accepted for £10,061 19s 4d (£10,061.96) and the the work was carried out in the following year.

NER BUS SERVICES

In November 1912 the NER began to run road buses from Durham to the Sacriston area to compete with private road services. Sacriston was two miles from Witton Gilbert station and only four from Durham itself, and there were over 2,000 people in that district. The service ceased during World War I (1915) but recommenced in 1920. The service started on 11 October 1920 was from Durham to Langley Park via Sacriston and Witton Gilbert, and on 1 June 1921 a new service began between Durham and South Moor (Stanley) via Lanchester and Annfield Plain. It is hardly surprising that the railway traffic declined in this period, as may be seen from the following figures:

| | Passengers | |
	1920	1921
Lanchester	50,001	32,729
Witton Gilbert	74,292	39,982
Aldin Grange	54,599	36,798

90   THE RAILWAYS OF CONSETT AND N.W. DURHAM

Receipts at Witton Gilbert showed a very substantial fall from £5,117 in 1920 to £2,950 in 1921. Worse was to follow and within ten years the roads had claimed so much of the traffic that the service was probably barely profitable.

BLACKHILL MPD

Originally named Benfieldside, this motive power depot was opened in 1876 at a cost of about £961. It had been built mainly to house an engine for the Crook passenger service to obviate a locomotive having to travel to and from Waskerley shed seven miles away. It housed two engines and was only to assume other than very local significance when the sheds at Waskerley and Annfield Plain were closed in 1940. The MPD was located just south of the site of the old Lanchester Valley station (where the station house still remains), and was latterly named Consett (officially 'Consett Junction'). It had a locomotive allocation of two 0–6–2Ts in 1923, twelve engines in 1941 and sixteen engines by 1947.

END OF KNITSLEY VIADUCT

The long wooden viaduct at Knitsley cost £440 to paint in

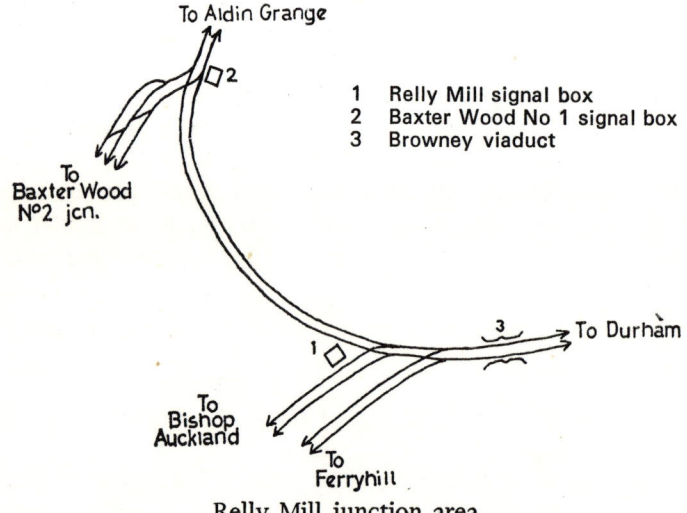

1 Relly Mill signal box
2 Baxter Wood No 1 signal box
3 Browney viaduct

Relly Mill junction area

1874 and 1889. By 1915 it was in need of major repairs; a NER minute of 18 March 1915 stated that the bridge required 'renewal' but an embankment was to be formed instead as allowed by the NER Act of 1913. At the same time it was intended to improve the curve at the south end of the bridge, the estimate of the costs involved being £16,000. Because of the war the only work done in 1915-16 was the extension of two occupation bridges at each end of the viaduct for over £1,000, but during 1919 the long embankment was formed, burying the decaying trestle bridge. The work was finished during 1920, and thus disappeared one of the main railway sights in county Durham.

CHAPTER FIVE

The Struggle for the Derwent Valley

LNWR ROUTE TO NEWCASTLE?

In 1859 while the NER was wondering whether to abandon the plan for its Lanchester Valley branch as described in Chapter 4, the company was faced with a project aimed at reaching Newcastle from the south west. This project utilised the valley of the river Derwent and had every appearance of being backed by powerful railway interests, particularly the London & North Western Railway, and also the North British Railway. Although the NER had no monopoly of Newcastle it felt every reason to regard it as one of the major hubs of its network. The company was even at that time in the process of working out amalgamation details with its fellow user of Newcastle Central station, the Newcastle & Carlisle Railway. There soon developed great rivalry for a railway in the Derwent valley, as the NER was forced to seek its own line through the district to forestall the rival plan.

In 1844 during the 'Railway Mania' there had been a plan for a Newcastle, Shotley and Weardale Junction Railway which had come to nothing. This scheme envisaged a railway in the Derwent valley linking the N & CR with the S & D (former S & T). The 1859 scheme named the Newcastle & Derwent Valley Railway, was essentially similar to this plan in its basic details, being a line planned to run from the south end of Scotswood Bridge (N & CR) to Hownes Gill (S & D). The route of the line closely followed the river Derwent, climbing steadily through Rowlands Gill, Westwood, Benfieldside and Blackhill, terminating at the east end of Hownes Gill viaduct. The route was of necessity steeply graded for its thirteen and a half miles, and had been surveyed by Thomas Bouch. The great threat of the scheme to the NER was in that it was supported by the LNWR, who saw it as a part of the new Liverpool—Newcastle route, using also the South Durham & Lancashire Union Railway from Tebay to West Auckland (then under construction) and the S & D by running powers. The S & D also were initially favourable to the scheme, as they had some hopes of running their own trains into Newcastle, while the North British company were in a period of rapid expansion and saw no reason to limit their ambitions to Northumberland in N E England.

The N & DV promoters intended to seek running powers from Scotswood Bridge into Newcastle, and to have their own station just west of the central station at 'a station to be formed at or adjoining the western end of the present station of the Newcastle & Carlisle Railway Company in or near Neville Street'. The plan for the line was deposited with the local authorities in November 1859, but they were not alone. The NER had rushed its surveyors into the Derwent valley as soon as it knew of the project, and in a remarkably swift time it had prepared its own route, and the plans were deposited at the same time as the rival ones. Both parties were seeking parliamentary sanction for their line during 1860, and the struggle was likely to be bitter.

It was obviously crucial for the NER to keep powerful rival interests out of one of the centres of their system, and it led to great difficulty in amalgamating with the N & CR, despite the wishes of most shareholders and directors of that company. As the N & DV plan relied on running powers into Newcastle over the N & CR, the promoters and supporters of the scheme obviously opposed the plans of amalgamation between NER and N & CR. In fact during 1859 a working agreement between the two companies had been upset soon after being established, largely due to North British interference in the Carlisle company's affairs.

So the year 1860 was a critical one for the NER. The Lanchester Valley situation had at last been resolved, and preparations were advancing for its construction, and the NER envisaged its own Derwent valley branch as a continuation northwards of that line from Consett. The NER Derwent valley branch was similar to the N & DV scheme in its route, even to the extent of having a junction with the N & CR at the south end of Scotswood Bridge, and seeking running powers over the three miles to Newcastle. The N & CR of course supported the NER and opposed the N & DV plan, while the latter opposed the NER—N & CR amalgamation attempt, a Bill for which was also presented in 1860.

When the N & DV Bill was ready to go into parliamentary committee the promoters suddenly discovered that the Stockton & Darlington Company was hesitating to support their plan. This was undoubtedly a result of the NER secretly approaching the S & D with a proposition for amalgamation, a move which soon gained favour with most of the S & D Board. The N & DV promoters therefore could not show in Parliament that they had the support of the railways which would provide the link between the line and the London & North Western Railway at Tebay, as the South Durham & Lancashire Union company was closely allied with the S & D. As a result of this, the preamble of the Bill was declared not proved.

Any pleasure felt in the NER camp was short-lived as the widespread opposition from the N & DV group of supporters caused the NER Bill to fail. The N & CR amalgamation Bill was also assailed in a similar fashion, and was declared not proved, and to add a bit more gloom the Lanchester Valley Bill for extension of time was, as recorded, also defeated. The only glimmer of hope for the NER was the growing support for their cause from the S & D group, as it must have been obvious to the S & D that if the N & DV plan succeeded, there was a possibility of the S & D being approached by the LNWR regarding leasing or amalgamation, and the majority of the board seemed to prefer association with the NER as a better policy, or lesser evil.

On 1 January 1861 a new traffic working arrangement between the NER and S & D came into effect. The N & DV promoters decided to abandon any further reliance on the S & D and enlarged their own project. The enlarged plan was named the Newcastle Derwent & Weardale Railway, and Thomas Bouch surveyed the whole route. Not only did the scheme involve extending the Derwent valley line from Consett to West Auckland to connect there with the SD & LU to Tebay, but the N & CR was avoided by having an independent line into

Newcastle with a branch to a projected shipping place on the Tyne, as well as thirteen other branch lines of varying lengths. The scheme was a bold one, and would have been very expensive, involving capital of £450,000. Besides the main line, over thirty miles long, the main branch was perhaps that from the Crook area to the West Hartlepool Railway near Byers Green, the West Hartlepool company being in close collaboration with the LNWR. This particular branch threatened the small West Durham Railway, which immediately amassed its support behind the NER as a result. Some of the other NDW branches included one to join the NER at Gateshead, to the N & CR at Derwenthaugh, to the S & D at Hownes Gill, to Tow Law ironworks, to Winlaton Mill from south of Swalwell, and to the S & D in the Bishop Auckland district. There was even a branch to the Shotley Grove paper mill near Consett. Obviously, besides being primarily a through route, the new project intended to tap all of the local industries en route. Further, the scheme included running powers for the LNWR from Tebay. The LNWR was also very interested in the port of West Hartlepool, hence the branch to join the West Hartlepool Railway, and it had produced a Bill of its own to enable it to buy lands and build warehouses at West Hartlepool and to acquire up to a quarter of the share capital of the West Hartlepool Railway. The LNWR therefore was making a determined effort to break into N E England and reach the major centre of Newcastle and the growing port of West Hartlepool. In fact two-thirds of the share capital of the NDW scheme was subscribed by the LNWR and the North British Railway. The latter thought it had a good chance of obtaining much traffic from the NDW line and of indulging in trade with enterprises such as the Consett ironworks, although it had not yet secured an entry for its traffic into Newcastle by a means independent of the NER. One of the main reasons for the LNWR pressure behind the NDW scheme was the Euston company's long-standing grievance against the NER sending its Liverpool traffic by the Lancashire & Yorkshire route, instead of by the LNWR Leeds—Stalybridge line. As a result the LNWR thought it should seize this chance to try to obtain its own Newcastle—Liverpool route, even if the line was heavily graded. It was at best quite a direct route. The chairman of the LNWR made a speech in which he told his shareholders of 'the necessity of promoting the line to the Derwent valley'.

1861 CONFRONTATION

The Newcastle Derwent & Weardale Bill and the NER Blaydon & Conside Bill were duly presented in Parliament during 1861. The course of the NER line was unchanged from its previous presentation. The route of the NDW from Newcastle was by way of a bridge across the river Tyne at Redheugh, and then past Dunston, Swalwell and along the Derwent valley, mainly following the east bank. The route in the valley required gradients of up to one in seventy. The line duplicated the Newcastle & Carlisle Railway's Redheugh branch between Dunston and Swalwell, and also ran parallel to the Stockton & Darlington line from Consett through Tow Law and Crook to Bishop Auckland.

The NDW company was to have its own station in Newcastle as well as having use of the Central station also. Besides the LNWR running powers over the NDW (including running powers to the Lancaster & Carlisle Railway – the LNWR subsidiary), the North British Railway was also to be granted running powers although its nearest line was nineteen miles away, beyond Hexham. The LNWR was also, of course, seeking running powers between Tebay and West Auckland over the SD & LU line, and over the Eden Valley Railway from Clifton, near Penrith, to Kirkby Stephen on the SD & LU.

In Parliament, therefore, it was really a struggle between the LNWR, NBR and West Hartlepool companies, against the NER, N & CR and S & D, and smaller companies such as the West Durham Railway. Evidence of the parliamentary rivalry can be found in the reports of the House of Commons Committee on the NDW Bill on 10 June 1861, and extracts are given in Appendix 4. Mr W. Dunn, a director of the N & CR 'objected very strongly to the facility powers sought in the present Bill over his line' and his company denounced the scheme as 'useless and unnecessary'. The NDW was to curve across the N & CR line west of Forth goods station, Newcastle, on land which the N & CR had reserved for other purposes. The NDW would then join the N & CR four hundred yards west of Forth. The N & CR was opposed to this proposal to cross or join their line. Another N & CR speaker saw the support of the LNWR and NBR for the Bill as 'out of their own self-seeking aims – the support of the North British sprung from the policy of aggrandisement pursued by that company'.

Mr Dunn was questioned by the NDW opposition on the rival NER Bill, and in particular its proposed junction with the N & CR at the south end of Scotswood Bridge, Blaydon. Mr Dunn said that the N & CR had no objection to the NER branch joining their line at Blaydon, and he 'thought it very convenient'. He was then reminded that in 1860 the N & CR had objected to the Newcastle & Derwent Valley Railway's proposed junction at the very same point as being 'a most inconvenient point'.

Mr Rodwell on behalf of the S & D said that the Hownes Gill—West Auckland section of the line was 'perfectly unnecessary'. He added that last year Mr Bouch had said that the best way to improve rail communication from Hownes Gill was by making certain alterations to the S & D. The evidence given in favour of this particular part of the line was 'of the vaguest character'. A mining engineer and coal viewer was called in to confirm that mineral deposits were adequately catered for by existing lines.

On 21 June 1861 the Commons approved the preamble of the NDW Bill and rejected the NER Bill, leaving the latter on the brink of defeat. In the House of Lords the NER pressed home its objections to the NDW scheme, particularly mentioning the heavy gradients all the way between Newcastle and Tebay for Liverpool trains, steep gradients up the Derwent valley, even steeper ones from Consett to Crook, and further heavy gradients over the Pennines via Stainmore. The running of expresses over such a route would be difficult, slow and expensive. There were other considerations, too, such as the absence of large towns on the whole route besides Bishop Auckland, which with 7,000 inhabitants was the main centre. The House of Lords decided the NER case was sensible and it rejected the NDW Bill on the 27 July. It was reported that the NDW promoters 'could scarcely believe their ears when they heard the decision'.

The NER had parried the threat for this year, and it was to pursue its respite by diplomacy, which enabled the threat to be removed altogether. In the meantime there was still the N & CR amalgamation Bill to be decided, and the opposition to it had not diminished. Such was the lateness of the Session however that it was decided to withdraw this Bill as there was no time for it to succeed in the circumstances.

The NER began to be diplomatic with its rivals later in the year and in early 1862. The NDW scheme had relied on running powers over the SD & LU line, which tended to favour the NER. At first the matter was not very successful for, although the S & D company had fostered the SD & LU line and regarded it as its protégé, its attempt to secure this by amalgamation was thwarted when the Bill on this was thrown out by Parliament on 10 June 1861 (only eleven days before the Commons' success of the NDW Bill). When the SD & LU opened for mineral traffic for most of its course between Barnard Castle and Tebay on 4 July 1861, the S & D worked all its traffic as arranged between the companies, and there was nothing the LNWR could do about this. The NER negotiated with the LNWR soon after this period, and discovered that the London company seemed quite prepared to abandon the NDW plan if the NER allowed it a reasonable traffic interchange between the systems, especially if it could send some of the NER Lancashire traffic via the LNWR from Leeds. It even appeared that the LNWR would be satisfied with similar interchange facilities at Carlisle if an agreement could be reached on the subject of NER—N & CR amalgamation. As for the North British company, the main objective was for it to be able to run its trains into Newcastle and establish its own through route from Newcastle to Edinburgh via Hawick. If it could achieve this it appeared that it would also be prepared to abandon the NDW project. As a result of these tentative soundings the NDW project was to vanish quietly into history during 1862.

NER 'BLAYDON & CONSIDE' BRANCH

In the 1862 Session no NDW Bill was presented, while the NER Blaydon & Conside Bill made its third appearance. The N & CR amalgamation Bill was again presented, and there was also a Bill to enable the S & D to lease the SD & LU. To enable the Bills to succeed the NER made concessions to the LNWR and

NBR. The former was granted every facility for exchanging traffic with the NER at Leeds, Carlisle and other places, while the NBR was to be granted running powers over the N & CR line between Hexham and Newcastle (and to Redheugh). The NER even managed to secure for itself running powers over the NBR main line from Berwick to Edinburgh, which was a measure of the Scottish company's desire to reach Newcastle.

The Bill to enable the S & D to lease the SD & LU was passed on 30 June 1862, and the two NER Bills became law on 17 July. As a result of the N & CR amalgamation Act (25-6 Vic c 145) the NER acquired over eighty route miles and an important cross-country link. North British trains began to run over this line from Hexham to Newcastle and soon afterwards to Redheugh, and for a brief time there were three colours of rolling stock on the section of line.

The Blaydon & Conside (later Consett) Act (25-6 Vic c 146) was not followed up by any rapid preparations for construction and nothing was done for two years. In the first place there was no longer the threat of a rival scheme, while the construction of the new line was likely to be very expensive. Further, the Lanchester Valley branch had just been completed to Consett, and so the NER decided to wait before proceeding with the new line. Another factor was the status of Consett ironworks. It is notable that it was only in April 1864 that a new company, the Consett Iron Co was formed to take over the ironworks, giving a new firm foundation to the industry, and soon after this preparations for building the new railway commenced. The line would provide a shorter route to Consett for West Cumberland haematite ore.

RAILS IN THE DERWENT VALLEY

On 29 July 1864 tenders were received to construct the branch. Nine were submitted, ranging from £150,036 to £198,000. The lowest, that of Messrs Morkill & Prudham of Duns was accepted. One of the tenders was from B. Lawton of Newcastle, the constructor of the Lanchester Valley branch, who tendered at £155,924 6s 2d (£155,924.31). T. E. Harrison, the NER engineer, examined the Morkill & Prudham tender and approved it in detail in September. For this work he had previously ordered some 1,950 tons of rails, 848 tons of chairs and 26,400 sleepers. The rails weighed 82lb per yard.

The length of the line was approximately eleven miles between Scotswood Bridge junction and Blackhill. At the latter place there was to be a new station beside the Durham road, and the line would meet the extension built north of Consett

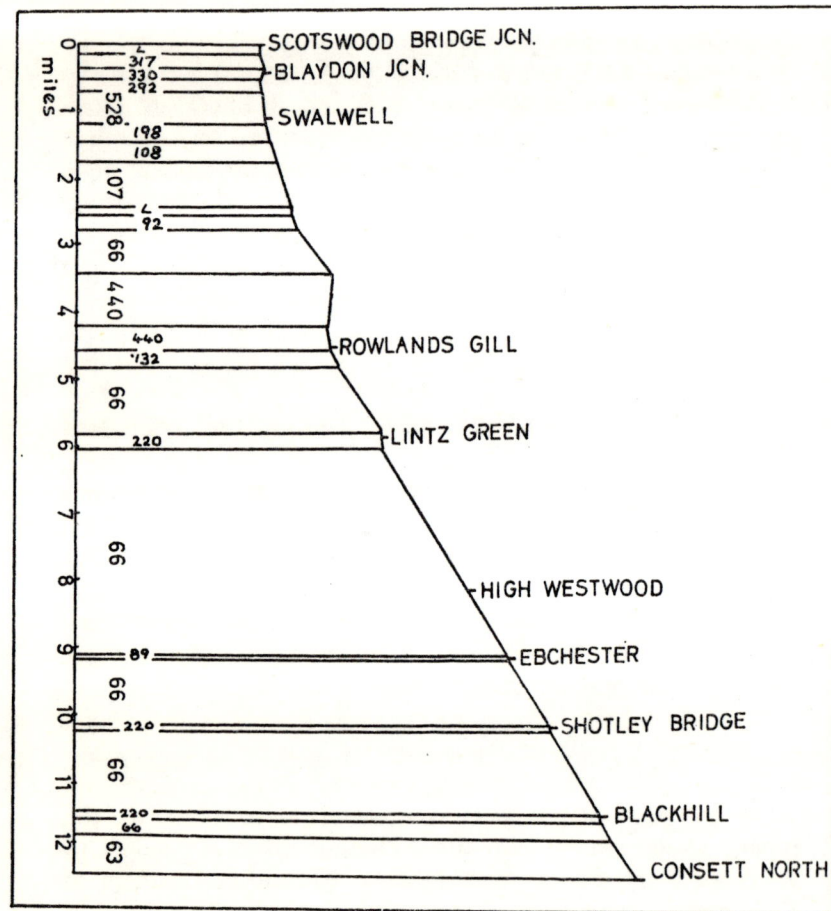

Gradient profile of Blaydon & Consett branch railway

station to serve the Shotley Bridge Iron Company's 'tin works'.

The largest settlement close to the line's route, besides Blaydon, was the township of Swalwell, about a mile from the approach junctions to Scotswood Bridge. Swalwell had almost 1,500 inhabitants, while the rest of the region traversed by the line, the Derwent valley district, was rather sparsely populated except for small pockets of settlement such as at Winlaton Mill and Shotley Bridge. Consett itself had 5,000 inhabitants by 1861. However, within several miles of the new line there were fairly populous areas around Burnopfield, Dipton, Pontop and Medomsley. The Pontop branch had no passenger service so that the increasingly populous villages of the Tanfield, Stanley and Annfield Plain districts could be expected to make use of the new line's passenger service.

Some of the heavy engineering works on the line may be cited. Near to Scotswood Bridge junctions (one junction towards the bridge and one towards the Redheugh branch facing Blaydon) was the Derwent viaduct, made of sandstone with three sixty feet arches. One clause in the Act stated that the NER had to 'deposit at the Admiralty office plans, sections and working drawings of the said bridge and works connected therewith for the approval of the Lord High Admiral . . . and approval to be signified in writing under the hand of the Secretary of the Admiralty'. This was because the bridge was to be only half a mile south of the Tyne and crossed theoretically navigable waters. Another bridge was necessary in Swalwell to take the line over the Hexham turnpike and to carry the line from its embankment (over a mile long) across the Tyne floodplain to the eastern slopes of the Derwent valley.

Near Rowlands Gill and Lintz Green further feats of engineering were required. To the north and south of Rowlands Gill the railway crossed from the east to west banks of the river Derwent, in order to pass through the village and to avoid the extensive grounds of Gibside Hall on the east side. These crossings required large viaducts. Lockhaugh (or Gibside) viaduct, 500ft long, had nine arches and was built largely of sandstone but with bricks beneath the arches. Rowlands Gill viaduct was mainly of red brick but had stone abutments, and had seven arches. Both bridges reached a maximum height of 80ft above the river, and had 60ft spans. Between Rowlands Gill viaduct and Lockhaugh viaduct a very deep cutting was required just south of the latter bridge which reached 60ft in depth and was about half a mile long. The construction of this cutting required some quarter of a million cubic yards of soil to be removed – the soil being largely boulder clay of the variety which is tenaciously sticky when wet and rock hard when dry. Morkill & Prudham had to use gunpowder to remove it, indicating that the weather at this particular time was fine. Incidentally this type of clay proved excellent for brick making, and when the railway was built a brickworks was set up at Rowlands Gill; the brickworks remains to this day.

Over a mile south of Rowlands Gill viaduct another deep cutting was necessary at Lintz Green, and here rock had to be removed, and stone retaining walls up to about four feet high built for a quarter of a mile. Two further large viaducts were necessary near Lintz Green. The Fogoes viaduct over the burn of that name was built mainly of red brick with six arches each of 60ft span, reaching 90ft above the stream. A quarter of a mile to the south and reached by a high embankment was the largest viaduct on the line. This reached a height of 120ft above the deep Pont Burn valley and had ten arches each of 60ft span, making it over 600ft in length. This bridge was constructed mainly of white firebricks, but as with the Fogoes, it had stone abutments. Both bridges were built to carry a single line. The Derwent and Lockhaugh viaducts were also single track, but Rowlands Gill viaduct was wide enough to carry a double line.

Two further engineering works were a high embankment to the north of Ebchester and a deep cutting partly through rock just north of Blackhill. The line had thus a fair number of major engineering requirements.

In August 1865 when preliminary work had been going on for only a few months, Morkill & Prudham complained to the NER about the 'unfair conditions proposed to be enforced upon them by the company's engineer' (Harrison). Whatever this reason was, the NER did not pay much attention to the complaint, for the company told Harrison 'to call upon Messrs Morkill & Prudham to carry out the above contract'.

The contractors did their work well, using a large number of Irish navvies, and the work was in its last phase in early

1867. On 24 May it was agreed to erect telegraph equipment on the line and on 18 June goods traffic began. The station at Blackhill was under construction by this time and here the line met the Lanchester Valley Blackhill extension end-on. The other stations, except one at Swalwell, were also being built, and it perhaps indicates the state of the contractor's finances at this time that the passenger buildings were ugly squat single-storey white (or cream) firebrick structures. The station houses were more distinctive, angular, three-storey buildings of interesting, but perhaps not very handsome appearance. Ebchester stationhouse, however, was a more conventional two-storey design.

Blackhill station, which was to be named Benfieldside after the parish in which it was situated – a fact not wholly meeting with local approval – it was estimatel in January 1867 to cost £9,577 13s 4d (£9,577.66½). It was the main station on the line. The other stations were to be at Swalwell, Rowlands Gill, Lintz Green, Ebchester and Shotley Bridge (originally named Snows Green). Rowlands Gill and Lintz Green stations were to have two platforms, as a length of nearly two miles of double track was laid from just north of Rowlands Gill to the north end of Fogoes viaduct to provide ample passing room for trains. The other stations were to have single platforms. The construction of Swalwell station was deferred and in November 1867 the NER obtained an acre of land for this station by exchanging an acre of its own nearby to the landowner. When the line was opened for passenger traffic on 2 December, all stations except Swalwell were ready.

Some conditions for staff may be cited. Rowlands Gill: stationmaster at 20s (100p) per week with house; no other booking clerk. Ebchester: Mr Smith 'now at Carr House station which is to be closed' appointed stationmaster at 20s (100p) per week, with house; no clerk or porter. Snows Green: stationmaster at 17s (85p) per week with house; no porter or staff. Benfieldside: stationmaster at £100 per year (the former goods assistant at Carr House); house included; two passenger porters at 17s (85p) per week each, and a booking clerk at 20s per week.

As stated in Chapter 4, the passenger service was combined with the Lanchester Valley service giving a Newcastle—Lintz

Green—Benfieldside—Lanchester—Durham service, that is, the 'Consett branch' service. The link line at Blaydon to the Redheugh branch facing Blaydon station was not used by passenger trains, but it was in its early years extremely busy with Carlisle—Consett iron ore traffic as well as Consett products bound for the Carlisle line. Double track existed from the outset for some 300yd south of Scotswood Bridge junction, to simplify the approaches to the Carlisle line. The branch crossed both the Blaydon Main colliery wagonway and the Garesfield wagonway without a connection.

OPENING AND EARLY SERVICES

The opening of the branch to passenger traffic on 2 December 1867 was recorded at length in railway journals and newspapers of the time. The *Newcastle Courant* described the opening day activity: 'At 10.20 am the party comprised of some of the railway officials and gentlemen otherwise interested in the success of the new line started from the Central station, Newcastle, and proceeded on to Benfieldside station where they were met by Mr E. Charlton and others and escorted to the offices belonging to the Consett Iron Company (Limited) where a substantial luncheon was provided. The completion of the line has been looked forward to by the people of the district as a great boon. It gives them direct access to Newcastle on the one hand and to Durham on the other and from thence northward and southward in all directions. To the people of Newcastle also the line will be of immense convenience. It opens out a new district in which a vast amount of business is to be done and it will be of immense convenience. The line passes through one of the most picturesque districts in the counties of Northumberland and Durham. It passes by the river Derwent and through the woods of Gibside, Lintz Green &c until it reaches Conside where it is at a very considerable elevation above the sea, the rise from the Tyne to Conside being continuous.

'The viaducts are lofty and longitudinally great. The sum for which the works were let by contract to Messrs Morkill & Prudham was £163,000. This is the first line that Messrs Morkill have constructed in this district.' This cost – greater than the sum tendered – was because at first the NER envisaged the whole branch as a single line of rails and only on 23 December 1864 was the 'subject of Blaydon & Conside branch as a double line brought before Board; a committee appointed to consider subject and report – first meeting on Friday, 6 January'. On 15 January the committee recommended doubling between 4 miles 8 chains and 6 miles 10 chains, and this was approved, the additional expense being estimated at £10,000.

The *Newcastle Courant* commented on the branch: 'Whatever may be the opinion as to the general policy of constructing branch lines there can be no doubt that the NE company have acted wisely in constructing the Derwent valley branch. Cheaply though well and substantially constructed, it will develop a traffic that will not only prove remunerative for the capital invested in the branch but will also prove a valuable adjunct to the main NE line.'

The *Newcastle Daily Journal* alluded to the scenic attraction of the Derwent valley: 'The scenery opened out by this branch is of a very beautiful description and in the summer will no doubt be much frequented by tourists.' And the *Railway News* stated: 'The line passes through one of the most pretty and picturesque districts in the kingdom. The ride from Newcastle to Shotley Bridge and thence onwards to Durham presents a series of panoramic views of the most beautiful description.' Shotley Bridge village itself was regarded as a spa until the 1920s, and no doubt some traffic was of visitors seeking 'the cure'. For long the NER ran excursion trains to Shotley Bridge.

The line was indeed most scenic and many years after its opening the LNER Sentinel steam railcars allowed passengers to see it to best advantage. Unfortunately the later BR diesel railcars were not to see service on the line, which was certainly the most picturesque in northern Durham.

The gradients on the line were not heavy for the section between Scotswood bridge and Swalwell, but steepened to reach an almost continuous 1 in 66 from Rowlands Gill southwards to Blackhill (Benfieldside).

In 1873 the NER ordered 'block signal cabins' to be established on the Consett branch. The most interesting of the boxes was the very tall brick box at Rowlands Gill. This allowed the signalman to see over the Shotley Bridge road bridge, which crossed the line between the box and the station, and to see the signals at the viaduct end of the station.

The first service for passengers comprised three trains each way on weekdays. The trains left Newcastle at 6.10am, 10.20am, and 5.15pm, taking 51 minutes to reach Benfieldside. Trains left Benfieldside (from Durham) for Newcastle at 8.58am 12.53pm, and 8.38pm. On Saturdays there were extra 'market trains' leaving Newcastle at 4.0pm and Durham at 7.0pm. By 1869 there were four trains each way on the branch (only three on the Lanchester line). There were two extra trains each way

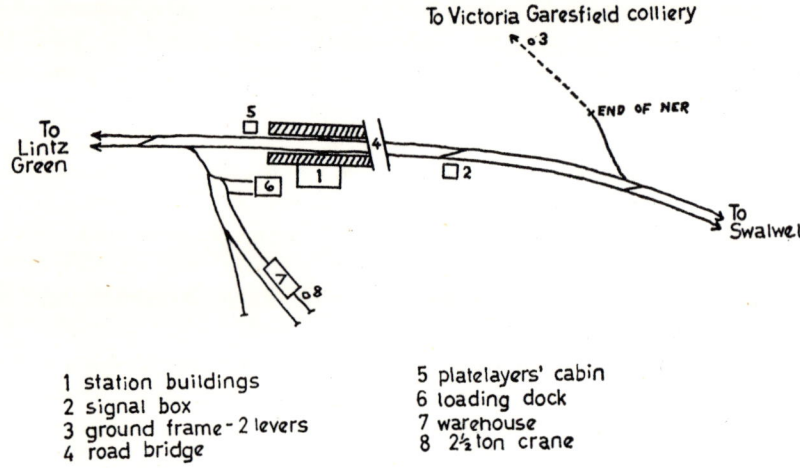

1 station buildings
2 signal box
3 ground frame - 2 levers
4 road bridge
5 platelayers' cabin
6 loading dock
7 warehouse
8 2½ ton crane

Rowlands Gill station

on Saturdays. Swalwell station was opened early in 1868, and Snows Green was renamed Shotley Bridge in the same year. In December 1869 third class carriages became standard on the Consett branch trains, following a request for this from the Consett Local Board.

On 19 November 1869 the NER considered a letter from Messrs Morkill & Prudham 'pressing for a settlement of their account for architectural works on the Blaydon & Conside Branch', and it was resolved that 'the offer of £2,000 previously made be increased to £2,200 on condition they accept this as full payment of their claims in connection with the Blaydon & Conside Branch'.

THE STRUGGLE FOR THE DERWENT VALLEY 107

Passenger services on the line were to grow almost continously up to World War I. In 1874 the fares on the trains were as follows:

Single		First	Second	Third
Newcastle to	Swalwell	10d(4p)	8d(3½p)	4½d(2p)
,,	,, Rowlands Gill	1s 5d(7p)	1s 1d(5½p)	7½d(3p)
,,	,, Lintz Green	1s 9d(9p)	1s 4d(6½p)	9d (4p)
,,	,, Ebchester	2s 4d(11½p)	1s 9d(9p)	1s 0½d(5p)
,,	,, Shotley Bridge	2s 6d(12½p)	1s 10d(9p)	1s 1½d(5½p)
,,	,, Benfieldside	2s 8d(13½p)	2s 0d(10p)	1s 2½d(6p)

An echo back to the Newcastle Derwent & Weardale scheme was the listing of connections at Benfieldside in the timetable – for Bishop Auckland, Barnard Castle, Tebay and Penrith.

From the start, coal traffic was important on the branch and was to increase greatly. Coke traffic from the Consett ironworks to Cumberland made use of the line in February 1869 and the NER considered an application from the iron company for a reduction in the rate for coke from Consett to Workington. In 1870 there was local coal traffic on the line from the Lintz and South Garesfield mines (via a short branch from Lintz Green station), from Garesfield colliery (near Rowlands Gill), and Hamsterley colliery (north of Ebchester). This latter pit was of the greatest importance at that date, supplying some 20,000 tons of coal and coke to the line during the year, and thus providing the NER with £2,780 in receipts.

On 27 February 1871, the NER noted that the Post Office had asked for the 'use of Conside Branch trains, Durham—Newcastle, for mail bags at £60 per annum instead of merely the use of one train each way between Benfieldside and Newcastle for which they pay £50 per annum'. (The two trains so used were the first Newcastle—Benfieldside departure, and the evening Benfieldside—Newcastle train.) It was resolved that 'the Post Office be offered the use of all the trains on the branch at £100 per annum'.

In March 1872 a tender of £480 8s 1d (£480.40) was accepted for painting all Consett branch stations. In 1870 £20 was contributed by the NER towards a new road being made to Ebchester station, and in 1872 a new road to Benfieldside station was made by the Consett Iron Co and in connection with this the NER provided an entrance to the southbound platform there for some £50.

PASSENGER TRAFFIC DEVELOPMENT

Expansion of passenger traffic is best illustrated by the following statistics for 1886 and 1906:

	1886		1906	
	Passengers	Receipts £	Passengers	Receipts £
Swalwell	42,979	1,059	82,038	2,329
Rowlands Gill	31,672	1,471	103,897	4,976
Lintz Green	29,870	1,624	32,898	1,872
Ebchester	31,206	1,156	58,880	2,407
Shotley Bridge	14,774	918	25,022	1,392
Benfieldside (Blackhill)	72,915	4,490	128,045	8,701

In 1901 there were 97,693 passengers at Swalwell, but traffic declined after this date owing to horse buses operating into Newcastle through Dunston and Gateshead. At Lintz Green station traffic was severely affected when the Newcastle—Annfield Plain passenger service began in 1894 (recorded in the next chapter). Many passengers from the Tanfield and Stanley districts, who had relied on Lintz Green station as their nearest passenger service, thenceforth used the new line close at hand, and passenger traffic at Lintz Green declined. The station had 45,121 passengers during 1893, and the total slumped to 36,307 in 1895, and was not to revive. The vast increase of passengers at Rowlands Gill can be largely attributed to mining expansion in that district, particularly around High Spen and Victoria Garesfield.

Steady growth of the passenger train service matched the increasing traffic. By 1880 there was a Sunday service on the branch, but this was not extended on to the Lanchester branch. By 1907 there were eleven trains daily on weekdays from Newcastle to Blackhill, and eight in the other direction, as well as certain extras and short journeys. Typical of the latter was the 5.15am train from Rowlands Gill to Newcastle. There were no 'expresses' or trains omitting a call at any station and all trains called at each station. The Sunday service consisted of three trains each way, two of which continued on to or from the Lanchester branch. Normally the branch trains were worked by Wilson Worsdell's Class O 0–4–4T and the older Fletcher Class BTP 0–4–4T. The latter also appeared from about 1907 in the guise of steam autocars with the locomotive coupled to a coach at each end, and operations by these autocars increased in succeeding years. In 1911 there were three workings each way by autocars on the line.

By 1914 the passenger service had reached its peak, with twelve trains from Newcastle to Blackhill and nine in the other direction, together with numerous extras and short workings. The line had a very heavy passenger traffic and Rowlands Gill remained the busiest station with the exception of Blackhill. The situation remained favourable until 1920 when, as on the Lanchester Valley line, decline began at a rapid pace. Motorbus services in the Derwent valley began to affect the traffic severely, which was further reduced by the fact that most of the valley stations except Rowlands Gill were not centrally situated in the villages they served.

The prosperity and decline may be judged from figures for 1919 and 1921, although inevitably worse was to follow:

	Passengers	
	1919	1921
Swalwell	86,068	45,845
Rowlands Gill	130,633	84,181
Lintz Green	38,408	22,759
High Westwood	132,322	92,876
Ebchester	40,285	35,346
Shotley Bridge	46,290	42,441
Blackhill	190,621	165,771

The new station at High Westwood was opened on 1 July 1909, and there was heavy traffic for the next decade. In 1908 the NER's traffic committee had recommended the construction of a station here, just over a mile north of Ebchester. The new station was better placed to serve the colliery village of Chopwell, two miles away, and the nearby colliery villages of

Hamsterley and Westwood. The cost of the station was estimated at £2,625 including £100 for land and £1,200 for the buildings. A tender of £1,005 1s 7d (£1,005.08) from a contractor at Birtley was accepted, but this tender was then withdrawn and the contract was awarded to A. Tench of Blaydon at £1,040 4s 2d (£1,040.21). The line at this point was also doubled for almost a mile, and the station had two platforms mainly of wooden construction. The work came to almost £735 more than tendered, due to the doubling of the line to simplify traffic operation. The new station had no goods traffic but had 84,375 passengers in 1910 and 94,064 in 1914. Ebchester station suffered some decline as a result, the passenger traffic there falling from 74,499 in 1908 to 30,997 in 1910.

GOODS AND MINERAL TRAFFIC

Coal traffic was, as with so many railways in Durham, of great importance to the Blaydon & Consett branch. Besides the mines at Hamsterley and near Lintz Green, the collieries at Axwell Park (near Swalwell station) and Victoria Garesfield (including coke ovens) were of significance. The latter was reached by a colliery-owned one and a quarter mile branch running from just north of Rowlands Gill station, the junction facing north. In 1872 the Consett Iron Co opened its colliery and coke ovens at Westwood, near Hamsterley, and there was soon heavy traffic. In 1886, Westwood sent 80,420 tons of coal and coke on to the line, providing the NER with receipts totalling £23,941 7s 10d (£23,941.39). Of this traffic, 72,504 tons of coke went via Blaydon to Carlisle bound for the West Cumberland iron industry. Nearby Hamsterley colliery also engaged in this Carlisle-bound traffic, for in the same year 13,822 tons of coke (out of a total coal and coke traffic for the year, of 27,472 tons), went from Hamsterley to Carlisle.

The Lintz and South Garesfield collieries' traffic (the latter also known as Friarside colliery) reached the branch by a steeply graded link from east of Lintz Green station that joined the branch at the north end of the station. The traffic from these pits had previously used the Pontop & Jarrow and Lintz wagonways, as recorded earlier. On 29 May 1874 the NER resolved to lay a siding for the Friarside and Lintz traffic, to be constructed for 'the purpose of preventing the shunting of this traffic on the main lines of the Consett branch'. The estimated cost of this short NER line was £2,000. It joined the Consett branch immediately north of the station and followed the branch for over a quarter of a mile before veering eastwards to the mines. The work involved a new bridge over an occupation roadway to carry the single line of rails. J. Lawton of Newcastle constructed an embankment carrying the siding to the mines for £1,071 13s 2d (£1,071.66), while the NER did the rest of the work for some £1,030.

Other collieries close to the railway included the Blackhill drift, south of Blackhill station, and the Lilley (or Lily) drift at Rowlands Gill. The latter used the branch for most of its traffic up to about 1896 when an 'endless rope' was opened to convey the coal northwards up the valley side to Blaydon Burn coke ovens, two and a quarter miles away. The coal then reached the N & CR at Blaydon. There was also a brickworks at the Lilley drift, which gave traffic to the line, and this brickworks is still in use, using road transport. There was another large brickworks near Swalwell station (Hannington's) reached by a siding. In 1907 there was 3,079 tons of brick traffic at Swalwell as a result, and also 920 tons of clay. At Shotley Bridge a gasworks was supplied chiefly with coal from Medomsley colliery by rail via Blackhill. Nearby was Shotley Grove paper mill (closed in 1905) and there was a second paper mill at Lintzford near Lintz Green. The latter, owned by Messrs Annandale up to 1912, used the railway for nearly all of its traffic. In 1923 the Lintzford mill became a printing ink works, and so it remains. The Shotley Bridge flour mill closed in 1920.

Axwell Park colliery, Swalwell, required additional sidings for its traffic by 1911, and these were laid for an estimated £865, out of which £800 was paid by the colliery company.

Station goods traffic was usually greatest at Rowlands Gill, excepting the immense traffic at Blackhill. In 1920 Rowlands Gill's traffic amounted to 28,761 tons of goods forwarded and 24,319 tons received. At Ebchester the comparative figures were 8,380 and 6,029 tons. There was no regular goods traffic, except coal traffic, at Shotley Bridge. Blackhill's goods traffic in 1920 totalled something like 500,000 tons.

There was a reasonable milk traffic on the railway also, from the Derwent valley area farms to Tyneside. Livestock traffic was not important, except at Blackhill, where there was an auction mart not far from the station. The Cumberland iron ore traffic to Consett ironworks had died out by 1880.

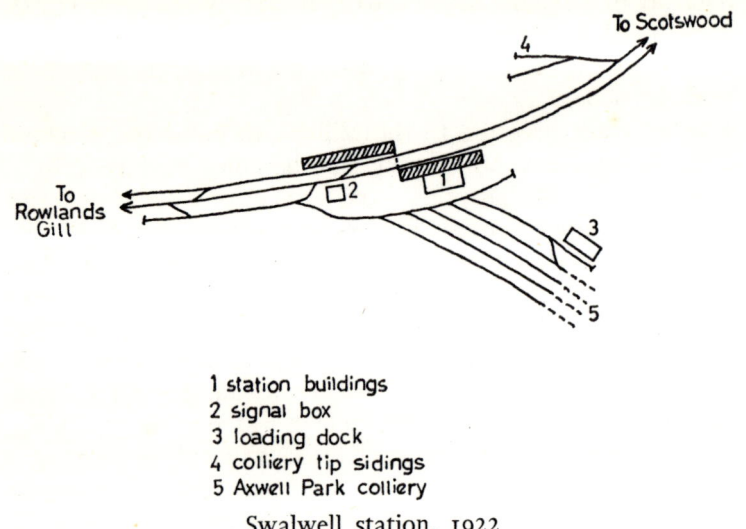

1 station buildings
2 signal box
3 loading dock
4 colliery tip sidings
5 Axwell Park colliery

Swalwell station, 1922

SWALWELL—ROWLANDS GILL WIDENING

Traffic growth by the 1900s had made the long single track sections on the Blaydon & Consett branch something of a nuisance. To improve the situation it was resolved to double the whole section from north of Swalwell to Lockhaugh junction at Rowlands Gill (beside the Lilley drift colliery). In 1898 electric staff working had been introduced on the two single track sections of the line (and also between Consett and Lanchester) but doubling was the best solution and this decision was made in September 1903. Powers were authorised in the NER Act in 1905 and tenders were invited in the same year. The 1903 estimate for doubling the four miles of line was £42,896, which included the heavy cost involved in widening the Derwent and Lockhaugh viaducts. On 11 May 1905 the tender of H. M. Nowell of Newcastle for £31,000 was accepted. Not only

THE STRUGGLE FOR THE DERWENT VALLEY

did the viaducts at Swalwell and Lockhaugh need widening to take a double line, but the various deep cuttings, including the particularly deep one at Lockhaugh, also needed widening. This was no easy task. The valley slope section south of Swalwell required much use of stone-retaining walls and drainage works to prevent slipping on to the line, and a considerable length of embankment was needed near Lockhaugh on the valley slope to carry the extra line. £100 was paid for land for widening Lockhaugh cutting to allow reasonable slopes to prevent slipping. It was reported during this work that 'Mr Nowell offered to remove the earthwork and deposit it at a point where an embankment is required on the same line for £3,442 7s 0d [£3,442.35]' (saving the NER 1s 0d [5p] per cubic yard on 2,000 yards on the contract). The two viaducts were widened, using sandstone and firebrick in the manner of the original structures, and subsequently it was easy to assume they had originally been built as double track. The bridge over the Hexham road at Swalwell was widened using stone and steel girders, and Swalwell station received a second platform of wood, staggered from the original. The work was completed officially on 5 January 1908 after over two years during which traffic was disrupted as little as possible.

OTHER IMPROVEMENTS

Nowell also constructed for the NER an eastwards-facing curve at Blaydon from the Swalwell direction to the Redheugh branch, and this opened in 1908. This double track loop allowed coal to reach Dunston and Derwenthaugh without reversing at Blaydon. Earlier in 1897-8 a curve had been built from south of Scotswood Bridge junction to join the Redheugh branch facing east (the 'Blaydon Loop'), the reason for which is given in Chapter 7.

At the other end of the branch many improvements and alterations were made at Blackhill station over the years. A carriage shed was built in 1873 and an additional shed and a warehouse were built in 1874. On 6 December 1877 the Consett Local Board requested a footbridge at the station to replace the level crossing. The NER demurred and on 28 March 1878 the company received a query from the Board of Trade on allega-

For the Information of the Company's Servants only.

B.—No. 29.

NORTH EASTERN RAILWAY.

NORTHERN DIVISION.

ADVICE OF EXCURSION AND SPECIAL TRAINS

AUGUST 11 to 14 inclusive.

NOTE.—Mr. Reid, Newcastle, will provide Guards, and Inspector Pringle Carriages and Vans, except where it is specially stated to the contrary.

MONDAY, AUGUST 11th.

No. 1. SPECIALS—EBCHESTER AND BENFIELDSIDE TO REDCAR AND SALTBURN, *via Team Valley Extension and Hartburn Curve.*

Consett Iron Company's Workmen.

Probable Number, 3,500 Adults, 1,500 Apprentices.   Fares, 3s. Adults; 2s. Apprentices.

Outward Journey—Ebchester to Saltburn—

	1. a.m.	2. a.m.	3. a.m.	4. a.m.	5. a.m.	6. a.m.	7. a.m.	8. a.m.
Ebchester ... dept.			5.30	5.45	5.55	6. 5	6.25	
Shotley Bridge ,,			5.36	5.51	6. 1	6.11	6.31	
Benfieldside ... arrive			5.41	5.56	6. 6	6.16	6.36	
,, ... dept.	5.20	5.30	5.45	6. 0	6.10	6.20	6.40	6.50
Durham ... arrive	6. 0	6.10	6.25	6.40	6.50	7. 0	7.20	7.30
,, ... dept.	6. 5	6.15	6.35	6.45	6.55	7. 5	7.25	7.40
*Ferry Hill ... ,,	6.25	6.35	6.55	7. 5	7.15	7.25	7.45	8. 0
*North Stockton ,,	7. 0	7.10	7.30	7.40	7.50	3. 0	8.25	8.40
Redcar ... arrive	7.45	7.55	8.15	8.25	8.35	8.45	9.10	9.25
Saltburn ... ,,	8. 0	8.10	8.30	8.40	8.50	9. 0	9.25	9.40

Return Journey—Saltburn to Ebchester—

	1. p.m.	2. p.m.	3. p.m.	4. p.m.	5. p.m.	6. p.m.	7. p.m.	8. p.m.
Saltburn ... dept.	6. 0	6.10	6.20	6.30	6.40	7.10	7.20	7.30
Redcar ... ,,	6.20	6.30	6.40	6.50	7. 0	7.30	7.40	7.50
*North Stockton ,,	7. 5	7.15	7.25	7.35	7.45	8.20	8.30	8.40
*Ferry Hill ... ,,	7.40	7.50	8. 0	8.10	8.20	‡8.55	9. 5	8.15
Durham ... arrive	8. 0	8.10	8.20	8.30	8.40	9.15	9.25	9.35
,, ... dept.	8. 5	8.15	8.25	8.35	8.45	9.20	9.30	9.40
Benfieldside ... arrive	8.45	8.55	9. 5	9.15	9.25	10. 0	10.10	10.10
Shotley Bridge ,,	8.50	9. 0	9.10	9.20	9.30	10. 5	10.15	10.25
Ebchester ... ,,	8.55	9. 5	9.15	9.25	9.35	10.10	10.20	10.30

* Cord stops.

† Follow 6.20 p.m. Ordinary Train if it is running to time.

‡ This special must proceed the 5.55 a.m. up ordinary train, which must be kept back to the extent of 5 minutes.

THE STRUGGLE FOR THE DERWENT VALLEY 115

tions made by the Consett Local Board of the 'danger to passengers at Benfieldside station level crossing.' The NER ordered its engineer to plan a footbridge. In 1902 a new footbridge was erected as a covered way for £550, replacing the 1878 structure. In 1884 a general waiting-room was built at the station, followed in 1889-90 by an extensive series of alterations and additions to meet the increasing passenger traffic at a cost of

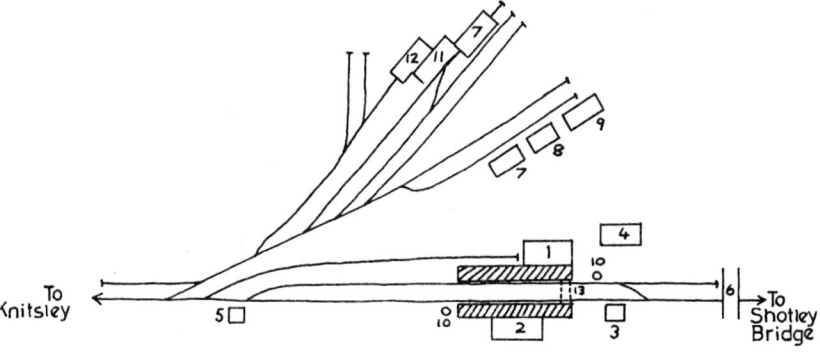

1 station buildings
2 waiting room
3 signal box
4 water tank
5 Blackhill South signal box (closed c1898)
6 Durham road bridge
7 warehouses
8 coke dock
9 cattle dock
10 water cranes
11 loading dock
12 coal depots – 8 cells
13 covered footbridge

Blackhill station

£1,192. In 1911 one platform was extended and the Crook bay platform lengthened. A coal depot built in 1879 for some £440 was enlarged at later dates. A new signal box of typical NER brick design was erected in 1898 and 'Blackhill South' box was later closed.

On 19 January 1882 it was ordered that water pipes and hydrants be laid down 'to protect goods warehouse, station and cottages at Benfieldside in case of fire' for some £84. On 20 April 1882 the Consett Iron Co asked the NER to pay a third of the cost of a new street at Blackhill, called Hawthorn Street. The NER replied that it was not prepared 'to bear any part of the expense of forming the street'.

Little major change took place at other stations except for

that already described at Swalwell. At the rather remote station of Lintz Green, the Lanchester Highway Board requested the NER in 1883 to improve the lane beside the station into a 'cart and carriage way' and dedicate it to the public. The lane crossed the railway just south of the station by an overbridge. The NER refused to do this but a few months later made some concession and agreed to erect steps from each platform to the

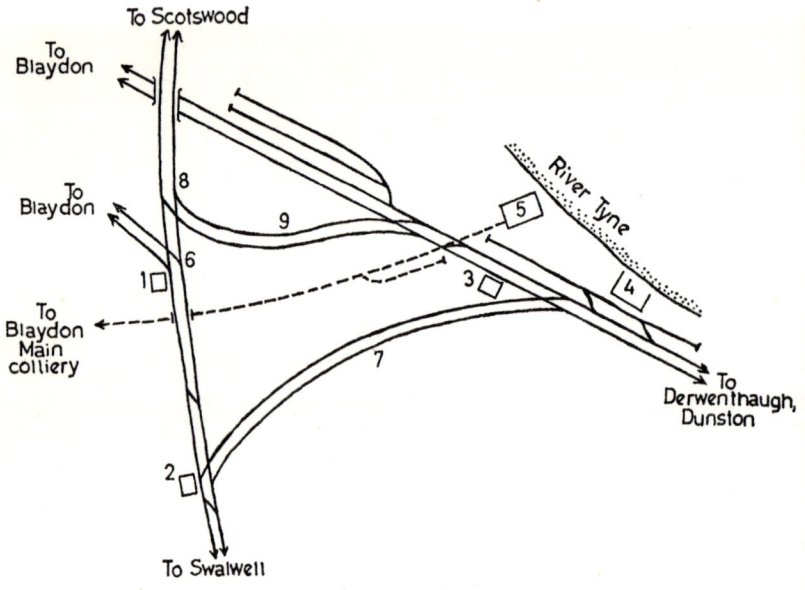

1 Blaydon South signal box
2 Swalwell North signal box
3 Blaydon Main signal box
4 Consett Iron Co staiths etc.
5 Blaydon Main cokeworks
6 Blaydon junction
7 Blaydon south east curve
8 Blaydon Loop west jcn.
9 Blaydon Loop

Junctions east of Blaydon

lane on each side of the overbridge at a cost of £160. Iron railings and gates were also supplied, so that passengers leaving the station had the benefit of excellent stone staircases and handrails, before reaching the (usually) muddy unmade lane leading to the nearest main roads over half a mile away. In fact in November 1882 the NER had planned to build a goods warehouse and mineral depots (three coal cells, one lime cell) at Lintz Green, and had requested that the inhabitants of the district should make the lane into a good road dedicated to the public. The estimated cost of the goods facilities was £1,300. This was to be done, however, only if the road were made. Thus, as neither party was prepared to make the lane into a reasonable road, the goods improvements did not come and passengers continued to suffer on the rutted lane. This quiet station came briefly to national attention on a day in 1911 (see Chapter 10) when its stationmaster was murdered.

Much of the goods traffic on the branch was worked by locomotives from the Blaydon engine shed after its opening in 1900. For half of the line's history its mineral and goods traffic was worked by 0–8–0 engines, especially the Raven Class T2 (LNER Q6). Blaydon shed often had a large batch of these locomotives, as outlined in Chapter 9.

CHAPTER SIX

Pontop Branch Progress

SOME MINOR ADJUSTMENTS

From 1860-80 there was not a great deal of change on the old Stanhope & Tyne line between Consett and Stella Gill. Locomotives worked the Consett—East Castle section as well as the Pelton and Stanley levels, where they had replaced the original horse haulage.

The line remained single track over the whole ten miles between Consett and Stella Gill until 1874, except for sidings at collieries beside the line. However, in the early 1870s the pressure of traffic in the Annfield—Stanley district forced the NER to double part of the line. In 1872 the NER refused to permit the South Moor colliery company to run its own locomotives on the line from Louisa colliery to Oxhill, an attempt by this colliery company to improve its flow of traffic. Then in November 1873 the NER resolved to double the two and a half miles of lines from Annfield to Stanley bank top for an estimated £9,500. On 12 December 1873 the tender of G. E. Forster for £1,936 for the works was accepted and work began in early 1874. In 1873 an incline was opened from Stella Gill to serve nearby Pelton colliery, the NER paying one half of the £1,200 cost, and the colliery company paid the NER £100 annually for working the traffic.

The Consett Iron Co (Derwent & Consett Iron Co before 1864) appears to have operated some of the mineral traffic on the S & T line west of Annfield inclines up to the NER—S & D amalgamation of 1863 and even thereafter into the 1880s. The S & D had converted a boiler house at Carr House into a locomotive shed in 1857 (ordered by the company on 10 November 1856), and after 1863 engines from Carr House and Waskerley sheds could work over the line east of Carr House. Carr House shed was replaced by Blackhill in 1876.

In August 1861 the NER was asked to build a one and a quarter mile branch to D. Baker & Co's new Pontop Hall collieries at Pontop, from near Leadgate. The NER agreed providing Baker laid the formation; the NER would lay the rails etc for some £1,800. The line was laid in 1862, and was known as the Pontop Hall colliery branch. It was worked by the Derwent & Consett Iron Co and a letter from the iron company to the NER in December 1862 reveals the situation: 'Derwent & Consett Iron Co offered to continue to work the Pontop Hall colliery branch in connection with the line from Annfield—Carrhouse, provided NER increases the amount paid to them for this from £800 to £1,000 a year, from January 1 1863 and arrangement terminable on three months notice either way.'

In 1864 the Ann pit was sunk at Pontop Hall, afterwards known as the South Medomsley colliery, and the line from South Medomsley junction, Leadgate, became the South Medomsley colliery branch.

Further west, the Medomsley branch was also worked by the Consett Iron Co, which owned Medomsley colliery. In March 1882 the iron company requested the NER to lower the level of the branch railway in connection with certain siding extensions at Medomsley colliery. This was agreed and the iron company paid the cost. In January 1882 a farmer claimed £14 from the NER for the loss of six sheep killed on the branch by an engine and wagons of the Consett Iron Co on 10 November 1881, a claim which was settled 'on the best terms' according to NER minutes.

At Consett the NER was continually providing extra sidings for the Consett Iron Co traffic. In 1873, for instance, £830 was spent on new sidings, and during 1883 a total of £2,200 was spent to provide additional sidings to a new steel plant.

By the early 1870s the NER had begun to consider improving the operation of traffic on the S & T line east of Consett, and the first consideration was to replace the two Annfield inclines so that locomotives could be used for the whole line west of Stanley Bank top. The company probably incurred severe hindrance to and expenses from the traffic operations between Consett and Stanley as a result of the two Annfield inclines.

Although an Act was passed on 29 June 1875 (38-9 Vic c 93) authorising a line 'one mile four furlongs eight chains and two yards in length' bypassing the Annfield inclines on the south side of the ridge, nothing was done at this time.

LOCAL PRESSURE FOR IMPROVEMENTS

At the beginning of the 1880s the NER was assailed by a concerted effort from the towns and villages between Consett and Pelton to achieve a passenger service on the railway in their area, either on the existing line or by building a locomotive worked line. Because of the growth of coal mining the population of the whole region had expanded considerably during the previous forty years. For example, Tanfield chapelry had 7,000 people, Kyo parish (Annfield Plain) had 2,500, and Pelton parish had over 3,000 inhabitants. This populace had to travel several miles to reach passenger stations on the main line at Chester-le-Street, Plawsworth or Birtley, on the Blaydon & Consett branch at Rowlands Gill, Lintz Green or Ebchester, or at Lanchester on the Lanchester Valley branch. Indeed the main function of Lintz Green station, which had little habitation nearby, was to serve the Tanfield and Stanley districts which lay three to five miles away to the south east.

Typical of the kind of local pressure was a meeting held at the co-operative store at Leadgate on 7 October 1880, when it was unanimously decided to send a 'memorial' to the NER to improve the local railway facilities and allow a passenger service. At about the same time similar meetings were held at Consett, Annfield Plain and in the Stanley district. A joint petition from these various places was presented to the NER on 27 January 1881 'praying for a passenger railway from Birtley to Benfieldside' and signed by 8,011 people. Part of this petition read as follows:

'That a mineral line of railway belonging to the North Eastern Railway Company passes through the district and that the western portion of the same from Benfieldside to East Castle, with the intended alteration (for which parliamentary powers have been obtained) to Annfield Plain could easily be made available for the conveyance of passengers, and that a slight deviation of the existing line to the north from Annfield

Page 121: *NOTABLE VIADUCTS*
(above) *Hownes Gill;* (below) *Fogoes, near Lintz Green*

Page 122: *IRON ORE TRAINS IN STEAM DAYS*
(above) Class O1 2–8–0 heads a Tyne Dock—Consett ore train at West Stanley, banked by a T3 0–8–0; (below) 9F 2–10–0 No 92060 passing South Pelaw junction. Another 9F is banking the train

Plain by way of Kyo, Shield Row, Beamish, Pelton and Ouston forming a junction with the Team Valley railway at or near Birtley station would meet the convenience of the main portion of the population. The route of the proposed new railway does not present any engineering difficulties and that the probable cost of making the same, compared with the revenue likely to be derived from the passenger traffic as well as a large increase to the mineral and merchandise traffic by intersecting several private railways and opening out several industries that have been discontinued on account of the expense of transit of goods by road, will amply justify the North Eastern Railway Company in promoting the proposed new line.'

Other points made in the petition included the observations that the heavy passenger traffic concentrated at Chester-le-Street and Birtley stations often required relief trains to be run to Newcastle, and that the NER had opened branch lines in 'more remote and less remunerative areas'. This last point is interesting but the fact remained that there was in fact a railway serving the area and a new line built to replace the inclines would not have replaced the old line for minerals, since the latter had collieries all along its length. Further, a locomotive worked line could only have been made with very heavy gradients and also, contrary to the claim in the petition, it would have required a certain amount of heavy engineering. Nevertheless the matter appears to have received close attention from the railway company, and later other events brought a similar scheme to fruition.

ANNFIELD—EAST CASTLE

In the meantime the NER resolved to pursue its dormant scheme for a line bypassing Annfield hill or ridge and replacing the two inclines. A new Act was passed to allow this on 19 June 1882. The new route curved around the south side of the Annfield hill and was about two miles in length, longer than the route planned in 1875. Work began in late 1883 and the line was opened to traffic on 1 January 1886. The line included about half a mile at 1 in 64 and a longer stretch at 1 in 103, and was built as a double track. Parts of the old route were left open to serve certain collieries at East Castle at the north end (with junctions to the new line at Castles West and Castles East), and South Derwent and South Pontop collieries at the south (from Annfield junction). The inclines were dismantled.

At about the same time a new locomotive depot was established at Annfield, situated on the spur leading to the former Loud Bank incline. This replaced an older shed which had housed the few engines working the line to Stanley bank top before 1886. The new Annfield shed was enlarged in 1893.

WEST DURHAM & TYNE PROJECT

The West Durham & Tyne Railway project of 1885 is of great importance, for although it did not succeed, it was the spur behind great improvements in the NER system in northwest Durham. As with the Sacriston & South Shields scheme of twenty-five years previously, the main reason for the new project was the grievance of coal owners at the allegedly high rates charged by the NER on coal to Tyne Dock. The promoters of the scheme wanted their line to run from the Pelton area to Dunston-on-Tyne, where new large staiths could be built. The aim was to give the collieries of the Pelton district cheaper transportation of their coal to the Tyne, and lower dock dues. A few years earlier such a plan would not have been possible owing to the mudflats and other navigational difficulties in the Tyne between Gateshead and Dunston, but the river authority of the Tyne had recently improved the navigational possibilities. In particular, the old Tyne road bridge had been replaced by a hydraulic swing bridge so that vessels of 1,500 to 1,600 tons could reach Elswick, opposite Dunston.

The West Durham & Tyne Railway was planned to run from Pelton Fell (close to Stella Gill on the Stanhope & Tyne) to Dunston through Birtley, following the river Team valley to Dunston. It paralleled the NER main line for some of this distance, and had links with four NER lines and two wagonways. The disturbing feature for the NER was the promoters' cool proposal to seek running powers over the NER between Pelton (Stella Gill) and Rowley, through the Stanley and Annfield coal areas and past Consett, and also from Lamesley (north of Birtley) to Tyne Dock and to Newcastle Central station.

Clearly the promoters were not just seeking a local line to take Pelton coal to Dunston, but intended to create a substantial rival to the NER in North Durham. Naturally the larger company completely opposed the whole plan.

Both sides made their claims in Parliament during 1885, when the West Durham & Tyne Bill was presented. The NER case was that it had provided good facilities and reasonable rates to the north-west Durham coal industry for many years, and that it had not raised its charges for a quarter of a century, even during the period of great mining prosperity in the 1870s. The House of Commons Committee had no adverse comments to make on the NER but it adopted a democratic ideal that the coal owners in question should have the option of sending their coal to Dunston instead of Tyne Dock if they wished and if it was to their advantage. The Bill was therefore approved.

As at other times in its history, it appeared that the NER was about to lose its case but it managed to avert such an event. In the House of Lords it adopted a compromise approach by stressing the existing rail facilities it provided in the region, and stating that with minor additions to this network it could provide a relatively direct link between Pelton and Dunston without the necessity and great expense of building an entirely new railway. The Lords Committee was suitably impressed when they had studied the maps and plans, and accepted the NER case on the condition that the works be done as soon as practicable and that new staiths be erected at Dunston. The West Durham & Tyne Bill therefore failed. Whether this was regarded as a tragedy by its promoters, led by Sir George Elliot, is not recorded, but it is not impossible that the eventual result was what the coal owners had hoped for. The parliamentary expenses would have been well worth while when the result was the desired route to, and new staiths at Dunston, paid for by the NER. An outline of the major railway improvements made in the Dunston district is given in Chapter 7.

THE SOUTH PELAW—ANNFIELD PLAIN DEVIATION LINE

Although the West Durham & Tyne scheme had been primarily concerned with obtaining improved rail facilities for coal traffic, it had also been the intention of the promoters to run a passenger service for the Stanley and Annfield Plain areas in particular, to Newcastle Central station. The NER very fairly decided to take this into account, being aware of the local feeling on this subject, and so a general improvement of the railway from Stella Gill to Annfield Plain was decided upon. The district was surveyed for a locomotive worked line to parallel the existing S & T line, which would meet the needs of the region for all kinds of traffic. The new deviation line was eventually planned to run from South Pelaw, about half a mile east of Stella Gill, to Annfield Plain, through Pelton village, Beamish and Shield Row, a distance of six and a half miles. The junction with the existing route at Annfield was to be a few chains east of the junction between the two routes to East Castle mentioned already.

In addition to this major new line there was to be a spur line from South Pelaw to join the Team valley main line south of Birtley to allow coal traffic to get to Dunston and passenger traffic to Newcastle.

The 'Annfield Deviation' ran from South Pelaw junction in a westerly then north-westerly direction, running westwards again through Beamish and turning south-westwards from Shield Row to Annfield Plain, never being over a mile north of the old S & T route. It therefore skirted the high parts of the plateau which the S & T had crossed with resulting heavy gradients; even so, the new line needed gradients of as steep as 1 in 35 and 1 in 50, and very little of it was at less than 1 in 100. It was at gradients of between 1 in 50 and 1 in 60 for most of its course. The 1 in 35 section, west of Shield Row, was about a quarter of a mile long, and through the Beamish district there were several miles continually at 1 in 51 and 1 in 55. These heavy gradients were the penalty incurred in providing an alternative route to the inclines to the south. The Bill to sanction construction of this line was presented to Parliament during the 1887 Session and received the Royal Assent on 23 May 1887.

The line was to be of double track, and have stations at Pelton, Beamish, Shield Row (for the Stanley and Tanfield districts) and Annfield Plain. The latter was to replace the existing goods station of the same name (which had been named Annfield until October 1884) and was to be situated on the 1886 route to East Castle. There was already talk of doubling the line from East Castle to Consett, to allow a passenger service all the way to Consett, and this will be mentioned later. Another reason for this consideration lay in a proposal made by the Consett Iron Co in 1885. The NER received a letter from W. Jenkins of the iron company on the cost of transit of haematite ore from Tyne Dock and Sunderland to Consett blast furnaces and asking 'the lowest rate at which ore could be conveyed from or near Dunston-on-Tyne to Consett as they contemplate landing the ore direct from vessels which have brought it from Spain at a quay on the Tyne at or near Dunston'. This letter of April 1885 was referred to the NER general manager and may have played a part in the Annfield Plain deviation decision, as well as in the East Castle—Consett widening proposal. It can be added here that the Consett Iron Co did not make Dunston their ore terminal after all.

At the beginning of 1890 tenders were invited for constructing the line. The NER estimate for the works was £107,000, and the lowest tender received, that of Messrs Whitaker Bros of Horsforth near Leeds for £92,055 18s 8d (£92,055.93) was accepted. Apart from the gradients, some heavy engineering was also necessary for the new line in contrast to the statement made in the petition of 1881 quoted earlier. Works included a half mile embankment from near South Pelaw to Pelton, another embankment at Pelton village, a long, deep cutting at Beamish, a half mile long embankment at Annfield Plain and short cuttings and an embankment at Shield Row and Stanley. Beamish cutting was the major engineering effort, being about a mile long and having an average depth of twenty-five feet. About 250,000 cubic yards of spoil were removed in constructing it. In the picturesque Hell Hole wood west of Beamish, the line skirted the Beamish burn valley and afforded a fine view northwards towards Ravensworth. Iron girder bridges were mainly used to cross the numerous lanes and roads but some overbridges were built entirely of brick or stone. Preliminary work began during the year. The total amount expended on the line and land etc at the end of 1890 was £95,222.

In June 1890 the NER considered the construction of new passenger stations and decided that they should be single-storey structures almost entirely of wood (excluding the station houses). It was decided that the verandas should have a less fragile covering than glass (wood again), and the stationmaster's and porters' houses should be placed 'where practicable' near colliery buildings. This decision was not final, for in September the district engineer and architect's report on the same subject said that wooden stations would be as costly as stone ones and unlike the latter, would require painting and be subject to decay. 'We would therefore suggest that the stone buildings be erected.' Nearly a year later with work on the railway well under way the NER resolved this question. On 6 August 1891 it was reported that 'Mr Harrison and the architect having reported further with reference to the character of the station etc buildings on the new Annfield Plain and Team Valley line' – resolved – 'that the stations, warehouses and signal cabins be built of wood'. Mr C. A. Harrison was divisional chief engineer. During 1891-2 the NER gave £20 per annum to the Navvy Mission Society on behalf of the men employed in building the railway. (In 1892 slow progress was reported 'owing to scarcity of men'—Directors' report.) Work was nearly complete in the early part of 1893 and the official opening for goods traffic was on 13 November 1893. The line had no connections with any other lines between South Pelaw junction and Annfield East junction, but several lines crossed it at various points. The Beamish wagonway crossed it by overbridges at Beamish and Pelton, while the West Stanley—West Shield Row wagonway (branching from the S & T at West Stanley) also crossed it by an overbridge almost five miles west of South Pelaw junction. At South Pelaw, where the line left the old route to Stella Gill, climbing at 1 in 56 to Pelton station, there were four main tracks as well as sidings. The curve to the main line, about three quarters of a mile long, was opened on 16 October 1893 at the same time as new lines near Dunston and Dunston staiths were opened. The junction of this spur with the main line was named Ouston junction. A few years later, the whole of the main line, from Ouston junction to Low Fell junction south of Gateshead, was widened to four tracks to meet traffic pressure, mainly of coal from the Stanley area to Dunston. This was authorised by an Act of 6 August 1897 and opened in 1900. Stella Gill goods station was closed in 1894, being replaced by

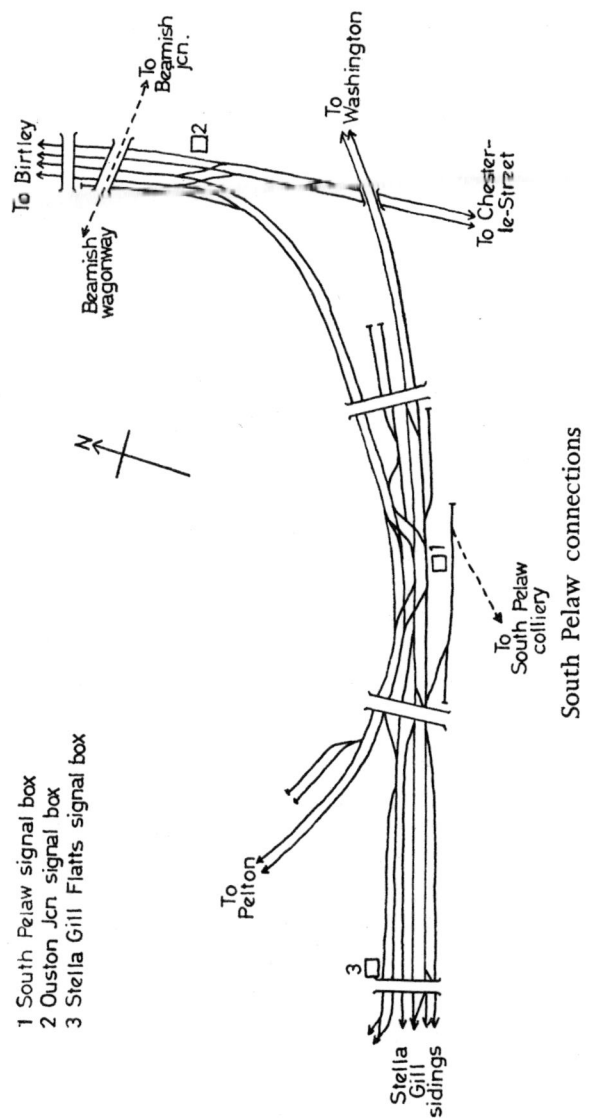

South Pelaw connections

1 South Pelaw signal box
2 Ouston Jcn signal box
3 Stella Gill Flatts signal box

the new station at Pelton, a mile west of South Pelaw, although a mineral office remained in use there.

The Newcastle—Annfield Plain passenger service began on 1 February 1894, on which day the new stations at Pelton, Beamish, Shield Row and Annfield Plain opened. Soon after its beginning, the service was operated by brand new 0-4-4 tank engines of Class O designed by Wilson Worsdell, which were to see long service on the line. On the main line these trains called at Gateshead West, Bensham, Low Fell, Lamesley and

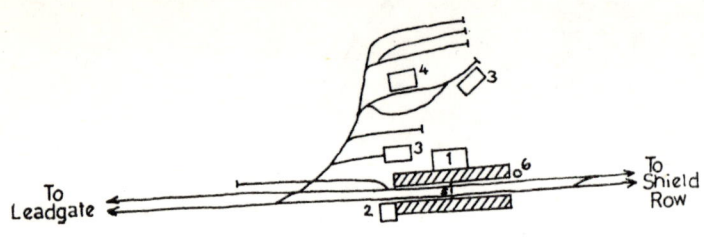

1 station buildings
2 signal box
3 loading docks
4 warehouse
5 footbridge
6 water crane

Annfield Plain 1894 station

Birtley stations. The new service was a considerable boon to the mining areas it served and passenger traffic was to grow rapidly in succeeding years. In the railway age, any populous area deprived of a convenient passenger service became isolated and so the new line filled an overdue need. This may be illustrated by an announcement in the *Durham Chronicle* for 2 February 1894 by the Beamish, Pontop & Consett Agricultural Society. At the annual general meeting of the Society 'it was unanimously resolved to hold the next yearly show at West Stanley on Wednesday August 15, this course having been rendered practicable by the opening of the new passenger railway through West Durham as far as Annfield Plain'. This was not an obscure society, for miners were generally keen gardeners (and, by the way, also pigeon fanciers, a fact often shown by pigeon 'baskets' on local station platforms on this and other branches).

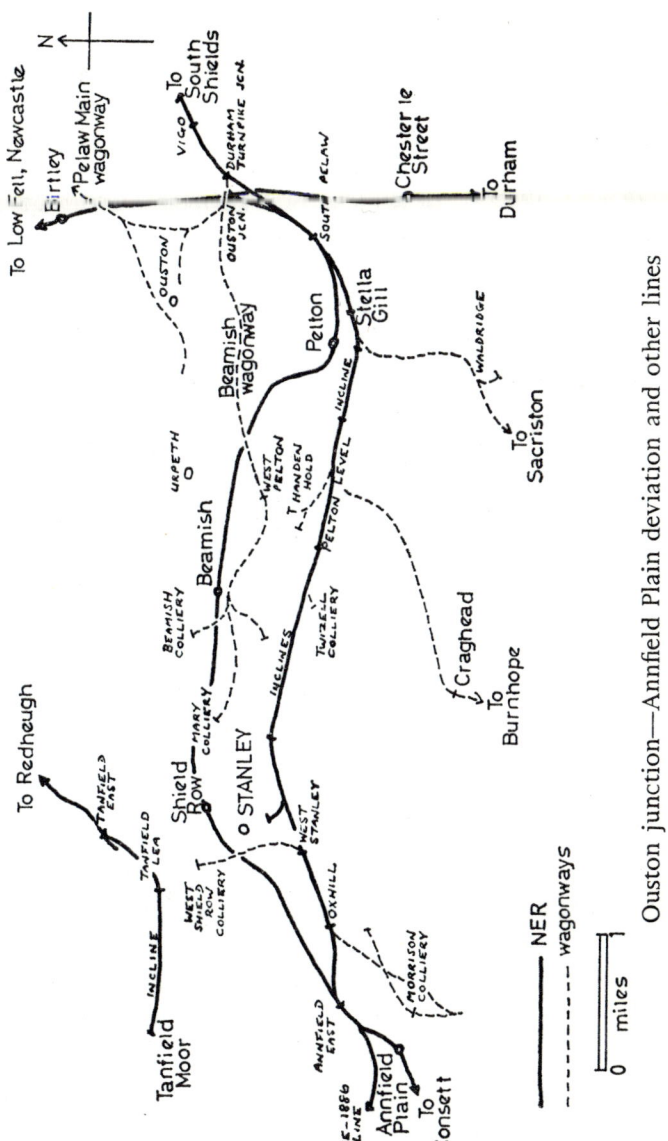

Ouston junction—Annfield Plain deviation and other lines

After completion of the line, the NER received notice in December 1893 from Whitaker Bros that they 'alleged a loss on their contract for the line and applied for an allowance'. They had tendered to build Annfield Plain station for £5,241 18s 5d (£5,241.92), while the NER estimate was £8,161 14s 10d (£8,161.74), and so their loss is perhaps not surprising. The cost of other architectural work on the new line was £12,116 10s 2d (£12,116.51), of which total signal boxes comprised £897 0s 4d (£897.02); station buildings cost £3,384 8s 7d (£3,384.43); and stationmasters' houses and various cottages took £6,051 14s 1d (£6,051.70).

IMPROVEMENTS NEAR CONSETT

In the late 1880s the Consett Iron Co had gone in for steel production and the resulting increase in traffic forced them to arrange an enlargement of their sidings facilities with the NER. In February 1890 these improvements were estimated at no less than £36,500, of which £15,000 was to be paid by the iron company. Initial sidings alterations were awarded to T. D. Ridley of Middlesbrough, who tendered for £13,659 in April, and this work was begun soon afterwards. Also ordered by the NER was a new spur between the S & T line to join the Lanchester Valley line in the vicinity of the old Lanchester Valley passenger station at Consett. In fact this link line had been planned in 1882, and tenders for its construction were advertised for in 1883 at the same time as for the Annfield—East Castle line. Nothing further was done, and in 1890 the work was 'not to be begun till powers are obtained in a Bill of this Session'. Powers were obtained and the line was built by T. D. Ridley who tendered at £10,160 17s 3d (£10,160.86). It was about thirty-five chains long, reaching 1 in 49 gradient, and was double track. It crossed the Lanchester Valley line and the 1868 Hownes Gill loop by a stone and girder overbridge, and joined the Lanchester line close to the old passenger station. Its junction with the S & T was named Consett East junction, and a typical NER brick signal box was erected here. This short but important connecting line opened in 1893, and cost £764 0s 7d (£764.03) more than the tendered figure.

With the opening of the new line from Ouston junction to

PONTOP BRANCH PROGRESS

Annfield Plain via South Pelaw in 1893, the single track section from East Castle through Leadgate to Consett must have be-

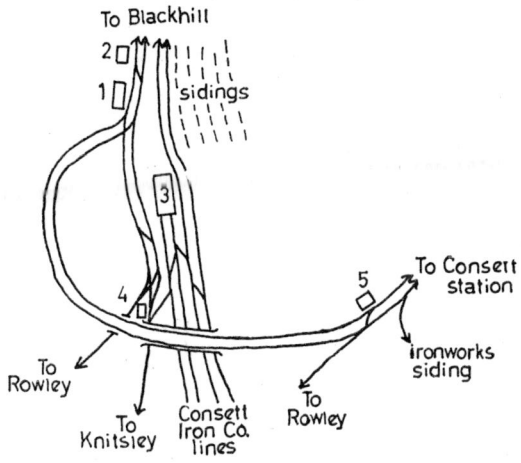

1 Consett 1862 station
2 Consett North signal box
3 Consett (Blackhill) MPD
4 Consett South signal box
5 Consett East signal box

Junctions at Consett (simplified)

come a bottleneck very quickly. In May 1894, when the NER was ready to invite tenders for the widening work, the Consett Iron Co raised the objection that 'the proposal to convert the line between the points referred to into a passenger line is likely to interfere with the Consett Co's traffic'. The NER therefore entered into negotiations with the iron company on the matter and the further delay so irritated the Consett Local Board that it took action. In July a deputation from the Board went off to York to meet the Way and Works Committee of the NER and asked them to proceed with the improvement of the railway to allow passenger trains to run from Annfield Plain to Consett as early as possible, 'the line being much needed for the accommodation of the district'. The NER explained to the delegation that the delay was due to negotiations with the Consett Iron Co on coal traffic and it expected 'probably within the present month' to advertise for tenders for constructing the line. In fact a draft advertisement was issued on 5 July 1894 and tenders for construction were received on 26 July. In October 1892 the estimate for the widening work was £59,621 for engineering, £18,500 for architectural works and £6,500 for land. The 1896 revised estimate was £42,786 for the engineering work, and the lowest tender, that of J. D. Nowell & Sons of London for £36,917 5s 5d (£36,917.27) was accepted. Architectural work on the scheme including the new Consett and Leadgate stations was now estimated at £12,764, and the tender of A. J. Cooke of Stockton for £11,887 7s 2d (£11,887.36) was accepted for this (Nowell had put in a tender at £12,950 for this work).

No time was lost and work began in August 1894. On 3 January 1895 the divisional engineer reported to the company that 'good progress has been made with this work'. Basically the work comprised the provision of a second line of rails but this entailed a number of new bridges, including a pair at Carr House and Leadgate which replaced level crossings. The alignment was altered slightly in some locations. Both new stations made much use of wood in their construction following the pattern established on the Annfield Plain deviation line. Disruption of traffic was inevitable, which the Consett Iron Co had feared but for which they were no doubt compensated, and the alternative lines to Consett were more heavily utilised. Work was completed in August 1896, and on 17 August the Newcastle—Annfield Plain passenger trains were extended to Blackhill using the 1893 curve from Consett east to north junctions.

In 1897 the NER had to meet two claims put in as a result of the widening. A school at Brooms near Leadgate claimed £1,475 for land taken for the work and compensation for 'severance and injurious affection'. The NER approved £150. A jury assessed the claim and awarded the school £220. The 'Travellers' Rest beerhouse' at Consett wanted compensation as the closure of Delves Lane level crossing had affected its trade, or so it claimed. It wanted £550 and the NER gave £325.

The local press had a certain amount of comment on the new passenger service, which was the fourth to use Blackhill if the Lanchester Valley and Blaydon & Consett services be considered separately. The *Newcastle Daily Journal* for 13 August

1896 had an article entitled 'The Annfield Plain & Blackhill Railway', which began: 'On February 1 1894 the North Eastern

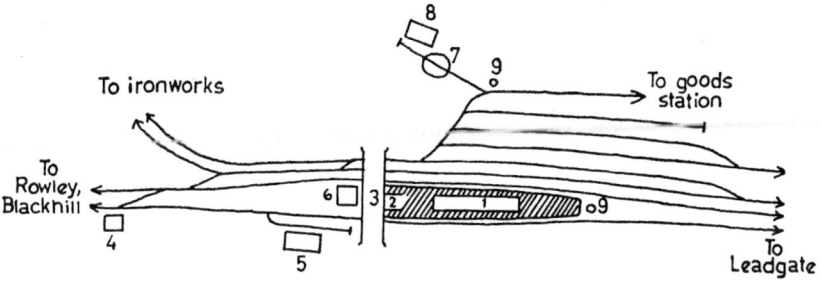

1 station buildings
2 ramp
3 Delves Lane bridge
4 Carr House West signal box
5 loading dock
6 mineral office
7 turntable
8 water tank
9 water cranes

Consett 1896 station

Railway Company opened for goods, mineral [sic] and passenger traffic a new line connecting Annfield Plain with the main Team Valley route. The branch has proved an inestimable boon in many respects. To tradespeople it has given access to several populous districts and to the residents of those parts it has afforded an easy means of reaching Newcastle. The heavy Saturday bookings indicate the extent to which the facility has been taken advantage of. But the company has now completed a further extension in this direction and on Monday next there will be put into ordinary public use a stretch of rails by which a circle will be practically constituted, the latest addition to the system of the company connecting Annfield Plain with Blackhill station. The length of the new line is about $6\frac{1}{2}$ miles. The Annfield and Blackhill line has involved a very large expenditure. The gradient in several parts is extremely heavy being at one place 1 in 50. From Annfield Plain a gradual rise is experienced and hence to Blackhill there are alternate ups and downs, the line being almost in the form of a switchback. The erection of numerous bridges has been found necessary.'

The first train on the opening day was the 6.10am from

Newcastle to Blackhill, and there was no formal opening ceremony, but the *Durham County Advertiser* stated that the train was 'freely patronised'. The first service comprised five trains each way every weekday, but there were several additional trains on certain days on the section east of Annfield Plain. On 19 August the new service was fully tested when the Beamish Pontop & Consett Agricultural Society held its annual show at Consett, the showground being closer to the new Consett station than to Blackhill.

ENGINE SHEDS

Stella Gill engine shed, housing eight locomotives, dated from 1858, in which year a new shed was authorised at Tyne Dock. This had opened by 1862 and expanded considerably during the 1870s. In October 1893 a shed was authorised for Pelton Level, west of Waldridge incline, to handle traffic coming down the inclines and from the wagonways to Burnhope and West Pelton. The tender of Kell and Groves of Chester-le-Street for £492 4s 11d (£492.24½) was accepted on 5 April 1894, and the small shed was opened later in the year. Usually a handful of engines, mostly of the shunting tank type were based at Pelton Level. Annfield shed was enlarged in 1893 in anticipation of the opening of the South Pelaw—Annfield line. This shed normally housed locomotives only for goods and mineral workings.

TYNE DOCK IRON ORE

The famous Tyne Dock—Consett iron ore traffic began in 1880, although for many years afterwards a certain proportion of iron ore also came from Sunderland. (For many years the ore was mined in northern Spain.) Sunderland ore usually reached Consett via Durham and Lanchester (although in later years it could be sent via Washington and South Pelaw), while the Tyne Dock iron ore travelled on the S & T route throughout until recent years. Its journey was made easier when the S & T inclines were bypassed. Ore trains required banking up the severe gradients from South Pelaw junction as far as South Medomsley, just east of Leadgate. They also required assistance up the initial gradient from the Tyne (Tyne Dock Bottom) to Tyne Dock shed a half mile to the south, before traversing the level section to South Pelaw. The powerful NER Class T3 0-8-0 engines (LNER Class Q7) were particularly suited to working the ore trains and many of the class were based at Tyne Dock for many years. The Tyne Dock ore trains are still running to Consett, but their route from the Tyne to South Pelaw has been changed, and double heading with diesel engines has replaced steam. However the trains still have to struggle up the steep slopes west of South Pelaw, and often reach a low speed.

PASSENGER GROWTH 1894-1920

From the start passenger traffic at all stations, including Pelton to Consett, grew rapidly up to the years after the World War I. The stations at Shield Row and Annfield Plain, which served the most populous districts (excluding Consett itself), showed a particularly marked growth in traffic. This may be judged by a simple comparison of passengers booked in various yearly periods, for instance in 1898, 1903 and 1913:

Station	1898	1903	1913
Pelton	45,614	63,706	78,316
Beamish	32,149	49,536	66,524
Shield Row	81,997	117,099	170,308
Annfield Plain	60,042	82,520	114,212
Leadgate	56,673	71,975	67,733
Consett	50,040	66,641	79,041

Only at Leadgate was there any decline. Receipts in 1913 ranged from £2,146 at Leadgate to £7,084 at Annfield Plain and £12,399 at Shield Row. For all six stations in 1898 the receipts were £14,526; in 1913 the total was £31,014. At Shield Row the receipts in the first full year of operation (1895) were £3,506, a figure which grew steadily almost each year afterwards, totalling £9,659 in 1907 and £16,640 in 1919.

The train service was also improved and augmented. By 1911 there were eight trains each way on weekdays between Newcastle and Blackhill or Consett (some trains terminated or commenced at Consett), but further trains ran on the Newcastle—

Annfield Plain section, and other additional trains on the line on specific days. Steam autocars appeared on the line from about 1907. There were two Sunday trains each way in 1911 and on alternate Sundays there was an additional train between Blackhill and Lamesley. The Sunday service had been started in 1898, and by 1917 there were three Sunday trains each way, two each way being over the whole line, the third being Newcastle—Shield Row in one direction and Annfield Plain—Newcastle in the other direction. The weekday service at this time consisted of nine trains from Newcastle to Blackhill or Consett, and ten the other way, with various additional trains especially on Saturdays when traffic was heaviest. Steam autocars had no duties on the line by this date, although they remained on the Derwent valley branch.

There was no great diminution in traffic until 1921, but then the decline was severe. The decline matched that mentioned for the Lanchester Valley and Blaydon & Consett lines in particular. The number of passengers at Annfield Plain dropped from 119,944 in 1920 to 76,495 in 1921, and receipts dropped from £11,843 to £7,713. The same sort of decline occurred at the other stations, and at Shield Row there was a fall of nearly 50,000; 138,664 passengers had been booked in 1920 while in the following year the figure was 89,760, and receipts fell by over £5,000. The motor age was having its first serious effects and worse was to follow. At least the NER, which became part of the LNER from 1 January 1923, did not survive to witness the tremendous decline in passenger traffic on its Annfield Plain branch by the 1930s. If it had it may well have wondered whether its expenditure in the nineties had really been worth while.

MAINLY COAL

Coal traffic continued to dominate the scene between Consett and the South Pelaw area right up to the 1920s. The numerous collieries and a smaller number of coke ovens passed traffic on to the railway in vast quantities every year for all sorts of destinations. In 1885 there were some thirty major collieries or coke ovens making use of the S & T line between South Pelaw colliery at the east end, and collieries of the Consett Iron Co

Page 139: *COAL TRAINS*
(above) *A T2 climbs the 1 in 56 towards Pelton from South Pelaw, passing a K1 with a coal train from Stella Gill, 22 April 1955;* (below) *3MT 2–6–0 No 77010 with Inkerman colliery train, Tow Law, 4 September 1963*

Page 140: *T2 0–8–0 ACTION*
(above) *No 63371 arrives at Gateshead from the Dunston line, with coal empties, 19 May 1964;* (below) *another T2 leaves Burnhill junction for Consett, with the goods train from Weatherhill. The Weathcrhill and Waskerley line is behind the engine*

around Consett itself at the west. Some of these establishments sent very great tonnages on to the railway. Medomsley colliery, for instance, sent 156,786 tons of coal and 19,831 tons of coke in 1885; in the same year the coal and coke traffic from West Stanley colliery was 53,846 tons, coal from Eden colliery, Leadgate was 82,177 tons and South Medomsley colliery near Leadgate supplied 52,338 tons of coal and coke. The total receipts from these four collieries alone was over £23,784 so the large annual income from coal traffic throughout this region by the NER can be imagined.

Traffic from the Consett ironworks passed on to other branches besides the Pontop line, but it is convenient to record that in the 1900s total iron and steel traffic was over 200,000 tons per annum. In 1913 it was over 227,000 tons. The company's brick works at Consett provided a steady traffic, including 3,545 tons during 1906. Brick traffic was also a feature at other places on the Pontop line. At Pelton the brick tonnage was 6,027 tons in 1906 and 3,989 tons in 1907, and there was a smaller traffic at Leadgate and Beamish. Both Shield Row and Beamish had a small traffic in building stone at the same period. The main item of traffic at Annfield Plain station in 1913 was 3,620 tons of sand and loam. Livestock traffic was not of great significance and is summarised below for the years 1897 and 1907. There was no livestock traffic at Leadgate, and none at Pelton prior to 1906:

	1897 head	1907 head
Pelton	0	2,334
Beamish	175	583
Shield Row	1,858	4,983
Annfield Plain	1,286	2,838
Consett	51	92

Station goods traffic forwarded and received is detailed overleaf for 1899. This excludes livestock and major minerals (coal, coke, limestone, lime):

	Goods Forwarded tons	Received tons
Pelton	6,335	42,967
Beamish	636	14,294
Shield Row	375	14,934
Annfield Plain	12,838	42,699
Leadgate	1,445	6,450
Consett	1,671	18,656

Before the opening of the South Pelaw—Annfield Plain deviation line in 1893, there were only two goods stations between these points on the S & T line. These were Annfield Plain (Annfield until 1884), which handled general goods but not minerals, and Stella Gill, which handled both. In 1889 the traffic at these stations was as follows:

	Minerals tons	Goods Forwarded tons	Received tons
Stella Gill	157	3,523	21,533
Annfield Plain	0	3,726	42,643

The vast coal traffic at Stella Gill sidings is not included, the 157 tons consisting of coal and probably also some lime for retail sale.

In 1906 the NER began a steam wagon road service from Newcastle Forth goods station to Stanley to provide a quicker goods service for that populous area. Mr K. Hoole has described this in an article: 'this traffic had previously gone out on the pickup goods the following day but it could now be delivered on the same day as it arrived in Newcastle. However traffic on this service did not exceed 4 tons 6 cwt per day and expenses were high. The wagons were frequently breaking down and often had to be left standing overnight: consequently the service was withdrawn on 27 February 1908.'

A relic of the days of the S & T is still visible at East Castle, near Annfield Plain. These are the old Annfield lime kilns which remain in a surprisingly well preserved state in view of their long period of dereliction, and are close to the 1886 deviation line from East Castle to Annfield Plain. Decay has not yet toppled part of an inscribed stone block bearing the words 'Railroad Co' and 'T. E. Harrison. Engineer, 1835'. In Annfield Plain itself is the 'Stanhope & Tyne Railway' hotel beside a level crossing, closed in 1959, the line ending beside the road as a siding. Another 'railway' hotel is the 'North Eastern' hotel, still present outside Blackhill station.

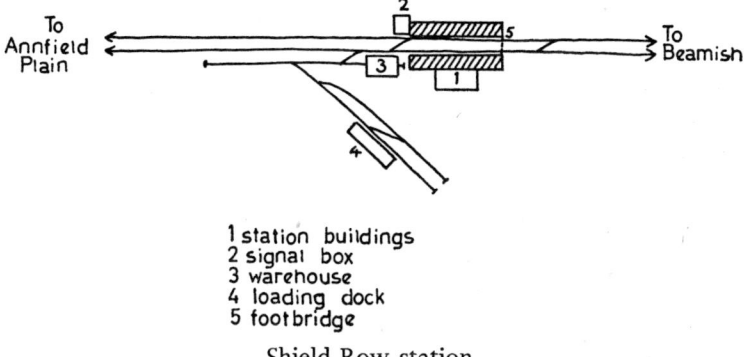

1 station buildings
2 signal box
3 warehouse
4 loading dock
5 footbridge

Shield Row station

CHAPTER SEVEN

Tyneside Consolidation

DUNSTON EXTENSION RAILWAY

Following the West Durham & Tyne affair, the NER went ahead with its improvements in the Dunston-on-Tyne area. Work on the new Dunston staiths commenced on 26 August 1890, and they were to be reached by a two and a half mile double track line from the Team Valley main line at Low Fell. This line was named the Dunston Extension Railway and it was constructed in 1890-2. £72,273 had been spent on the line up to the end of 1890. The line included a long embankment, and a girder bridge across the river Team on the approach to the staiths. A loop connected the line to the former Newcastle & Carlisle Railway Redheugh branch (Dunston East junction) and the loop also had a girder bridge over the Team. The junction faced westwards. The 'severe weather which has prevailed' interfered with the works in the winter of 1890-1, but the NER directors reported on 5 February 1892 that 'the new railway from Low Fell to Dunston has been completed, but owing to difficulties arising from bad foundations, the erection of the Shipping Staiths at Dunston has been much delayed until towards the end of this year'. However on 10 February 1893 the directors were only able to report that 'all the new works under construction have made satisfactory progress except the Shipping Staiths at Dunston, in regard to which progress has been slow. It is expected that these Staiths will be ready for traffic in May next.' The staiths and the Dunston Extension line were opened officially on 16 October 1893, from which date coal traffic from the Pelton and Stanley districts began to travel to Dunston in increasing quantities. The staiths were 1,709ft in length with three shipping berths about 260ft apart. There were two sets

TYNESIDE CONSOLIDATION

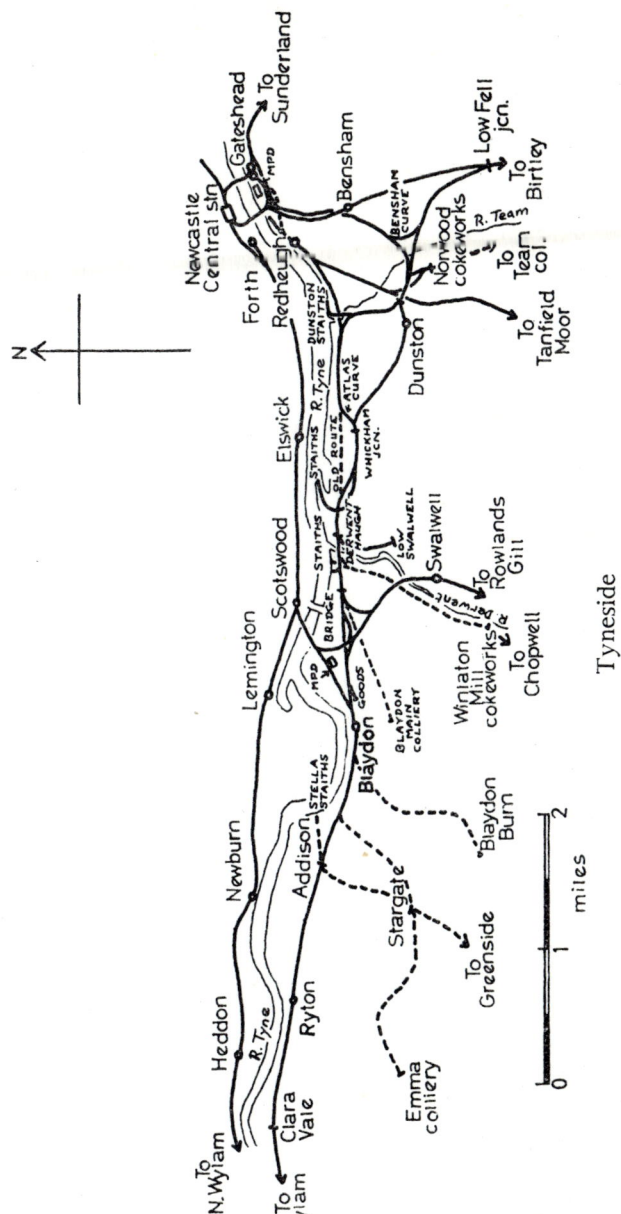

Tyneside

of side-tipping spouts to each, the lowest thirty-five feet and the highest forty-three feet above high water level. The staiths were extended in 1899-1900.

One result of the opening of the staiths was that the old West Dunston staiths, near Derwenthaugh, gradually declined in importance and were largely redundant within ten years. Dunston staiths have remained in use to this day although their present traffic is much less than in the pre-1914 days. In November 1905 the quay wall at the staiths collapsed and had to be rebuilt.

The junction of the Dunston Extension with the main line at Low Fell, facing south, provided a new route from the south to the Newcastle & Carlisle line which avoided Newcastle. The route curved considerably near Dunston staiths and along the Tyne, and within a decade the NER resolved to improve the route by constructing a more direct line through Dunston.

THE DERWENTHAUGH BRANCH

An Act of 2 August 1898 empowered the NER to construct the Derwenthaugh branch, a two-mile line from Dunston to east of Derwenthaugh, providing a direct route for through traffic from the Low Fell junction to the Newcastle & Carlisle line at Blaydon. The line was built in 1903-4, and opened on 29 August 1904. It was a double track line and included a short deep cutting in Dunston with a short embankment further to the west. The new line left the Dunston Extension at Norwood junction, and a new goods station for Dunston was opened twenty-one chains west of the junction on 1 March 1905. Just east of Norwood junction, incidentally, the Dunston Extension embankment crossed the old Tanfield branch with no connections between the lines. Further to the east a short branch served Norwood colliery and coke ovens, and the ovens are still in operation today. A spur line from the ovens joined the Tanfield branch, facing north, at Teams: this was part of the Team colliery wagonway from mines in the Team valley, to Dunston.

On 22 April 1907 a new loop from Dunston to Gateshead was opened from Norwood junction to near the Gateshead MPD, burrowing under the main line tracks at Bensham by a

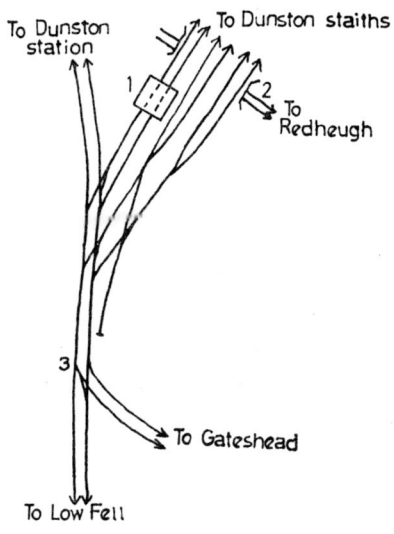

1 Norwood signal box
2 Tanfield branch
3 Dunston Extension jcn.

Norwood junction

short tunnel. This improvement allowed traffic from Dunston and the Newcastle & Carlisle line to reach Newcastle easily or travel along the Sunderland branch. The King Edward bridge across the Tyne from Gateshead to Newcastle had been opened on 1 October 1906 to augment the traffic-saturated High Level bridge. On 1 January 1909 a Newcastle—Dunston passenger service began, operated mainly by steam autocars. Dunston station was thus opened for passenger traffic, and comprised an island platform between the two running lines, with a ramp to the nearby road overbridge as the passenger entrance. The service ran to Newcastle using the 1907 loop line to King Edward Bridge junction.

Dunston was a populous industrial district and the service was quite successful. Some idea of the passenger traffic at Dunston station may be judged from the following figures:

Year	Number	Receipts (£)
1909	43,152	410
1910	42,559	359
1911	44,780	374
1912	49,631	418
1913	65,122	642
1914	73,082	832
1920	48,699	791
1921	54,798	921

During the World War I, Dunston station was closed on 1 May 1918 as an economy measure and reopened on 1 October 1919. Road transport was a growing factor, however, and motor omnibuses competed with the Dunston—Newcastle passenger trains. Even in 1914 traffic receipts at Dunston were less than the expenses: £1,096 against expenses of £1,180. The passenger service was withdrawn and Dunston station closed to passengers on 23 May 1926.

Other traffic at Dunston included minerals, parcels and milk. General goods traffic was small and was accredited to Gateshead goods station. Parcels receipts were £110 in 1909 and £794 in 1920. Mineral traffic totalled 2,906 tons in 1914, and milk traffic was 528 cans (5,280 gallons) in 1920.

The old Redheugh goods station beside the Tyne and dating back to N & CR days had a heavy goods traffic up to the early 1900s when the opening of the new lines in Dunston tended to divert traffic to Gateshead. Thus in 1904 goods traffic at Redheugh was 268,476 tons, but by 1908 it had fallen to a mere 13,441 tons. Much of the traffic at Redheugh was of minerals, chiefly coal. In 1885 mineral traffic had been 87,092 tons and other goods 81,187 tons. Not all the mineral traffic was coal, however. As there was only one shoot, the NER decided in March 1883 to provide a second lead ore shoot at the quayside for £40-£50 because of 'the inconvenience and delay in transferring lead ore from truck to keel'.

Further west, Derwenthaugh goods station, also dating from N & CR days, had a heavy traffic, although receipts were less than those at Redheugh. In 1885 mineral traffic at Derwenthaugh was 19,475 tons and goods traffic 7,390 tons. Traffic here

TYNESIDE CONSOLIDATION 149

included coal (some from nearby Low Swalwell colliery), bricks, iron and steel and rails, there being an iron foundry nearby. The old N & CR coke ovens had been sold by the NER to private interests shortly after 1862. In 1906 iron and steel traffic at Derwenthaugh was 14,804 tons and rails 14,045 tons. Brick traffic totalled 4,797 tons in the same year, and there was also a traffic in clay.

In 1900 traffic receipts at Redheugh were £30,622 and expenses £1,540 while the respective amounts at Derwenthaugh were £8,978 and £191. However, traffic at the latter was much greater than the receipts suggest. In 1906 Derwenthaugh had a mineral traffic of no less than 375,650 tons, and goods traffic was 60,718 tons forwarded and 81,499 tons received. This massive traffic produced receipts totalling only £8,993. Coal traffic here declined subsequent to the closure of the West Dunston staiths nearby, whose traffic was diverted to the new Dunston staiths. The Consett Iron Co also had its own staiths west of Derwenthaugh, and these were enlarged at the turn of the century. Derwenthaugh coal traffic fell from 334,821 tons in 1909 to 21,290 tons in 1910. The approach line to the West Dunston staiths was also closed; this was about three-quarters of a mile long and had an embankment, and bridges over the Redheugh branch and over various sidings.

ATLAS CURVE AND BLAYDON LOOPS

The loop lines at Blaydon have been referred to in Chapter 5. The 'Blaydon Loop' itself was only 26 chains long, it was sanctioned in 1894 and opened in 1898. It allowed traffic from the Derwenthaugh and Dunston direction to run into Newcastle over Scotswood bridge without the need to reverse to Blaydon itself.

The line was built as a result of the experience of August-November 1893, when the strike of Yorkshire and Midlands coal miners caused a huge demand for north-east coal from those regions. Much came from Northumberland, and soon traffic was so heavy that some trains were diverted from Newcastle to Blaydon and back to the main line via Dunston, as the three-track High Level bridge could not meet the traffic efficiently. Thus for some time there was a stream of coal trains arriving at Blaydon from Newcastle and having to reverse before proceeding on to the Redheugh branch. The Blaydon Loop allowed future traffic to run through from Scotswood towards Derwenthaugh and provided an alternative route to the High Level bridge. Actually the opening of the four-track King Edward VII bridge from Newcastle to Gateshead in 1906 made the Blaydon Loop less essential in this respect, but it formed part of the regular route for goods trains between Forth station Newcastle and the south.

The loop line from the Blaydon & Consett branch at Swalwell North to the Redheugh branch at Blaydon Main, west of Derwenthaugh, was opened on 24 February 1908, allowing traffic from the Consett direction to reach Dunston without reversing at Blaydon. This line, the Blaydon south-east curve, was double track, as with the Blaydon Loop. At about this time the Blaydon Main wagonway, which joined the Redheugh branch at Blaydon Main junction, fell into disuse following closure of the colliery and was later dismantled.

The Redheugh branch itself was affected by the decision to construct an electricity power station at Dunston beside the Tyne in the early 1900s. The power station was to be built on land crossed by the Redheugh branch between Derwenthaugh and Dunston, and the NER had to arrange for a diversion of the railway to the south of the site. The result was the Atlas curve from Dunston west junction to a point on the Derwenthaugh branch (Whickham junction), and the line was twenty-seven chains in length. It was a double track line and was opened on 16 June 1908. The old route disappeared except for sidings at the Derwenthaugh end, and a siding into the new power station from Dunston west junction. Exchange sidings were laid in the power station grounds. Between Whickham junction and Derwenthaugh (three-quarters of mile), four tracks were provided to prevent any hold up to traffic on the Derwenthaugh branch and the new Atlas curve.

There was never a regular passenger service on the Derwenthaugh branch west of Dunston station, but occasionally the line was used by diverted passenger trains. Mr J. S. Maclean recorded the diversion of N & CR line trains via Dunston after a derailment at Elswick during World War II while he was in a Newcastle—Carlisle train headed by Pacific No 2748 *Colo-*

rado. The line was also used by trains diverted into Newcastle. from the south, via Blaydon Loop.

A final addition to the Dunston area network came in 1922-3 when a short loop line was opened between the Dunston Extension and the Dunston—Gateshead loop in Bensham (known as the Bensham curve), which especially allowed goods trains from the south to reach Newcastle without travelling over the busy two-track main line from Low Fell to Gateshead. Such trains could run from Low Fell junction to the Bensham curve, and then by the Dunston—Gateshead loop to the King Edward or High Level bridges. Occasionally passenger trains were also diverted by this route, usually due to wagon derailments north of Low Fell junction.

Adjacent to the Dunston Extension line just north of Low Fell junction, sidings were laid down on the west side of the line for the exchange of traffic from mainly the Dunston area with the main line (Low Fell sidings). On the other side of the line and below the main line embankment was a permanent way depot for railway stores and materials, and a steam crane was based there. This depot and the sidings are still in operation today.

NEWCASTLE & CARLISLE LINE SERVICES

From the Dunston area it is necessary to return to the N & CR main line and examine briefly services after 1862. The passenger service was expanded continuously up to World War I, and for long afterwards it remained the busiest passenger line in north-west Durham. It was also probably the most interesting line with a variety of motive power, including the North British stock. The NER Newcastle—Hexham service was usually operated by tank engines from the 1870s with the Fletcher BTP 0-4-4T, Worsdell A 2-4-2T and O 0-4-4T arriving to assume major roles. Tender engines predominated on the Carlisle service and NBR trains (see also Chapter 9).

In 1890 the NER passenger train service on the N & CR through Blaydon and Ryton consisted of fourteen trains from Newcastle and sixteen into Newcastle on weekdays, with additional trains especially on Saturdays. On Sundays there were only two trains in each direction. The weekday trains had a variety of destinations, but Hexham and Carlisle were the most common. Some trains did not call at the smaller stations on the line, including Ryton. There was one train each way between Newcastle and Blaydon.

The NBR service in 1891 consisted of three trains in each direction. The 6.15am train from Newcastle to Galashiels and the 11.0am from Newcastle to Riccarton called at all stations to Hexham, but the 4.15pm Newcastle to Galashiels train was an express to Corbridge. In the other direction two of the trains similarly stopped at all stations east of Hexham, while the third stopped only at Blaydon between Corbridge and Newcastle. One of these trains was a through train from Edinburgh, calling at Ryton at 9.19pm and Blaydon at 9.25pm, having left Riccarton at 6.50pm. There were no NBR Sunday trains on the line at this time.

By 1913 there was virtually a half-hourly Newcastle—Hexham passenger service from 8.00am to 9.00pm, and a Newcastle—Carlisle train almost every two hours on weekdays. The North British service had altered to two trains each way between Newcastle and Hexham, and there remained no Sunday service. Passenger traffic growth was marked at both Blaydon and Ryton stations, as the following figures indicate:

	1885	1897	1914
Blaydon	165,228	259,816	296,884
Ryton	64,555	89,247	144,826

Passenger receipts at Blaydon rose from £3,931 in 1885 to £8,381 in 1914; at Ryton the comparable figures were £2,118 and £6,115.

For goods traffic the good position of Blaydon made it a major centre, with traffic interchange between Carlisle, Consett and Dunston lines. Ryton on the other hand had no regular goods traffic, which was handled at Blaydon, two and a quarter miles away. Total goods traffic at Blaydon was 105,823 tons in 1885, and 132,481 tons in 1905. Goods receipts in 1910 were £15,413. Total traffic receipts at Blaydon in the same year were £22,586 and station expenses £3,214. At Ryton in this year receipts totalled £5,446 and expenses £514.

Items of traffic of importance at Blaydon included bricks,

clay and sand, chemicals, glass, manure, iron and steel and metals. Livestock traffic brought receipts of £303 in 1910, while parcel receipts were £594. Local coal traffic was especially important, as it so often was in north-west Durham. Just to the west of Blaydon was Addison colliery and coke ovens, while the colliery wagonway ran from near Blaydon to Blaydon Burn colliery. The Addison—Stargate wagonway was extended for almost two miles to serve a new pit at Greenside after 1904. This line connected with the Stella—Emma line at Stargate. (The Stella—Stargate section closed just after World War II.) Some of this local traffic went to Stella staiths near Addison, but much went on to the NER. In 1889, Towneley colliery, Ryton, provided 16,700 tons of coal traffic to the NER (receipts £7,154). Nearby Stargate colliery gave the NER 23,554 tons of coal traffic during 1894, while Addison colliery and coke ovens supplied 32,623 tons in the same year. By 1893 a new colliery west of Ryton had entered production at Clara Vale beside the N & CR line, and during 1894 a total of 26,991 tons of coal and coke was carried by the NER from this mine. The receipts were no less than £11,710. Coal was black gold for the NER.

BLAYDON MPD

The Newcastle & Carlisle Railway Co had a locomotive depot at Blaydon for its early years, but the NER erected a new large shed in the 1890s. Blaydon was an obvious site for a major locomotive depot in view of its location in relation to the other local railways. Besides the Consett branch of 1867, in 1875-6 a new line was opened from Scotswood to Wylam along the north bank of the Tyne (Scotswood, Newburn & Wylam Railway), increasing the number of lines in the Blaydon district. Even before the 1890s the number of goods sidings at Blaydon had been gradually increased and the NER stated that 'Blaydon is a central point for traffic from the Carlisle line and from the Consett Branch, and it is a place at which arrangements could be made for certain of the trains to pass through Newcastle without going into the Goods Station'. With the sidings being continually expanded and locomotives having to be based at Blaydon to shunt the traffic, in June 1897 the NER resolved to erect a new locomotive depot there. This was to consist of two round sheds housing 48 engines, with a 50ft turntable at each. Nearly £400 was spent on preparatory work by the end of 1897.

The contract to construct the sheds, coaling stage, workshops, offices, fitting shop etc, was awarded by tender to J. & W. Simpson of Blyth for £24,000 (NER estimate £27,200) in March 1898. 'In addition £1,045 to be spent by the Engineer on new water and gas mains, 9 inch drains, and plates for the water tank.' The NER estimated 'that the saving in working which would be effected would roughly speaking, amount to about £4,000 per annum'.

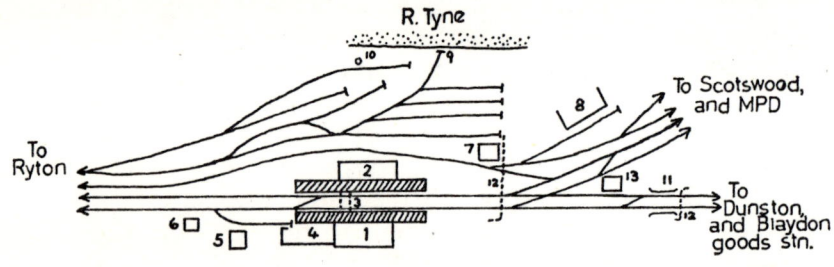

1 station buildings
2 waiting rooms
3 covered footbridge
4 loading dock
5 stationmaster's house
6 ground frame - 5 levers
7 water tank
8 Brett's oil & grease works
9 jetty
10 5ton crane
11 level crossing
12 footbridges
13 signal box

Blaydon station

The depot was opened in April 1900, and was situated beside the N & CR line between Blaydon station and Scotswood bridge, on the south side of the line. It housed both goods and passenger locomotives and was one of the major depots of the NER. In 1920 its allocation was 67 engines and the number had risen to 84 by 1930. Throughout BR days it had shed-code '52C'.

STATION ALTERATIONS

A complaint on the state of the accommodation and request for improvements at Blaydon station was made by the local board of health in 1881, and this request was granted. A second, extensive rebuilding came in 1910-11, and new buildings of red brick were erected comprising passenger accommodation and staff offices. The new structures had a handsome façade on Tyne Street. Ornamental cast-iron columns supported 290ft long glazed platform canopies, and a substantial covered footbridge linked the two platforms.

Ryton station never altered much throughout its history, but it did acquire a foot subway to link the platforms. On the N & CR. line, footbridges or level crossings were more usual.

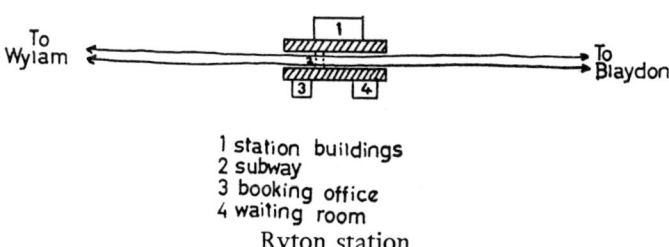

1 station buildings
2 subway
3 booking office
4 waiting room

Ryton station

CHAPTER EIGHT

Trains and Traffic to the Nineteen Seventies

POST-1923 PATTERN

During the late 1920s and throughout the 1930s passenger traffic on all lines gave way to road transport but goods traffic remained steadier. Coal traffic continued to be heavy over most of the lines, and although several small collieries closed between the two world wars – and some before – it was only in the post-1945 period that massive colliery closures in north-west Durham seriously diminished railway traffic. This pattern of decline may be briefly described for each of the lines.

FORTY YEARS ON THE LANCHESTER VALLEY

The serious effects of bus competition, including NER buses, were soon apparent on the Lanchester Valley branch, and the regular passenger service on the line was to be one of the first in the region to disappear. Passenger traffic in 1919 had totalled 185,753 passengers; in 1928 the total was only 28,631. Knitsley station had been re-opened for passengers on 30 March 1925 and for goods on 25 May 1925, and on 11 July 1927 Aldin Grange station was renamed Bearpark. The stationmaster at Witton Gilbert commented in his returns for 1928 that 'passenger traffic is adversely affected by increased bus services here to Newcastle, Chester-le-Street, South Shields, Consett and Durham etc'. His colleague at Lanchester was more forthright: 'Decrease in passenger traffic owing to poor and inadequate train service, and road competition'. In 1930 the basic service on the line consisted of only four trains from Durham to Blackhill and five the other way, with a fair number of additional trains on Saturdays. On Sundays there were two trains out of Durham

Page 157: *THE BLAYDON DISTRICT*
(above) *View east from Blaydon station to junction;* (below) *Class P3 (J27) 0–6–0 No 65855 crosses Derwenthaugh bridge with coal empties from Stella to Sunderland*

Page 158: MPD SCENES
(above) *Waskerley shed with Class B 0–6–2Ts, 1935;* (below) *No 63400 simmering at Blaydon shed, 1960*

to Blackhill, and only one in the other direction. To emphasise the paucity of the service the times of the Durham—Blackhill trains may be cited. Daily departures from Durham were at 7.14am, 12.08pm, 2.43pm and 5.25pm, with no later train than the latter except on Saturdays. The additional Saturday departures were at 1.55pm, 7.00pm, 8.45pm and 9.55pm, but the 7.00pm and 9.55pm ran only to Lanchester. The morning service on the branch was particularly bad.

In 1932 the station traffic and receipts were as follows:

	Passengers	Receipts (£)
Knitsley	2,677	126
Lanchester	5,986	426
Witton Gilbert	15,086	534
Bearpark	9,407	142

By 1938 the number of passengers on the line had fallen to only 15,303, with total receipts of £819, and on 1 May 1939 the service was withdrawn. The official explanation was terse and to the point: withdrawal was due to 'the heavy expenditure involved and the lack of public patronage', words that might be repeated innumerable times for countless railway lines since that date.

All the stations remained open for excursion traffic and all except Bearpark still handled goods traffic. Weekend excursion trains to such coastal resorts as Tynemouth and South Shields and further afield had been a feature of this and other lines in the Consett area. The branch remained a valuable link southwards from Consett steelworks and Consett—Ferryhill (for Teesside) goods trains were a regular feature of the line until closure. Local coal traffic from Bearpark, Langley Park, Lanchester etc continued.

Only in the 1960s was there further decline, hastened by Dr Beeching's arrival as chairman of British Railways. Excursion trains disappeared, and one by one the three stations were closed to goods traffic: Witton Gilbert on 30 September 1963, Knitsley on 9 March 1964 and Lanchester on 5 July 1965. In 1963 the limestone traffic from Coxhoe near Durham to Consett had switched to road transport, so that by 1965 the main traffic was steel from Consett southwards, and some local coal

K

traffic. This was not enough to save the line already earmarked for closure when the Tyne marshalling yard at Lamesley near Low Fell was opened a few years earlier, on 28 June 1963. Consett—Teesside traffic could be routed via Annfield Plain to the Tyne yard and then southwards on the main line, an obvious move in the search for rationalisation and economies. Local coal traffic could use the roads. The branch was therefore closed on 20 June 1966 and subsequently dismantled. The spur lines at Baxter Wood also went, and all that remained was a short section of line from Consett south junction, leaving about 200yd of siding.

Three years later the station at Knitsley still looked remarkably intact, despite the attentions received from vandals. Both station nameboards in faded paint remained more or less intact thirty years after the ending of the regular passenger service.

RUN-DOWN WEST OF CONSETT

The Parkhead—Rookhope railway of the Weardale Iron Co closed as early as 1923 but the rails remained *in situ* until World War II. On 1 May 1939 the passenger service between Tow Law and Blackhill was withdrawn (at the same time as for the Lanchester Valley line), and on 18 May the through route was severed by the closing of the line from a point south of Burnhill junction to about two miles north of Tow Law. The rather bleak district between Tow Law and Consett had never provided a sizeable passenger traffic, and in 1931 there had been only 4,982 passengers at Burnhill and 2,548 at Rowley. This contrasted with 20,720 passengers at Tow Law and 23,462 at Crook in the same year. The latter figures, incidentally, show a considerable decline in traffic over the preceding ten years owing to bus competition. In 1938 there were a mere 753 passengers at Rowley and 2,560 at Burnhill providing receipts of only £61 and £96 respectively. It is therefore not surprising that withdrawal of the service soon followed.

Passenger trains from Darlington then ran only to Tow Law and the closure of the line to Burnhill junction meant that henceforth these trains were usually operated by Darlington engines. Waskerley shed lost much of its importance and was closed on 9 September 1940. All traffic from the Waskerley line now had to be sent via Consett, necessitating reversal at Burnhill junction. Mineral traffic continued to flow from Stanhope Kilns and Parkhead (renamed Blanchland in 1923) stations, and traffic at Rowley was not inconsiderable; in 1934 goods traffic at Rowley was 19,393 tons, mainly of stone from nearby quarries.

The war delayed further contraction, but on 28 April 1951 British Railways closed the Crawley and Weatherhill inclines, leaving the terminus of the railway at Parkhead and Weatherhill where the extensive sand quarries continued in production.* This traffic, with some fluorspar traffic from the same district, was henceforth the main traffic on the branch. The Stanhope Kilns limestone and lime traffic, which had been declining for some years, had to use the roads or the Wear Valley branch railway. Consett steelworks was obtaining limestone from Coxhoe and Frosterley, and some of the Weardale traffic arrived at Rowley by road to reach Consett by rail. A government depot at Burnhill provided traffic – mainly of explosives!

In 1952 the disused Burnhill junction—Blackfield (Tow Law) line was lifted, and in 1953-4 the shed and other buildings at Waskerley were demolished, leaving a weighbridge and goods office. The village itself was declining in population. A few years later, the lay-out of lines at Burnhill junction was simplified, and the Burnhill junction—Rowley section was singled. Signalling on the line west of Consett was dispensed with.

At this time, contraction south of Tow Law began. In 1951 there were five trains each way on weekdays between Tow Law and Crook and another train each way on Saturdays, with no Sunday trains. But the Tow Law service was unprofitable, and on 11 June 1956 it was withdrawn; the Darlington trains ran only as far as Crook. Goods traffic at Tow Law continued, but in 1960 the closure of several local collieries led to the closure of the Sunnyside branch and was then lifted. Inkerman colliery, north of Tow Law, remained in production for some years later, providing the main reason for retention of the line north of Crook. Blair's steel products works, Tow Law, was another traffic source.

The railway era at Crook and district came to a sudden end

* Ashes limestone quarry closed in 1949.

during 1965. On 8 March 1965 the Bishop Auckland—Crook passenger service was withdrawn and on 5 July 1965, at one stroke, the whole line north of Wear Valley junction was closed. In 1966-7 the whole section was dismantled, and the formerly busy sidings at Crook became a derelict wasteland. Rails, signal boxes, footbridges, level crossings, some overbridges, all went, with the gaunt shell of Crook station remaining until burnt down in 1970. A housing estate now covers the former railway station area at Tow Law.

In its latter years diesel multiple units had worked most of the Crook passenger trains, but steam engines made appearances up to closure. An old LMS Fowler tank was an interesting performer. On 23 May 1964 a railway brake van tour of the Crook—Tow Law line was made, hauled by Ivatt 2–6–0 No 43129.

The last remnant of the line west of Consett thus remained the old Stanhope & Tyne line, to Parkhead and Weatherhill. A goods train from Consett to Weatherhill operated each day, and later until 1964-5, it was operated for a few times a week by a Class T2 0–8–0, then by a diesel. On 2 August 1965 goods traffic at Parkhead and Waskerley stations ceased, and Rowley station was similarly closed on 6 June 1966. On 29 April 1968 the Burnhill—Weatherhill section was closed, followed by closure of the remainder on 1 May 1969 facilitated by closure of the War Department siding at Burnhill. It was closed from the junctions at Consett (Consett south and Consett east), and the sand traffic from near Parkhead was then sent on to the Wear Valley line or the roads. The line was dismantled at the Parkhead end later in 1969 and completely lifted in the first months of 1970. A short length from Consett east junction was left as a siding. No longer therefore do rails cross historic Hownes Gill viaduct, and the railway village of Waskerley is almost a ghost village, haunted by the long memories of NER 0–6–2 tanks crossing the moors from Weatherhill. Hownes Gill viaduct has been designated of 'special architectural or historical interest' and should remain.

WITHDRAWAL IN THE DERWENT VALLEY

The passenger service on the Derwent valley line lasted

fifteen years longer than that on its southern extension (the Lanchester Valley branch), but the line was nevertheless the first to succumb in its entirety. Decline of the passenger traffic from the 1920s was, of course, quite marked. Bus services in the Derwent valley district developed extensively, and many of the stations on the railway suffered from their relative distance from centres of population, particularly Shotley Bridge, Ebchester and Lintz Green. High Westwood station drew much traffic from the Chopwell district on the other side of the Derwent, and buses took most of this traffic. Only Rowlands Gill and Blackhill stations were centrally placed in their respective settlements, and from them and from Swalwell station came most of the traffic. The decline in passenger traffic may be judged from the following figures:

	1923	1934
Swalwell	30,558	17,596
Rowlands Gill	74,283	22,421
Lintz Green	14,189	3,386
High Westwood	72,645	10,062
Ebchester	32,570	5,384
Shotley Bridge	40,185	7,948
Blackhill	173,714	40,408

Despite fare increases, receipts were naturally much lower in 1934 than in 1923; at Blackhill they had fallen from £17,094 in 1923 to £3,492 in 1934.

Goods traffic on the line was greatest at Rowlands Gill, with the exception of the large traffic at Blackhill. In 1934 traffic on the branch (excepting Blackhill) was:

	tons	wagons of livestock
Swalwell	9,827	3
Rowlands Gill	24,539	90
Lintz Green	6,651	0
High Westwood	0	0
Ebchester	3,355	2
Shotley Bridge	0	0

An important aspect of traffic at Rowlands Gill was timber,

much of it being sent to Liverpool. Milk traffic here and at Ebchester was large: 32,640 gallons from Ebchester and 2,610 gallons from Rowlands Gill went by rail in 1934, mostly to Tyneside. Even High Westwood station had milk traffic, incoming milk predominating, and 1,190 gallons arrived in 1934.

Typical excursion trains on this line may be cited for Whitsuntide 1937. On Whit Sunday there was a day excursion from Blackhill to Scarborough calling at High Westwood. On Whit Monday there was a half-day excursion from Blackhill, Shotley Bridge, Ebchester and High Westwood to Whitley Bay.

High Westwood was the last station to be opened on the branch in 1909, and it was the first to be closed on 4 May 1942. Possibly the timber buildings had deteriorated a great deal in thirty-three years and the LNER was unwilling to expend money on a station whose income had been steadily declining (£571 receipts in 1938). Traffic here was resigned to the buses.

After the war, traffic continued to decline, and the local collieries began to close. Westwood coke ovens had closed as early as 1922, but the serious closures came in the 1950s. Closure of the passenger service was not long delayed and was only to be expected in view of the lack of patronage. Sunday trains disappeared before 1950. In 1951 the service reached its lowest ebb, with only three trains from Blackhill to Newcastle and three in the other direction, one train in the latter case being on Saturdays only. This contrasted with a bus service up the valley about every ten minutes. Several of the trains ran in a circle from Blackhill to Newcastle via Annfield Plain, or from Newcastle—Annfield Plain—Blackhill—Rowlands Gill—Newcastle. Thus the 6.20am from Newcastle went via Annfield Plain to Blackhill where it arrived at 7.47am. At 7.54am it left for Newcastle via Rowlands Gill. Of the five daily weekday trains on the line, two did not stop at Shotley Bridge and Ebchester, and one did not call at Swalwell. In 1952 the state of the passenger traffic had reached such a level that there were only 7,716 tickets issued at Blackhill, 36 at Ebchester, 2 at Lintz Green and 754 at Rowlands Gill. The end was nigh, and on 21 September 1953 the stations at Shotley Bridge and Ebchester were closed to all traffic, followed on 2 November by those at Lintz Green and Swalwell, although the latter station retained goods traffic (as a public delivery siding) and excursion train

TRAINS AND TRAFFIC TO THE NINETEEN SEVENTIES 165

Tables 144—148

First BR timetable: Consett area, 1948

facilities. The last station was therefore Rowlands Gill, which was closed to passengers on 1 February 1954 when the Newcastle—Blackhill service up the Derwent valley was withdrawn. Blackhill still had the service via Annfield Plain and Consett until 1955, and remained open for goods thereafter.

Parcels traffic facilities at Swalwell were withdrawn on 2 May 1955, but no further changes affected the line, apart from some track rationalisation, until 7 March 1960, when Swalwell was closed completely. Meanwhile the local collieries such as Axwell Park, Victoria Garesfield, Lilley Drift and Hamsterley were shut down, and the way was ready for complete closure of the line. Much traffic on the line was of Consett Iron Co orientation, particularly of scrap from Tyneside shipbreakers' yards.

On 11 November 1963 Rowlands Gill was closed to goods traffic, bringing the whole line into disuse. In its last few years the line had in fact been little used between Rowlands Gill and Blackhill. The line was dismantled in 1964-5 from the junctions at Blaydon (including the curve to Blaydon Main) to Blackhill, at which place goods and coal traffic continued. The Blaydon Loop was left for some while longer, as if the authorities considered retaining this as the diversion route from the Dunston direction into Newcastle for which it was built. But this too was lifted in 1966, including the bridge over the Blaydon—Scotswood bridge road, where in the 1930s a passenger in an open-top double deck bus was killed by striking his head on the iron girders.

Thus disappeared a North Eastern Railway branch with a very interesting history, just a few years before the centenary of its opening, leaving the high viaducts as a monument to the past. No longer is heard the roar of a T2 crossing Lockhaugh viaduct above the serene beauty of the Derwent. Perhaps one can express regret that some part of this line was never taken over as a preservation project, for which some sections were admirably suited. However, with its route a nature trail, the superb vistas near Lintz Green and Rowlands Gill will not be lost.

LAST RAILWAY TO CONSETT

The oldest railway route to Consett and the line which

included the last-built, long section of railway in the area is the remaining railway to Consett. In this area there was once a complex of collieries, and the numerous mines of 1947 are now a mere handful, some of them not even using railway transport.

A description of the decline of passenger traffic in the 1920s would be virtually a repetition of what has been said of the other lines. Suffice it to say that the number of passengers at Shield Row station, for example, was 61,958 in 1923, 15,966 in 1933 and only 9,526 in 1938. Receipts for this station had fallen from £7,692 in 1923 to £1,179 in 1938. On 1 February 1934 Shield Row station was renamed West Stanley. This and Annfield Plain station retained the heaviest traffic on the line, however. Goods traffic on the line, with the exception of Consett, was greatest at Annfield Plain, which handled most of the traffic for the Stanley region as well as for its own neighbourhood. In 1933 traffic there was 26,745 tons, while that at Pelton was only 12,104 tons and Beamish 4,403 tons. The Consett and Blackhill traffic in 1933 amounted to a vast 372,990 tons, with receipts £134,874, somewhat greater than Annfield Plain's goods receipts of £3,797.

And what of the passenger train services? Normally worked by the 0–4–4 tank engines, the basic service in 1929 consisted of twelve trains daily on weekdays from Newcastle to Blackhill or Consett, and nine the other way. There were a number of additional trains, particularly on Saturdays, when the miners and their families flocked to Newcastle for shopping and entertainment and two Sunday trains each way. In the early 1920s card sharpers in the Saturday night trains frequently attempted to abstract the miners' hard-earned money. The number of trains slowly diminished as traffic fell off, and by 1941 there were eight trains from Blackhill or Consett eastwards and seven in the other direction. One must again say a word about excursion trains. On this branch especially there was a large enough local populace to make excursion trains very profitable, and the LNER advertised such trains frequently in the local press. Trains to the coastal resorts of Tynemouth, Whitley Bay and South Shields were common, but much longer excursions were also provided. For instance on 25 May 1928 there was an excursion from Shield Row to King's Cross, calling at Annfield Plain, Leadgate, Consett and Blackhill, leaving Shield Row at 9.06pm and Blackhill at 9.21pm running to London via Lanchester and Darlington. On 28 May 1928 there was an excursion leaving Shield Row at 6.05am to Edinburgh; another example is a Consett—Blackpool excursion calling at all stations to Birtley on 19 September 1931. Only in the early 1960s did excursion trains stop running from this district, leaving people to use the bus to reach Newcastle or Durham.

World War II boosted traffic on the line, particularly of coal and coke, and vital steel traffic from Consett made the town a target for German bombs. The railway itself was a target for the enemy who thought the number of lines visible from the air in the Beamish district represented a marshalling yard, and bombed the area severely. In fact it was merely the closeness of the Pontop branch and the Beamish wagonway and associated colliery sidings which created this impression.

In 1946 the old Stanhope & Tyne inclines west of Pelton Level were closed, following closure of several mines served by this line. The rails were lifted in 1952. At West Stanley itself, west of Stanley bank top, several mines continued in production, such as the Louisa colliery, and this section of line from Annfield east junction remained open. It was only in 1969 that the last of the Stanhope & Tyne inclines, the Waldridge incline, was closed. This followed the closure of Craghead colliery on 11 April 1969, the last pit using the line from Stella Gill, where all had once been such a hive of activity. The Handen Hold colliery, West Pelton, was another old-established pit which had used the Waldridge incline until the mid-1960s. At the time of writing the whole line from South Pelaw junction to Pelton Level awaits lifting. The last mine in this region, Sacriston, uses road transport.

The Newcastle—Consett—Blackhill passenger service was withdrawn on 23 May 1955 after several years of decline. Just after the war Sunday services disappeared, and by 1951 there were only four trains westbound on the line plus a Saturday extra, and three in the eastbound direction, again with a Saturday extra. This was the basic service at the end. Before withdrawal several of the stations had already been closed. Beamish was the first to go on 21 September 1953, remaining open for goods, and on 7 December 1953 Pelton was closed altogether. The very last regular passenger train, the 8.38pm from Newcastle to Blackhill, was hauled by 2–6–2T No 67657 upon which had been scribbled chalk slogans. The local press recorded that a few people had gathered at West Stanley and Annfield Plain to see the train for the last time, but at Leadgate only the stationmaster was on the platform. At Consett, 'passengers alighting . . . were welcomed by the singing of the station's porter, Tommy Carr'. Withdrawal of the service would mean a saving of £13,078 per year to the railways, said the papers. Thus Blackhill station, opened in 1867 and within thirty years a major passenger station with some 125,000 passengers a year lost its regular trains, and Consett disappeared from the national passenger network for ever.

In the early 1960s closure of the stations to goods traffic, except at Consett, was effected. Beamish was closed on 2 August 1960, West Stanley on 11 September 1961, and Annfield Plain and Leadgate both on 10 August 1964. West Stanley and Annfield Plain stations were demolished during May to June 1965. Only Consett station was left intact and the station buildings are in use as staff offices.

Wagonway branches and most sidings have almost vanished, most having succumbed in the 1950s. The main colliery lines closed during this period were the Waldridge and Sacriston wagonway (1955), the Medomsley branch (1959), and the South Medomsley and Craghead—Burnhope lines. The Medomsley branch, which had in NER days been so extensively used by the Consett Iron Co, was sold to that concern in 1924. In 1947 the National Coal Board took over operation of the branch until late 1959. Medomsley colliery then used road transport until it closed in 1962. A locomotive shed for the branch was situated at the Leadgate junction. Another line, of even greater antiquity, the Beamish wagonway, was closed before 1960 east of West Pelton, when a short connection was laid by the NCB to Handen Hold to allow Beamish coal to reach Pelton Level, and run via the S & T Waldridge incline and Stella Gill. Beamish 'Mary' pit had been modernised at great expense by the NCB in 1952 to give it a thirty year life; it closed in March 1966 and the Pelton Level—Beamish line was dismantled. At Pelton level itself was the modern NCB Grange Villa coal washery. Thus, apart from sidings at South Pelaw junction, the only sidings on the Pontop branch between there and Consett are at Annfield Plain, consisting of two sidings at Annfield junction where trains from the Oxhill branch are shunted, and a siding to Ransome & Marles' bearing works (opened 1953) west of Annfield Plain itself.

The bulk of traffic on the South Pelaw—Consett branch is now associated with the Consett steelworks. All of the works' iron ore and most of its coal arrives by rail, the ore from Tyne Dock and the coal mainly from mines in east Durham, such as Herrington colliery. Morrison colliery is the last local supplier of high-grade coking coal in quantity. Other Consett Iron Co traffic includes fuel oil and the outward flow of steel plates and other products. Coal traffic from Morrison colliery to places such as Norwood coke ovens at Dunston remains significant. Most of the traffic on the branch runs to the main line via Ouston junction, some trains being re-marshalled at Tyne yard, Lamesley. The South Pelaw—Washington line is still in use, albeit by few trains, but has occasionally seen heavier use, as for a few days following a derailment at Ouston junction on 9 February 1970. This section of the old S & T lost its importance in November 1966 when the Washington—Boldon colliery line was closed, and the iron ore trains were re-routed via Gateshead.

In recent years signalling arrangements on the Pontop branch have been somewhat simplified and a number of boxes abolished. The remaining signal boxes are South Pelaw junction Beamish, Annfield East,* Carr House East, Carr House West, Consett East and Consett North. The Oxhill signal box on the line serving Morrison colliery is still in use to control the level crossing on the busy Stanley—Annfield Plain road (see Chapter 10). The single track from Consett North to Blackhill goods (coal) station is now operated by one engine in steam (a diesel shunter, one train daily), and signals have been dispensed with. The only colour light signals in the region are between Ouston junction and South Pelaw, operated from Tyne signal box, Lamesley.

* a BR brick-built box – the NER box was destroyed by fire.

CHANGES ON TYNESIDE

The Newcastle & Carlisle line passenger service is now the last service in north-west Durham, excluding the NER main line from Durham to Newcastle, on which Chester-le-Street station* is still open. The N & CR service remained frequent and decline was much less marked than on the Consett area lines up to the 1950s. The Newcastle & Carlisle line, however, has a unique geographical position and has always been of more than local importance as a cross-country link between east and west coast main lines, and north-east England and western Scotland. That other service on the N & CR, the North British service from Newcastle into Scotland via Hexham and Bellingham, did lose its importance in LNER days, becoming a rustic byway. Nevertheless this service lasted until 13 October 1956, when the passenger service north of Hexham ceased. North British 'Scott' class 4–4–0s were for long the usual passenger locomotives.

Blaydon station retained much of its heavy traffic in passengers and goods, despite the growth of road transport. Ryton however, with no regular goods traffic and a station well off-centre for the settlement it served, declined somewhat. In 1929 there were 81,166 passengers at Blaydon and 13,238 at Ryton; the receipts being £3,408 and £426 respectively. Goods traffic at Blaydon provided £55,650 11s 6d (£55,650.57½). Thus the station receipts amounted to £60,586 at Blaydon and £637 at Ryton. In 1937 there were 104,403 passengers at Blaydon and 14,227 at Ryton. The actual goods tonnage at Blaydon was, in 1934, 136,096 tons forwarded and 134,067 tons received. This was a large traffic but it may be compared with that at Consett and Blackhill in the same year, which was no less than 318,785 tons forwarded and 199,878 tons received. Comparative receipts were:– Blaydon: £58,388; Consett: £181,810. This was really a measure of the traffic associated with the Consett Iron Co.

The actual Newcastle—Carlisle passenger service remained very frequent, with Hexham and Carlisle as the usual destinations, and Haltwhistle somewhat less common as a destination.

* Chester-le-Street station buildings were modernised in Nov–Dec 1970.

In 1938 service improvements on the line included for the first time a Newcastle—Carlisle express taking only 77 minutes for the 60¼ miles.

After World War II, as the motor age advanced, traffic declined more noticeably. At Blaydon the trains to Newcastle at one or two each hour were losing out to the buses outside the station, which ran almost every five minutes. At Ryton the station was just too far from most of the growing village to serve a useful purpose, and it was closed on 5 July 1954. It had the dubious distinction of being one of the first on the whole line to be closed. In 1951, however, there had been ten daily westbound departures and nine eastbound from Ryton, with a Saturday extra each way. Many more trains stopped at Blaydon: nineteen regular daily westbound trains, and sixteen eastbound, including North British line services. The earliest morning train westbound from Blaydon was the 6.04am to Riccarton Junction, which did not stop at Ryton. The earliest eastbound from Blaydon was the 6.27am, which originated at Hexham. Most of the trains were, in fact, to or from Hexham, covering what may be somewhat inaccurately called the 'commuter belt'. On Sundays there were nine trains each way, only three of which began or ended at Carlisle: one to Carlisle and two from Carlisle. As had been the case for very many years, no Sunday trains ran on to the former North British line. Another Scottish link was the summer only through train between Newcastle and Stranraer harbour, which in 1951 stopped at Blaydon. This train dated back to NER days, but in the past, and in the future, it did not always stop at Blaydon, running mostly as an express to and from Carlisle.

By the late 1950s, diesel multiple units worked many of the Newcastle and Carlisle trains, and steam soon disappeared from the services altogether, the NER shed at Blaydon becoming a diesel refuelling point.

As elsewhere the coal mining industry of the Tyneside fringe of north-west Durham had declined. Blaydon Burn colliery and the wagonway from Blaydon closed in 1956; the Garesfield wagonway closed completely south of Derwenthaugh coke ovens (Winlaton Mill) in 1960 following closure of Chopwell colliery in 1959 and High Spen (Garesfield) pit in 1960; finally, in 1962-3, the lines from Addison to Stargate, Greenside and

Towneley (Emma) were closed, after which the Emma and Greenside pits used road transport. In 1955 some 1,700 tons of coal daily were arriving at Addison from these wagonways, mostly from Greenside colliery. This closure meant the end of the Addison incline. Clara Vale colliery west of Ryton was closed not long after this, ending the local association of the N & CR and the coal industry, except for trains of coal to the new Stella South power station, near Addison, opened in the early 1950s.

At Blaydon there was a big decline in railway services when the branch to Blackhill was closed in 1963 and the Blaydon locomotive shed was closed in 1965; Blaydon goods yard became redundant in the same period when the Tyne marshalling yard south of Low Fell opened: these factors all led to the lifting of many sidings, transforming the aspect of the railway for the worse.

In the Beeching age it was inevitable that the immediate and long-term future of the Newcastle & Carlisle passenger service should receive close scrutiny. In the short term it was decided, in 1966, to close many of the stations, leaving about nine intermediate stations open. Unfortunately, Blaydon was not selected for retention. When the axe fell in 1967, Blaydon was reprieved by the Minister of Transport, probably because of the large population in the district. Even with a frequent bus service between Newcastle and Hexham, there must have been some people out of the thousands in the area who at some time wished to go by train to Carlisle or beyond. One question was that if there was no local station, would they go into Newcastle to return past the bus stop they had left over half an hour before? In the long-term view, things look bright, for there is the possibility that the east coast main line north of Newcastle may be down-graded and that much Scottish traffic will be sent to Carlisle from Newcastle. With the electrification of the west coast main line now decided, this is a possibility.

In early 1967 the line between Blaydon station and Scotswood was closed owing to railway bridge alterations at Scotswood in connection with the construction of the new Tyne road bridge nearby. A bus service was run between Blaydon and Scotswood stations, as passenger trains were re-routed from Scotswood to West Wylam junction through Newburn during this period. The arrangement lasted for several months. The normal service was resumed on 1 May 1967.

In 1969 Blaydon station became an unstaffed halt, in common with most of its fellow stations on the line. As a result the station buildings are decaying more than they did before, a fact which one would have considered to be scarcely possible. In 1967 colour light signals replaced semaphores at Blaydon, but semaphores remain between Blaydon and Wylam, colour lights having arrived at Wylam in 1969. Semaphore signals remain between Blaydon and Norwood junction signal box at Dunston, beyond which Tyne box colour lights occur. Several NER signal boxes remain in use in the Tyneside region. At Ryton, there is Peth lane box, with Addison box to the east; Blaydon signal box remains, and to the east are Derwenthaugh, Dunston West, Dunston East and Norwood junction boxes. Blaydon Main signal box, at the former junction between the Blaydon—Dunston line and the Blaydon south east curve, closed and was demolished in 1967. Remaining local goods and coal traffic at Blaydon is now shunted when necessary by a Gateshead 0–6–0 diesel.

END OF THE TANFIELD BRANCH

Traffic on the Tanfield branch slowly declined after World War I. By 1945 it amounted to only a third of the 1907 figure. In 1947 the Tanfield Moor colliery ceased production after several centuries of operation, and the LNER closed the Tanfield Moor incline. This was not lifted until 1957 by which time it was in an advanced state of dereliction. The remaining sources of significant traffic following this closure were Tanfield Lea (Margaret) pit and East Tanfield colliery. The latter ceased using rail transport in 1955, after which usually only one locomotive was needed on the line to handle traffic. On 24 August 1962 the death knell of the line sounded when Tanfield Lea colliery was closed. The railway was then closed south of Watergate colliery (Lobley Hill). The remainder succumbed on 18 May 1964 when Watergate colliery switched to road transport. The northern part of the branch then fell into disuse and was eventually dismantled, although even in early 1969 parts of the rusting lines remained near Teams crossing, Dunston,

Page 175: *TRAINS AT BLACKHILL AND CONSETT*
(above) *J39 No 64842 from 52C (Blaydon) shed with Newcastle train (via Consett) at Blackhill;* (below) *special train at Consett station, 1963, headed by K1 No 62027 of Consett (52K) shed*

Page 176: *DIESEL ERA*
(above) *Type 2 Nos 5111 and 5107 with Consett ore train near Beamish, climbing the 1 in 51/55 bank;* (below) *Type 3 No 6893 with coal train from Morrison Busty colliery at Oxhill crossing, 8 April 1969*

just north of the embankment carrying the Dunston Extension Railway. A few forlorn NER signal gantries and other relics also remained, but in 1970 construction of a new road on the course of the line has removed some of these mementoes. It was at Teams crossing on a sunny day in 1960 that NER 0–6–2T No 69109 was visible in spotless black livery simmering peacefully, before making its way to Redheugh and thence back to Gateshead. Unfortunately a camera was not to hand, and line and locomotive have gone.

That neighbour of the Tanfield branch, the Pontop & Jarrow (Bowes Railway) has now followed the path of decline. The major closure here was in 1968 when Burnopfield (Hobson) and Byermoor collieries were closed. The railway was closed and lifted west of Marley Hill in 1969. Marley Hill colliery remains in production but this has not prevented the closure of the line between there and Kibblesworth, lifted early in 1970. This has left a railway 'island' at Marley Hill, where now a single NCB Hunslet 0–6–0 ST tank engine (No 83) shunts coal wagons about before road transport carries the coal away. As this is written, the Marley Hill lines are to close on 13 August 1970. The line east of Kibblesworth colliery remains, including the two inclines in the Team valley which meet at a point beneath the east coast main line railway beside Tyne yard, combining the old and the new.

AN INEVITABLE DECLINE

The growth of motor traffic on the roads after the 1920s made the decline of the railways of north-west Durham inevitable. Motor buses and private cars, and road haulage lorries on short trips all played a part in the decline, not to mention the ailing coal industry. And finally the Beeching period of 1962-3 saw the final decline of the railways. To look ahead to the near future, further contraction seems unlikely, for the Newcastle & Carlisle line is secure and the Dunston district lines are busy with goods traffic, both of coal to Dunston staiths and power station and through traffic between Tyne yard and Carlisle. In July 1970, however, the Press described a new plan to beautify the banks of the Tyne in the Dunston staiths area. This mentioned the possible limitation of life of the staiths with the decline of the coal shipping trade. (Coal shipped at Dunston declined from 1,902,467 tons in 1955, to 699,900 tons in 1964. Moreover the older 'rival', Tyne Dock, ceased to ship coal in 1967.) Additional news about Tyne Dock is that it is to be replaced by a new iron ore terminal at Redcar, on Teesside, from late 1972. The ore will then have a longer journey to Consett, via Stockton, Leamside, Pelaw, Gateshead and South Pelaw.

The short Swalwell branch from Derwenthaugh is still in use, with coal traffic from a coal disposal plant at Swalwell, and some iron and steel traffic. The line to Consett is probably safe so long as Consett has its steelworks; the last part of the 'Main Way' seems secure as long as there is the cokeworks nearby.

CHAPTER NINE

Locomotives

LOCOMOTIVE SURVEY

The great problem that arises in attempting to describe the locomotive history of north-west Durham lies in the wealth and complexity of that history. From the days of the first Stanhope & Tyne locomotives at work on the east end of that line in 1834, to the present situation of British Railways diesels and a handful of industrial steam locomotives, there has been a complex period of locomotive history which needs a whole book to relate properly. Therefore the writer has tried to steer a path between on the one extreme a complete but generalised account of the main features of the locomotive history, and, on the other, details of notable locomotive changes and individual engines which at various periods occupied a foremost position in the area or on specific lines or parts of the region. There will be omissions and over-simplifications, but this must be unavoidable in such a survey.

Where appropriate NER classifications are given, with the LNER classification equivalent in brackets to simplify the presentation. The actual details of dimensions and performances of classes of locomotive will not usually be given as much has been written elsewhere on these matters.

EARLY YEARS

The seven locomotives owned by the Stanhope & Tyne company in 1837 consisted of six six-coupled engines, and one four-wheeled engine. They all bore names, as did all of the Newcastle & Carlisle Railway engines. The S & T engines were named after persons associated with railway or locomotive development such as, *James Watt* and *Robert Stephenson*. The N & CR locomotives had a more varied selection of names, such as *Comet* (the first engine on the line), *Hercules, Samson, Atlas, Tyne, Eden, Nelson* and *Wellington*. The S & T locomotive livery appears to have been a slate grey colour, N & CR engines were 'Indian red', and Stockton & Darlington locomotives had a complicated livery with green as the main component.

Mineral locomotives have always been important on the railways of north-west Durham, for reasons which will be appreciated from earlier chapters. In 1846 William Bouch designed the S & D 0–6–0 engine No 35 *Commerce*, whose design was more advanced than with previous engines. The boiler barrel was nearly fourteen feet long and the engine weighed twenty-six tons and had outside cylinders. Later improvements of the type by Bouch culminated in the famous 'long boiler' class (NER Class 1001), built by the S & D section in 1865-75.

As is well know, the era of Edward Fletcher as NER locomotive superintendent from 1854-82 was renowned for its wide variety of locomotive types and there were even differences between locomotives of the same nominal class. E. L. Ahrons wrote at the beginning of the 1880s that 'Mr Fletcher's standard Gateshead built goods engines are of the very few classes that merit the term "standard" ' although he added that the locomotives in the Gateshead district itself in 1882 were a 'ragged and variegated assortment'. However, during Fletcher's years most of the even wider variety of early engines inherited by the NER from its various components and predecessors and from companies taken over after 1854 (such as the N & CR), had been withdrawn from service. Here one must mention the S & D after the amalgamation with the NER in 1863. 157 locomotives were taken over by the NER as a result of this merger but the S & D section was allowed to go its own way almost as a separate entity for another twelve years or so; hence production of engines designed by Bouch continued. Several predecessors of the Fletcher 'standard' 0–6–0 (Class 398) were built for the S & D section in 1868 by Hawthorn Leslie: Nos 1207-8, 1210-11. Class 398 itself was built to a total of 324 engines from 1872-83. It is not surprising that so numerous a class found its way all over the NER network and many of the class were based in north-west Durham. Some examples will be cited later.

Several other Fletcher classes were prominent in the region for many years. These included the Class BTP 'bogie tank passenger' 0–4–4T type, Classes 675, 686, and 1440 2–4–0, and Class 708 0–6–0. The NER Gateshead locomotive works near the High Level bridge built some of these and many subsequent NER locomotives until engine building ceased there in 1910. The Class 1440 2–4–0s, fifteen in number, were common on Newcastle & Carlisle passenger trains for many years. The Class 901 2–4–0s, for most of their history a main line passenger service class, appeared on the branches west of the main line in their later years. No 693, a Class 686 2–4–0 built in April 1870, has been recorded as the first large NER engine allocated to the erstwhile N & CR, and was based at Carlisle. Fletcher built three 2–4–0s specially for service on the Consett branch passenger service with the heavy gradients on that line; these were Nos 21 and 680 during 1869, and No 139 in March 1871. Some of the old N & CR engines were rebuilt by Fletcher in various guises, some as saddle tanks. An example of a N & CR rebuild was N & CR No 33 *Alston*, built in 1850 by Robert Stephenson as an 0–6–0. It became NER No 481 in 1862, and in 1869 Fletcher rebuilt it at Gateshead as a 2–4–0 (Class 675) retaining the wheels and motion. N & CR 0–6–0s Nos 476 and 479 became 0–6–0STs in 1873 to bank on Redheugh incline (see page 187). There were other such changes.

On the various colliery wagonways there was a very wide variety of locomotives and some venerable machines lasted a very long time on such lines. On the Craghead wagonway for instance, the famous *Wylam Dilly*, built in 1813, worked from 1862 to 1879. Quite a number of tank engines built in the 1870s and 1880s for colliery companies survived to National Coal Board days in 1947.

The Consett branch between Newcastle and Durham was one of the lines selected by the NER on which to conduct experiments to find the most suitable type of brake for passenger stock after 1874. Until then handbrakes alone had been used. Several kinds of braking system were tested on various NER lines, and in 1876-7 the Westinghouse air brake and automatic brake were tried out on the steep gradients reaching 1 in

60 on the Consett branch, with good results. As a result of these and other tests the NER adopted the Westinghouse brake for its stock.

NER STANDARDISATION

The post-Fletcher age was largely one of standardisation on the NER with new classes of locomotives being built in large batches. Alexander McDonnell, locomotive superintendent in 1883-5 designed two main classes which saw service in north-west Durham. His Class 38 4–4–0 passenger engines, of which there were twenty-eight, were much in use on the N & CR line for over thirty years. These bogie engines were disliked intensely by most of the NER men because their operation was different from usual. McDonnell's Class 59 0–6–0 type totalled 44 units and was more popular, at least after McDonnell's departure from office. These engines bore some resemblance to his famous 0–6–0 class on the Great Southern & Western Railway, which, however, long outlasted the Class 59s. Maclean recorded in 1906 that the Class 59s were 'largely used for excursion traffic and slow passenger trains'. Several of the class ended their days in the moorland fastness of Waskerley.

The Worsdell period brought a long series of standard classes, and by the early twentieth century the Fletcher locomotives of Class 398 were disappearing. Most of the T. W. and Wilson Worsdell classes were represented in the region at certain periods.

Boiler pressure of Fletcher and McDonnell locomotives had usually been 140lb psi. T. W. Worsdell's Class A 2–4–2 passenger tank class, built in 1886-92 had 160lb psi boiler pressure, as had several succeeding classes. The 2–4–2Ts appeared on the Newcastle & Carlisle line trains, and there was a batch of them at Gateshead depot for many years. Class B 0–6–2T (1886-90) was constructed to a total of 62 engines, and many appeared on mineral shunting work at Waskerley, Blackhill (Consett) and other places. Indeed this class was associated with the Burnhill Junction—Stanhope line for many years. Class C was T. W. Worsdell's new 0–6–0 tender class, most of which were two cylinder compounds (Class C1 were the 'simple' engines).

There were 201 of Class C/C1, and their longevity was a tribute mainly to their number, some of them lasting to the 1960s. This class appeared all over the NER and was very well represented in north-west Durham throughout its existence. The standard T. W. Worsdell 0–6–0T shunter was Class E (1886-95), and there were 120 of these represented at most NER sheds. Probably a few of this class came to the Tanfield branch in the late 1880s in place of Fletcher tanks which had been on the line since 1881. In 1891, however, new Class L 0–6–0Ts arrived on this line. The Class F 4–4–0s (1886-91) worked main line trains in their early years, but later appeared on branch line services, particularly the Newcastle & Carlisle trains.

Wilson Worsdell succeeded his brother in 1890, and was soon building his own designs, such as Class L, although building of some earlier types such as Class C continued. New 4–4–0 Class M and Q (1892-7) for main line services appeared in their later years on some of the branch services. In 1894 appeared the Class O 0–4–4T of which building continued up to 1901, and this class was common in the region from the start. Sixty years later some of these engines were still working the branch passenger trains. Fletcher's BTP class was somewhat rebuilt by Worsdell to improve its rather dated appearance, and this class continued to share the passenger work on Newcastle—Hexham Newcastle—Blackhill—Durham and Newcastle—Annfield Plain —Blackhill services, with Class O in particular. A few of both 0–4–4T types were on the S & D lines, occasionally operating between Crook and Blackhill. From 1906 some of the BTPs were adapted as 'steam autocars' coupled to a coach at each end as a push-and-pull unit. These 'autocars' began operating on the Consett branch in 1907, and page 88 shows one at High Westwood.

Two 0–6–2T types emerged to supplement the Class B. In 1893-4, Class N (twenty engines) was produced, very similar to the earlier type, and in 1902-3 came the twenty engines of Class U. Both of these classes operated in the region, and the Class U type, first tried 'with success' on the Tanfield branch in 1902, figured on that line for the next sixty years, when the line was mostly closed and the last 0–6–2Ts withdrawn. At Bowes Bridge shed on the branch there were normally two

Class Us, and further examples were common at the parent shed at Gateshead.

The Class P family of 0–6–0 goods engines appeared in 1894. Improvements of the type to form Classes P1, P2 and P3 resulted in a total of 355 engines when the last of Class P3 was built in 1923. Inevitably many saw service in north-west Durham. Wilson Worsdell's standard 0–6–0T shunter, Class E1, appeared in 1898, and had a long history in the area. In 1899 the Class S 4–6–0s and Class R 4–4–0s for main line services came on to the scene. Some of the former appeared on the Carlisle line, and in their later years the Class R type operated some local passenger trains, particularly the Newcastle—Carlisle and Crook—Blackhill services.

THE NER 0–8–0S

The last of the Worsdell standard types built in any quantity, apart from new Atlantic passenger engines, was Class T 0–8–0 introduced in 1901. Some of the class had slide valves (Class T1) instead of the more usual piston valves. By 1911 there were 90 of these 0–8–0s, many of them engaged in mineral work in north-west Durham. Their boiler pressure was 175lb psi, and tractive effort was 28,000lb (tractive effort of a Class C 0–6–0 with Stephenson valve gear was at the most 20,840lb). In 1901 experiments were conducted at Tyne Dock with the brand new Class T engine No 2116. The locomotive hauled a 1,326¼ ton train of coal wagons, 569yd long – the longest loaded train which had ever been dealt with by the NER. The class was designed to haul trains up to 60 loaded coal wagons but because of its success, the normal load was increased to 72 wagons, a load of about 1,170 tons. The class proved itself eminently suited to hauling heavy coal trains over the steeply graded lines of north-west Durham. At the end of 1920 engines Nos 643, 651, 769, 785 were at Annfield Plain shed, Nos 1173 and 2116 at Tyne Dock, Nos 654 and 655 at Borough Gardens (Gateshead), and Nos 657, 772 and 1709 at Gateshead (Greensfield).

Sir Vincent Raven, Worsdell's successor as chief mechanical engineer, produced a new 0–8–0 type in 1913, which was to make an even greater impact on the railways of north-west

Durham. His Class T2 0–8–0 had a boiler pressure of 180lb psi and a tractive effort of 28,800lb. It had a driving wheel diameter nominally of 4ft 7½in whereas the T/T1 had a 4ft 7¼in driving wheel diameter (in fact the T2 wheel diameter *was* 4ft 7¼in). The first T2, No 1247 and many subsequent engines, were soon at work moving coal in north-west Durham. As is well known, the T2 was an outstandingly successful design and the powerful locomotives handled heavy coal trains almost with ease on the heavily graded sections of line. They were smooth riding engines and extremely versatile, able to negotiate winding colliery branches as easily as well maintained major lines. The class was to give over fifty years of service to the railways of this and other regions.

Building of T2s went on until early 1921, by which time there were 120 of them, many in sheds which worked the north-west Durham branches. In December 1920 there were eight of the class at Blaydon (Nos 2222, 2238, 2260, 2261, 2262, 2266, 2267 and 2269); 25 at Gateshead (Nos 1335, 2236, 2253, 2255, 2256, 2259, 2268, 2270, 2278-9, 2284-98); 21 at Borough Gardens (Nos 1250-2, 1257, 2221, 2227, 2234, 2245-7, 2271-7, 2280-3) and no less than 28 at Tyne Dock (Nos 1247, 1253-4, 1262, 1264, 1278-9, 1284-5, 1291, 1293-4, 1361, 1363, 2213, 2215, 2223, 2225, 2229, 2231-2 2240, 2242-4, 2263-5). A few more of the class were at Darlington. Subsequently, of course, some of the class moved round from shed to shed, but several examples appear to have spent the greater part of their lives in the region, including Nos 1253, 1293, 2222, 2261 and 2263 which ended up respectively as British Railways Nos 63346, 63363, 63379, 63418 and 63420. In 1923 there were thirty-two T2s and a solitary T1 at Tyne Dock shed.

The third NER 0–8–0 type was introduced in 1919. Class T3 comprised five three-cylinder engines with a boiler pressure of 180lb psi, 4ft 7¼in driving wheels, and a tractive effort of 36,965lb. Nos 901-3 were sent to Blaydon shed and Nos 904-5 to Gateshead. Later one of the latter pair was sent to Tyne Dock and tried on the Consett iron ore trains. It was successful, and the others were sent for the same duty. In 1924 the LNER built another ten of the class (which had become Class Q7) and these also went to Tyne Dock (Nos 624-6, 628-34). For much of their subsequent existence, all of the class was based at Tyne Dock to work the iron ore trains, and for other heavy mineral duties.

CONSETT REGION

Waskerley shed housed not only mineral engines but a few for the passenger service between Blackhill and Crook and beyond. These were usually Class 59 0–6–0s, but for a number of years there was a solitary 4–4–0. In 1920 it was Class F No 663 which lasted for a number of years, but was withdrawn in 1932. Before this period, old Class 1001 'long-boilers' and Class 398s were being taken out of service at Waskerley, as elsewhere. Long-boilers Nos 1079, 1272, 1281 and 1290 were withdrawn at Waskerley in 1914. In 1920, Waskerley and its sub-shed Blackhill had, besides the 4–4–0 mentioned, four Class 398, two Class 59 and five Class B. The latter were Nos 238, 345, 349-50 and 1105. Class P1 0–6–0s were engaged in much of the goods and mineral traffic on the Crook line, being based in the West Auckland area. A further two Class P1s were at Annfield Plain alongside the T/T1 0–8–0s and Class N 0–6–2T Nos 1648 and 1652. Durham shed which operated traffic on the Lanchester Valley branch as well as the main line and branches nearby, had a variety of locomotive types in 1923 consisting of one Class 398, one Class 59, two Class C, and three Class 1440. Although there remained 86 Class 398s in NER stock in 1923, they had all been withdrawn by March 1928, and McDonnell's Class 59 had gone by 1930. The Fletcher BTPs also vanished in the twenties up to 1929.

TYNESIDE REGION

By about 1920 the Newcastle & Carlisle line passenger trains were generally operated by 4–4–0s on the Newcastle—Carlisle trains, and Classes A, O and BTP, and a few 2–4–0s, for the Newcastle—Blaydon—Hexham 'locals'. The North British Railway passenger trains were usually worked by 4–4–0s, with 0–6–0s on goods trains. In earlier years 2–4–0s had been common. Local coal and goods traffic in the north-west Durham Tyneside district was handled by a wide variety of classes. Besides the 0–8–0s the most numerous types at local sheds were the 0–6–0s, and in 1920 Class C was prevalent at Blaydon and Gateshead, Class 398 at Borough Gardens (with no less than seventeen of these veterans) and Classes P and P1 at Tyne Dock. For passenger trains Blaydon had ten Class O tanks (Nos 405, 1169, 1691, 1702, 1765, 1783, 1840, 1868, 2094 and 2097) and Gateshead had six of the same type (Nos 1778, 1788, 1916, 1920 2093 and 2095) and also had the only BTP remaining in the area, No 624, which was withdrawn in 1923.

Some of the early 4–4–0s used on Carlisle trains and based at Gateshead included Class F Nos 18, 1324, 1538, 1543 and 1546; Class M Nos 1621, 1625, 1631, 1638, and Class Q Nos 1908 and 1929. No 1929 is depicted on a Carlisle train on page 34 in this book. Gateshead also had eleven Class A 2–4–2Ts in 1920, and eight of Raven's 4–4–4T introduced in 1913 for passenger work. There were also many more modern 4–4–2s and 4–4–0s for main line services.

On the Tanfield branch the first pair of Class U 0–6–2Ts in 1902 had been Nos 1112 and 1138. These, or Nos 1109, 1321, 1683 and 1716, were the usual members of the class at work on the line or at Gateshead shed. Several of these locomotives spent nearly all their lives in the district. Local shunting in Dunston, particularly at Dunston staiths, was undertaken mainly by the various 0–6–0T types. Before its closure, traffic up the Redheugh incline was normally worked by Class L 0–6–0Ts and Fletcher Class 476 0–6–0 STS. There were four '476s' – Nos 476, 479, 481, 487, built in 1875-83 for Redheugh banking duty when the rope haulage was ended. They soon were dubbed 'the camels'. The incline was closed in c 1907.

NER ROLLING STOCK

In the 1890s NER branch passenger rolling stock was usually of six-wheeled carriages with clerestory roofs but within a few years eight-wheeled stock was more common. Some of the more modern carriages were often used on the Newcastle & Carlisle trains.

In the early years of the present century the NER commenced to improve its mineral wagon stock. Until then 10 ton wagons were almost universal but 20 ton wagons began to be produced in increasing quantities. Even a 40 ton wagon for coal traffic was produced. In north-west Durham the 20 ton coal wagon with its wooden body became standard until the end of NER history, and there was little change in this and other aspects of rolling stock under the LNER.

LNER PERIOD: SOME NEW ARRIVALS

The grouping in 1923 brought new liveries and locomotive classifications, but for some years the district was not affected by new locomotive classes. The old stagers, the Class A (now F8), B (N8), C (J21), F (D22), O (G5), P1 (J25), Q (D17/2), T/T1 (Q5) and others, including the T2 (Q6) and T3 (Q7), dominated the scene. In the late 1920s withdrawal commenced of some of the early T. W. Worsdell classes, including the Class A from 1928 and Class C from 1929. This process continued gradually, although World War II delayed the process somewhat, as did nationalisation.

The withdrawal of these engines led to newer types arriving to replace them. By 1930 Blaydon shed had acquired some Class P3s (J 27) including Nos 1006, 1016 and 1227 to replace Class Cs. The steady disappearance of the older types is shown in the LNER records; thus in October 1932 Class C No 1338 was withdrawn at Blaydon, and in December 1933 Class B No 185 was similarly dealt with at Waskerley. No 349 of this class was withdrawn at Waskerley in 1937. Rapid withdrawal of 2-4-2Ts took place, Nos 21, 55 and 187 disappearing from Gateshead in 1928-30, and by 1938 this class was extinct. Blaydon acquired several of the 4-4-4 tanks for Hexham trains (Class D – LNER H1), including Nos 1330 and 1552.

Class B 0-6-2Ts predominated at Waskerley until the shed was closed in 1940, after which several were based at Consett. Class F No 777 arrived at Waskerley in about 1932 for the Darlington—Crook—Blackhill service and lasted until May 1935. As has been recorded by T. E. Rounthwaite in *The Railways of Weardale*, an experiment was then made with Great Northern Railway Class D2 4-4-0 No 4386 but this was sent back to York in July of the same year, probably because it was unsuitable for the heavy gradients. Class C 0-6-0s and some Darlington Class R 4-4-0s then operated the Crook—Blackhill service until its withdrawal north of Tow Law in 1939. The closure of Annfield Plain and Waskerley sheds in 1940 had the result of making Consett shed more important than it had ever been. At closure Annfield shed had five T2s and a P1. Previous to this the shed at Wear Valley junction, south of Crook, had closed on 8 July 1935 and the closure of Shildon shed in the same year had necessitated the re-opening of West Auckland shed, which had been closed in 1931. After 1935 therefore West Auckland and Darlington sheds provided the motive power for the line up to Consett (Tow Law from 1939).

Meanwhile there was an influx of new LNER-designed locomotives. On the main line Pacifics had arrived, but the newcomers for branch services were V1 2-6-2Ts for passenger work (No 465 arrived at Blaydon in May 1936) and Class J39 0-6-0s for passenger and goods work. In 1933-6 the Class D 4-4-4 tanks had been rebuilt to 4-6-2T (as Class A8), and several were at Gateshead and Blaydon. Some K3 2-6-0s were also in the same area.

New Class D49 4-4-0s had replaced old engines on Newcastle—Carlisle passenger trains, and several Class R (D20) 4-4-0s displaced from main line work also operated on this line. Newcastle—Carlisle goods work was entrusted to Gateshead-based NER Class S3 (B16) 4-6-0s, among other types. The LNER introduced small Sentinel Class Y3 0-4-0Ts on to shunting work at Dunston staiths in particular.

During World War II more J39s and K3s arrived on Tyneside. Some of the latter at Blaydon in 1943 included Nos 38, 1322, 1324 and 1332. In this year there was a large re-allocation of T2s from Blaydon to Teesside, notably to Newport shed; fourteen were moved in March 1943 and were partly replaced by Darlington T/T1s. Some of the latter were Nos 444, 474, 715, 1685 and 2125. Consett received P3s in the same year, including Nos 2347 and 2351.

THE LAST LNER YEARS: RENUMBERING

In 1942 the LNER had decided to renumber its locomotive stock. This was begun in 1946 and the old NER numbers vanished. Some examples of the new scheme may be given. The 0-8-0s were renumbered 3250-3339 (T/T1), 3340-3459 (T2) and 3460-74 (T3). The Class O 0-4-4T became Nos 7240-

7349, and the surviving Class Cs were renumbered between 5025 and 5123. In 1947 there remained five of the latter at Blaydon, and another two at West Auckland. Consett still had three Class Bs and the small shed at Pelton Level had Class N (N9) No 9424 (NER No 1652). No 9424 had spent almost the whole of the preceding thirty years first at Annfield Plain and then at Pelton Level. Built in 1893 it survived until 1955, moving to Tyne Dock at the end. For many years Pelton Level had operated two Class L tanks on its coal shunting work. By 1947 the batch of Class U (N10) 0–6–2Ts at Gateshead consisted of ten, which were Nos 9090-1, 9093, 9099, 9102-3, 9105-7, 9109 (old Nos 1321, 1667, 1697, 1132, 1317, 1706, 1699, 1707, 1711, 1716). At Bowes Bridge were Nos 9097 and 9100 (NER Nos 1109, 1138) which remained there for several more years.

Of the 0–8–0s in January 1947, there were a dozen T2s at Consett, seven at Borough Gardens, three at Tyne Dock and seventeen T/T1s at Blaydon. The latter shed had not yet recovered the T2 allocation lost during the war, but it had no less than 33 Gresley J39s. Nine K3s were at Gateshead. Tyne Dock depot had acquired a small army of 2–8–0s of both LNER Class 01/04 types and some LMS Class 8Fs (Nos 8529, 8556 and 8558). The fifteen Class T3s remained here, and there were also nine T/T1s. Withdrawal of the T/T1 engines commenced in 1946 and their rapid disappearance was completed by 1951.

Passenger locomotives at Blaydon in 1947 comprised seven Class Os (Nos 7255, 7259, 7265, 7277, 7323, 7325, and 7339) and two Class VIs (Nos 7638 and 7658). There were also two North British Class D32 4–4–0s allocated, Nos 2448-9, but these did not last many more years. These engines worked the former NBR Newcastle—Hexham—Riccarton junction service alongside the newer Class D30 which were based at Edinburgh, Hawick and sub-depots. In Tyneside surroundings the latter, the 'Scott' Class, looked distinctly 'different' beside old NER classes and modern LNER types. Regular performers at this period included Nos 2421 *Laird o' Monkbarns*, 2425 *Ellangowan* and 2440 *Wandering Willie* among others. To be sentimental it was pleasant to see the rugged but handsome D30s beside the most attractive NER D20s.

Gateshead shed had some V1/V3 2–6–2Ts, and eleven D49s, mainly for the Carlisle line. The latter included Nos 2742 *The*

Braes of Derwent, 2747 *The Percy*, and 2771 *The Rufford*. New Class B1 4-6-0s had appeared at Gateshead supplementing the Pacifics and V2 2-6-2s which had ousted NER Atlantics. The B1s were Nos 1011 *Waterbuck*, 1012 *Puku*, 1013 *Topi*, 1014 *Oribi* and No 1100.

Newcastle & Carlisle line passenger locomotives based at Carlisle Canal and Hexham also appeared in the region. Carlisle had six D49s including No 2731 *Cumberland*, and Hexham had Class O Nos 7245, 7268, 7313 and 7329. Carlisle also had five Gresley Pacifics for the Waverley route and it might be mentioned that on occasion, but particularly in the late 1950s, Pacifics sometimes worked on the passenger service to Newcastle. In the past it had not been unknown for ex-North British Atlantic engines based at Carlisle to appear on the service.

At the other end of the region, the small shed at Durham had several 0-4-4Ts, and a few V1s had arrived at West Auckland where there were also some of the Great Central designed A5 4-6-2Ts. Goods engines at West Auckland in 1947 included a pair of Class Ts, two Class Cs, a dozen Class P1s and a single Class N (No 9422 – NER No 1650). Some of the Darlington allocation which saw duty on the passenger trains to Tow Law include A5 Nos 9830-42, Class O Nos 7250, 7342; ten Class C (including Nos 5031, 5033, 5078 and 5090) and thirty-four Class J39s.

The LNER had taken into stock from 1925 into the early 1930s a number of Sentinel steam railcars, some of which appeared on the Newcastle—Blackhill—Durham service. These provided good views of the line scenery. In 1931 a diesel electric railcar was tried out and run from Blackhill to Newcastle via Annfield Plain, achieving a speed of 64 mph on the main line section. After the war the company planned to purchase some diesel mechanical railcars, especially for use on the Newcastle—Blackhill services. In December 1946 the plan was for ten such AEC railcars to be based at Newcastle, and in March 1947 the number proposed was eleven. Nationalisation intervened to forestall implementation of the scheme.

STEAM CLIMAX

The early years of British Railways saw a climax of steam history in the region. New designs of engines, albeit in small numbers, arrived to stand beside the old T. W. Worsdell 0–6–0s and Wilson Worsdell 0–4–4Ts. Chief amongst the newcomers were more B1 4–6–0s, Class K1 2–6–0s, and BR 3MT and 4MT 2–6–0s. There were also new Class E1 (LNER J72) 0–6–0Ts built in 1949-51, and J94 0–6–0 STS. The oldest engines held their own for a few years before the idea of 'modernisation' took firm root. In 1954 old Class C No 65090 (NER No 1562) was allocated to Blaydon alongside new 4MT 2–6–0 No 43126, and Nos 65062, 65064, 65088, 65091, 65097 were on duty at West Auckland beside 3MT 2–6–0 Nos 77000-4 and 77010-11. West Auckland also had 2MT 2–6–0s which were mainly used on the Stainmore line. Darlington shed possessed 2–6–4Ts of LMS (Nos 42083-5) and LNER (Class L1) types.

To replace the T/T1s as they disappeared, Blaydon re-acquired T2s in 1947-8, the latter including Nos 3353, 3376, 3385, 3391, 3398-9, 3403, 3412, 3432, 3444 and 3448. T2s Nos 63352, 63359, 63362, 63387, 63437 and 63453 had arrived at Tyne Dock by 1954 to join the fifteen T3s. Several Class WD 2–8–0s were based at Tyne Dock, and two had managed to find their way to Consett shed – Nos 90045 and 90054. Consett's main allocation was twelve T2s. There were sixteen T2s at Borough Gardens shed, Gateshead, which also possessed three B1s (Nos 61319-21). Another eight B1s were at Gateshead Greensfield. No 61238 *Leslie Runciman* had been there since delivery in October 1947, and No 61019 *Nilghai* had reached Gateshead after a spell at Heaton shed. Both of these locomotives moved to Blaydon a few years later. The other Gateshead B1s consisted of Nos 61011-3, 61022 *Sassaby*, 61100 and 61199.

The K1 2–6–0s were in evidence on all lines in the region on both passenger and goods (including minerals) services. Nos 62002, 62006, 62010, 62021-30 were at Blaydon and Nos 62001, 62005, 62007-8 and nine more were at Darlington. No 62008 of the latter frequently worked the Crook and Tow Law passenger service. No 62022 had the duty of working one of the last trains on the North British route from Hexham on its last day (13 October 1956). No 62022 headed the 11.10am Newcastle—Hawick train. J39 0–6–0s remained a numerous class on Tyneside, but withdrawal of the 0–4–4Ts had begun. Nevertheless there were four Class Os at Durham in 1954 (Nos 67258, 67263, 67298 and 67307); eight at Blaydon (Nos 67241, 67248, 67277, 67304, 67320, 67323, 67325 and 67339); one at Gateshead (No 67259) and another six at Hexham. No 67255 (NER No 1169) was at Blaydon when withdrawn in May 1951, and had been at that shed thirty years previously. V1/V3 tanks were still at Blaydon and Gateshead, the former shed having Nos 67636, 67639, 67653, 67656-8. A few Class Rs were in this area, rapidly reaching the end of their days. No 62349 was at Blaydon and Nos 62360, 62375, 62396 were at Gateshead. They were withdrawn in 1956-7. The only D49s in the area were Nos 62747 and 62771 at Blaydon. J94 saddle tanks on shunting duties at Blaydon were Nos 68010, 68035-6, 68038 and 68059, while No 68019 was at Consett. New Class E1 (J72) tanks at Blaydon were Nos 69023-6. Several of the Class Us at Gateshead were withdrawn from service in 1956, but others soldiered on.

The Consett iron ore trains from Tyne Dock had long been worked by the T3 0–8–0s, and they were assisted by several Class O1 2–8–0s (Nos 63712, 63755, 63760, 63856 and 63874) which had also been fitted with air pumps to supply compressed air for operating the doors of the iron ore hopper wagons. The ore trains were banked up the 1 in 40 from Tyne Dock bottom usually by an 0–6–0 shunter, and T2s often banked the trains from South Pelaw to South Medomsley (near Leadgate). The usual load was eight or nine hoppers. In 1955 BR Class 9F 2–10–0 No 92037 was tested on the ore trains, and soon afterwards ten of this class were allocated to Tyne Dock to work the trains. These were Nos 92060-6 and 92097-9. The T3s and O1s were largely released for other mineral and goods duties but they occasionally appeared on the ore trains thereafter.

DECLINE OF STEAM

After 1955 the veteran classes continued to be thinned out

in numbers. Class C No 65090 was withdrawn from service at Blaydon in 1955 but No 65033 was still in the area at Hexham. This engine managed to last until 1962, chiefly on Northumbrian branch lines, and is now preserved at the North East Folk Museum at Beamish. As NER No 876 it had been built in March 1889 and so reached the good age of 73. It had nearly ended its days in 1939, being withdrawn in that year, but was reinstated. The 0–4–4Ts disappeared in 1958, and one of the last in service was No 67329 (NER No 2100) latterly at Hexham, and was withdrawn in November 1958. A year later this engine was still in store near Darlington. Durham shed closed in 1958, shortly after withdrawal of its last 0–4–4T, No 67263 (NER No 1866). The V1/V3 2–6–2Ts on Tyneside were reduced mainly to secondary duties, such as shunting and pilot duties, after the closure of the Consett passenger services in 1954-5. Withdrawal of many other classes began or accelerated, including the 4–6–2Ts, K3 2–6–0s D49 4–4–0s, P1 0–6–0s and U 0–6–2Ts. On the Newcastle & Carlisle passenger trains, Pacifics, V2 2–6–2s and B1 4–6–0s appeared frequently, and diesel multiple units made their appearance by 1959.

In May 1959 Class U No 69105 moved from Pelton Level shed to Gateshead, joining the survivors of its class at that shed, largely for Tanfield branch duties. At Bowes Bridge were No 69097 and P1 No 65700. A J94 went to Pelton Level, although it was not long before a diesel shunter replaced it. In 1959-61 massive withdrawals of the J39 0–6–0s took place because of their relatively costly maintenance compared with P2/P3 (J26-7) 0–6–0s for example. The early 1960s brought withdrawal of all but the most modern BR classes, but it is well known that, ironically, the rapid decline of steam eliminated the BR types before some NER veterans, as will be related. In 1962 the last Class U 0–6–2Ts were withdrawn at Gateshead and Bowes Bridge sheds, these being Nos 69097, 69101, 69109 (NER Nos 1109, 1148 and 1716). Bowes Bridge shed was closed later in the year. At the end of 1962 all the T3 engines were withdrawn, but No 63460 (NER No 901) was set aside by BR for preservation, although it has yet to be exhibited. Withdrawal of the T2s began in 1963, apart from two damaged in accidents and taken out of service in 1960-1.

Steam was withdrawn from Blaydon shed on 4 March 1963

LOCOMOTIVES 195

and the engines including T2s and B1s reallocated. Diesel locomotives were beginning to become common in the region, and diesel shunters in particular had replaced many of the small tank engines. Gateshead shed was to become the diesel shed serving main line and all local Tyneside branches, and the other sheds in the area were gradually closed. In 1965 Blaydon shed was closed on 15 March, and on 24 May Consett shed also closed, but was retained as a signing-on point. West Auckland shed closed on 2 February 1965, and its locomotives were reallocated. During this year the line north of Wear Valley junction was closed completely. For several years the Darlington—Crook passenger service had been operated by diesel railcars, but steam locomotives made appearances almost to the end. No 42405, a Fowler 2-6-4T for example, was seen at Crook on a passenger train on 4 September 1964. Another 2-6-4T, No 42085, also made late appearances on this line. The goods and mineral traffic on the line to Tow Law in its last years was worked by T2s, Ivatt Class 4MTs, K1s and 3MTs, chiefly. On occasions a BR Type 2 diesel appeared.

STEAM FINALE

The years 1966-7 saw the last of the steam locomotives in both north-west and north-east Durham. These grimy locomotives, which had once such fine exteriors finished their days as they had begun with moving minerals. Gateshead shed had become fully dieselised and the B1s had largely vanished from the region. Tyne Dock shed had a collection of T2s, K1s and P3s, while Sunderland had the same types and also Class WD 2-8-0s. The main duty of these two depots west of Gateshead was the carriage of coal to the power stations at Dunston and Stella South. Many of the allocations at both places appeared on these coal trains in 1966-7, notably Tyne Dock Class K1 Nos 62007, 62023, 62025, 62060; Sunderland WD Nos 90321, 90361, 90417, and the following T2s from both sheds – Nos 63346, 63366, 63395, 63426, 63429, 63455, 63458 (NER Nos 1253, 1335, 2238, 2269, 2272, 2298, 2301). The P3 0-6-0s that appeared included Nos 65789, 65795, 65804, 65855, 65879-80, 65882, 65892, 65894 (NER Nos 938, 1227, 1007, 1226, 2357-8, 2360, 2390, 2392). A West Hartlepool T2 No 63387 (NER No

2230) made at least one appearance in February 1967 on a Stella coal train. Some of these engines survived until the end of steam on BR in the north east in August–September 1967, including No 63395, which was subsequently bought for preservation. One of the last P3s, No 65894, has also been preserved.

The end of steam power on the Tyne Dock—Consett ore trains occurred on 19 November 1966, when No 92063 was cleaned up for the occasion. A few of its fellows had already been withdrawn, notably Nos 92061 and 92099, and by the end of November 1966 only one of the ten 9Fs, No 92065, remained operational on goods traffic. It did not last much longer. Their place on the ore trains was taken by ten BR Sulzer Type 2 diesels, Nos D5102-11, which worked the trains in pairs. The old Stanhope & Tyne line between Boldon Colliery and Washington was closed at the time of this changeover, so that the ore trains were re-routed via Gateshead to reach South Pelaw.

Of the steam locomotives from north-west Durham that were re-allocated following shed closures, quite a number ended their days at the old NER headquarters at York. No 77002 with 77012 were the last of their class north of London, with several B1s they were withdrawn by July 1967. The B1s included Nos 61013-4 withdrawn in January 1967, No 61238 *Leslie Runciman* in February, No 61019 *Nilghai* in March and No 61012 *Puku* in July 1967. They were thus all survived by several NER P3s and T2s.

DIESELS AND INDUSTRIAL LOCOMOTIVES

The English Electric Type 3 is the commonest locomotive type, excepting shunters, in the area today. The line from Wylam to Low Fell through Blaydon and Dunston is used by Type 4 diesels on Tyne Yard—Carlisle goods trains, and Brush, BR/Sulzer and English Electric Type 4s are all to be seen. BR/Sulzer Type 2s, Clayton and English Electric Type 1s operate local coal and goods traffic in the Tyneside region.

Since 1945 the great decline of the coal mining industry in north-west Durham has seen the extinction of many mines, wagonways and locomotives. The NCB introduced modern 0-6-0STs, many of which have survived, while the old ex-company engines have disappeared except for a few old engines.

On the Garesfield wagonway between Winlaton Mill (Derwenthaugh cokeworks and the adjacent Clockburn drift mine) and Derwenthaugh (where the staiths were closed some ten years ago), there is a solitary diesel and several 0-6-0ST engines. The diesel was built by Vanguard Works in 1964 on the frame of a steam engine. Many tank engines have seen service on this line since 1947, and these have included two Kitson pannier tanks, of which No 41 (Kitson 2509) was built in 1883 and is in store. Three or four post-war saddle tanks are in current use and several other engines are stored. NCB 0-6-0ST – No 28 works the traffic at Morrison Busty colliery, Annfield Plain, and three engines were allocated to Marley Hill, Bowes Railway, one of which was in use in 1970 before closure of the line. Another tank, 0-4-0ST No 81, is on the NCB Railway at Lamesley (part of former Team wagonway) near Tyne marshalling yard. Another old NCB engine in store is *Twizell*, an 0-6-0T built by Robert Stephenson in 1891 and stored at Annfield Plain. Several other NCB tank engines shunt at Norwood cokeworks, Dunston.

Consett steelworks operated a fleet of tank engines up to the 1950s, but Hunslet 0-6-0 diesels now shunt the traffic. (Sentinel 0-6-0s are recent additions.) These locomotives can be seen on BR lines beside the 1896 Consett station, where they bring traffic from the works to the BR sidings for removal by an English Electric Type 3. They also shunt the sidings near the former MPD – the 'low yard'.

The two large power stations at Dunston and Stella South both operate steam locomotives. In 1970, there were four such engines at Dunston and three at Stella, all being 0-4-0STs. In addition there is a diesel shunter at both locations, that at Dunston being an Armstrong Whitworth locomotive dating from 1933. Finally, at the end of the old Newcastle & Carlisle Railway branch from Derwenthaugh to Swalwell, there is a coal-coke disposal point where the sidings are shunted by several 0-6-0STs.

Railways of Weardale provides details of the locomotives

used in the Stanhope area, at Ashes Quarry (Consett Iron Co); the Rookhope branch (Weardale Iron Co) and by the Weardale Lead Co at Rookhope and Stanhopeburn.

CHAPTER TEN

Accidents and Incidents

There have been no accidents in north-west Durham involving great loss of life, but there have been several destructive incidents. The steep gradients of the Ouston junction—Annfield Plain line have especially played a role in several of the accidents. For information on accidents I am indebted to the Ministry of Transport.

DERAILMENT ON KNITSLEY VIADUCT

On 21 December 1874 the last passenger train of the day on the Consett branch, the 7.55pm from Durham, left Lanchester at about 8.20pm for Benfieldside and Newcastle. The train consisted of a brake van marshalled behind the engine's tender, nine passenger carriages, another brake van, and at the rear an empty passenger carriage. The train was partially fitted with the Westinghouse air brake (three carriages and the leading brake van). It was a clear winter's evening, the ground was covered with snow and it was freezing hard. Driver Joseph Laing did not force the long train unduly up the 1 in 80 and 1 in 60 gradients, and it was travelling at a speed of about seven mph when it reached Knitsley viaduct.

The train rounded the sharp curve at the south end of the bridge and then ran on to the viaduct. Driver Laing suddenly felt that the train was pulling harder than usual, and looked back from his cab. He must have received a tremendous shock, for one carriage was well off the rails, and even as he watched it lurched sideways and fell over the parapet and off the viaduct. The train was quickly brought to a halt without further damage and it was found that all the leading carriages were off the rails, some leaning on the parapet. It was the third carriage which had fallen from the bridge, and the first two carriages, the fourth, and the first brake van were all derailed. Fortunately the carriage which had fallen some seventy feet from the bridge was an empty first class carriage. Two passengers in other carriages were slightly injured in the derailment.

Captain H. W. Tyler of the Board of Trade investigated the accident and in his report stated that it was caused by a wheel coming loose on its axle under the first carriage, and the consequent freedom of movement of the other wheel striking against the deep transoms between the longitudinal sleepers on the viaduct caused the axle to be torn loose on to the track. This obstruction caused the second carriage to become derailed and the third to fall from the bridge.

The very sharp curve on the approach to the bridge may well have loosened the wheel and in fact the curve was improved when the viaduct was replaced in 1919-20 (see Chapter 4).

ACCIDENTS AT OUSTON JUNCTION

On 9 February 1931 there was a serious accident at Ouston junction, where the curve from the Pontop branch connects with the east coast main line. Class T1 0-8-0 No 644 left Stella Gill with a coal train for North Blyth staiths and ran towards Ouston junction, where the signal was at danger. Instead of stopping, the engine and its twenty-one wagon train ran past the signal and gathered speed on the downward gradient. The brakes had failed. The points were set for a main line train and the coal train ran with great force into the buffers at the end of the 'runaway' siding. The fireman jumped from the footplate before the collision but the driver suffered severe scalding and bruising. The engine was derailed and embedded in the ballast at the end of the line, while the tender and one of the wagons were stood on end. The wreckage, which was considerable, did not affect the main line, but a breakdown gang worked all through the night to clear the worst of it.

By a coincidence there was another serious accident at Ouston junction on 9 February, in 1970. Another coal train, in this case from Morrison colliery at Annfield Plain to Dunston hauled by an English Electric Type 3 (Class 37) diesel, became derailed on the junction points and the wagons ran amok on both sides of the line. Unfortunately the guard in the rear cab of the engine jumped out when he saw the wagons leaving the track and was killed by the wagons which piled up beside the line. Traffic was disrupted on the main line as well as the branch for several days, and branch traffic was re-routed via Washington while some main line trains were diverted via the Leamside route.

SOUTH PELAW DERAILMENT

In late April 1942, Class T2 0–8–0 No 2286 was heading a coal train down the bank east of Annfield Plain when the brakes ceased to function. The train soon gathered speed on the steep gradients and rushed down through West Stanley, Beamish and Pelton, becoming derailed at South Pelaw junction. The engine overturned and the whole train was wrecked, and both driver M. Ridley and fireman W. Stanley were killed; the guard was luckily unhurt although his van was damaged. Traffic was disrupted for some days. A result of the accident was that the braking system on T2 locomotives was somewhat modified to guard against another such failure. Because it occurred during wartime this accident received very little attention from the Press, and details of it were scanty.

HELL HOLE WOOD LANDSLIP

There were severe snowstorms in north-west Durham in the middle of February 1941 followed by a thaw at the end of the month. During the early hours of the morning of 4 March the thaw caused the land above and below the railway in Hell Hole Wood, west of Beamish, to slip, undermining the formation and also covering the track to a depth of 30ft for a length of 30yd. Shortly after this, a light engine J39 (No 1577) and guard's van came down the line from Stanley, travelling slowly back to Tyne Dock. The crew, driver Phillips and fireman J. Craig of Tyne Dock shed, did not see the landslip until too late, and the engine ploughed into the obstruction. The track subsided, and both engine and van fell down the embankment course of the line and came to rest 70ft away and 45ft below the level of the rails. Luckily the crew received only slight abrasions and shock and the guard was unhurt. The men set off down the line and succeeded in warning an approaching train.

The line was closed until 7 March while workmen cleared the landslide and slewed the track on to firm ground. During this time passenger trains from Newcastle terminated at Beamish, and a service to West Stanley was run via Rowlands Gill and Blackhill. All goods traffic was diverted to other routes, and the iron ore traffic was routed to Consett via Rowlands Gill.

BEAMISH RUNAWAY COLLISION

On 9 December 1964 there was an accident at Beamish involving one fatality. A coal train was being shunted at Annfield Plain junction when part of it broke loose and ran away down the steep gradient towards Stanley. A signalman only just failed to derail the 23 runaway loaded wagons, which contained 500 tons of coal. The railwaymen at Annfield Plain hurriedly contacted signal boxes at Beamish and beyond in an effort to keep the line clear. Unfortunately there was another goods train near Beamish which could not be warned in time. The runaways roared through Beamish at 80 mph and crashed into the goods train which was travelling eastwards. The unfortunate guard of this train was killed, his van having its body scythed off its frame. All of the runaways left the rails and together with about half of the goods wagons, piled up into a mountain of rubble thirty feet high along the embankment. The front part of the goods train had been sent flying forwards with the impact, and driver Waller was taken to hospital with severe shock, but his fireman was unhurt.

It was several days before the line was cleared and reopened and meanwhile all traffic was diverted via Lanchester. Sixty railwaymen were engaged in the clearance operations. A police inspector commented that it was the worst accident he had ever seen, and certainly the destruction of rolling stock was considerable. On 11 December a private enquiry into the accident was held by senior railway officials.

TWO EVENTS AT BLAYDON

The 1870s were one of the worst decades for British railway accidents, and there were two serious but non-fatal accidents at Blaydon which are worth mentioning.

On the afternoon of 10 November 1870, the 4.40pm Newcastle—Edinburgh passenger train of the North British Railway collided with a stationary light engine just west of Scotswood Bridge, Blaydon, after passing from the down to up line owing to the points being incorrectly set at a cross-over. The accident would have been more serious if the NB train had been travelling more quickly. The *Newcastle Daily Journal* describes the event under the headline 'Alarming railway collision at Scotswood Bridge':

'An accident of a somewhat serious and alarming character occurred yesterday afternoon on the Newcastle and Carlisle Railway to the North British passenger train which leaves the Central Station at 4.40pm for Edinburgh. After the train had proceeded about 50 yards past Scotswood Bridge it ran from the down to the up line in consequence, as it is alleged, of the points having been left open, and before it could be stopped it came into collision with a locomotive which happened to be standing on the railway waiting until the line should be cleared in order to enter Newcastle. The train was travelling at the rate of ten miles an hour, and such was the violence of the shock that the tender of the stationary engine was smashed to fragments and hurled all over the line. The driver and stoker were at their post when the collision occurred and both were thrown with great violence upon the metals. Beyond a severe shaking, however, they did not sustain any serious injury though the stoker lay insensible for a few seconds in consequence of the stun he received. The passenger train did not leave the rails and escaped with comparatively little damage. One or two of the carriages were more or less broken, while all the lamps were smashed and the lights extinguished. The driver and fireman were thrown upon the tender of their engine and received only a few slight bruises. Most of the passengers of whom there were forty to fifty in the train were severely shaken, but none incurred serious hurts with the exception of an old lady who was much cut about the face, and Mr Hall, Birtley, whose nose was completely broken and severely cut. Mr Bell, surgeon, Newcastle, was also amongst the injured and although he had received a bad bruise on one of his legs, he lost no time in rendering his professional aid to other sufferers. After an hour's delay the line was sufficiently cleared to allow the train to proceed; but Mr Hall, who was travelling to Edinburgh was unable to continue his journey beyond Blaydon, whither he was attended by Mr Bell, and is now doing as well as can be expected. The rest of the passengers went on with the train.'

The NER was much disturbed by this accident as a few years earlier the Board of Trade had drawn the company's attention to the matter of points and the need for interlocking with signals. The North British also probably sent a communication on the matter to York. However, less than a month later there was an accident which, following so closely the Blaydon affair, really aroused the Board of Trade's ire. This was the Brockley Whins accident of 6 December 1870, involving a head-on collision on facing points, the pointsman having forgotten to re-set them. This caused five deaths and many injuries, and Colonel Yolland severely criticised the NER, and the latter began to pursue the interlocking principle more seriously.

The second Blaydon incident again resulted in no fatalities, but could easily have done so. Locomotive No 787 (a Fletcher 0–6–0 built in 1872) arrived at the sidings to the west of Blaydon station with the Sunday morning goods from Carlisle on 24 November 1878, and proceeded to shunt the wagons. At nine o'clock the quiet Sunday atmosphere of Blaydon and neighbourhood was shattered with a 'loud report' as the boiler of No 787 exploded, destroying the engine and a nearby house, and causing damage to private property which resulted in claims totalling £120 reaching the NER. Several people including the engine crew had narrow escapes from death. The *Newcastle Courant* describes the event concisely:

'The engine was in charge of John Hardy, driver, and William Hewitt, fireman, and at the time stated was standing on account of the 'boards' being against it. Joseph Hodgson, foreman in the mineral department at Blaydon, lives in a house close by the railway. He had a friend named Samuel Dodds who is employed as a lighter at Gateshead sheds staying with him, and when the engine stopped, the driver and fireman got off to speak to Dodds and went about five yards to do so. To this circumstance may be ascribed their safety. Some idea of the force of the explosion can be gathered from the following facts: – the dome was thrown 300 yards and landed at the opposite side of the river [in Northumberland]; a piece of metal has been found a quarter of a mile away; and houses 200 yards distant had the slates shaken out of their places. The house occupied by Mr Hodgson is a complete wreck, most of his furniture is destroyed, and he has been obliged to remove into another dwelling. Some of the escapes are almost marvellous. Mr Hodgson was feeding his poultry and had a pan in one hand and a wooden spoon in the other. A large piece of metal fell and broke the handles of both the spoon and the pan about half an inch from his hand. The engineman and his fireman were talking to S. Dodds who had his son in his arms at the time, and they were thrown down and received a severe shaking and were also slightly scalded. Mrs Hodgson was in the room where a door was blown past her and she escaped unhurt. The telegraph wires were blown down for a quarter of a mile on each side. Mr Hunter and a staff of men were soon in attendance and had them replaced by four o'clock.'

OTHER ACCIDENTS

On 13 September 1941 Class T1 0–8–0 No 781 was derailed into a bomb crater between Knitsley and Consett. The engine was only slightly damaged and its crew unhurt. The Germans had bombed Consett during the previous night.

On the many inclined planes in the region there have been occasional accidents usually because of rope failures. It was unfortunate that the opening of the Stanhope & Tyne Railway west of Annfield was marred by a fatal accident. Four wagons filled with forty to fifty people were being hauled up Weatherhill incline when a sudden jerk of the rope broke a shackle and the wagons began to run backwards, gathering speed on the steep hill. A railwayman at the foot of the incline was faced with the terrible choice of allowing the runaways to continue and to run away down the even steeper Crawley incline with dire results, or to direct the wagons into a siding at the bank foot where unfortunately there were four loaded mineral wagons. The man chose to switch the runaways into the siding, and in the violent collision two men and a boy were fatally injured.

A rather different kind of accident on an incline took place on 12 July 1851 on the Twizell incline on the Stanhope & Tyne line. A new locomotive of the York Newcastle & Berwick Railway had lately been based at Pelton Level, mainly to bank iron ore wagons to Consett up the inclines. On the day in question the engine was being sent to Annfield Plain to bring an 'iron pipe' to Pelton Level, and was pulled up Twizell bank tender first. Six men, including driver John Mann, were on the footplate or the tender. Eighty feet up the bank, the tender jumped the rails and dragged the engine off the line. Fireman Francis Minto and inspector John Swinburne jumped to safety 'plunging head-foremost amidst the coal rubbish'. The engine turned over twice on top of the other four men. Driver Mann and bankrider William Richardson were crushed to death instantly but the two others had only broken thighs. The inhabitants of the tiny colliery village of Twizell 'in an incredibly short time were at the scene of the disaster. The women, instead, as is too often the case on occasions like this, of giving way to useless exclamations of grief, set to work and seemed to render as much assistance as the men themselves. In consequence of the great weight of the locomotive and tender however – they weighing 17 to 18 tons – it was fully two hours before they could be lifted.' The inquest on 14 July was attended by Captain O'Brien (YNB secretary), T. E. Harrison (general superintendent), Mr Mackay (general surveyor of the line) and Mr Fletcher (inspector of the platelayers). The jury verdict was 'accidental death'.

A breakaway on the Fugar incline, Tanfield branch, in 1939 caused a destructive derailment of wagons, and left scars on a bridge carrying the Newcastle road over the line which were visible twenty years later.

The steep gradients of north-west Durham are not confined to the railways – there are many steep banks on the roads too, and on one of these, Blackhill bank near Consett, the railway company had the interesting distinction of suffering a bus accident. One of the twenty LNER road buses on the Durham—Consett area routes was climbing up this hill in May 1928 when it stalled and began to run backwards. The driver managed to bring it to rest against a property (not without damage) but no one was hurt. An action was brought against the company, but the case was dismissed, the court ruling that the mechanical failure was not the fault of the LNER. Today the main Consett—Newcastle bus route (via Shotley Bridge), for example, does not use the bank in its entirety.

THE SNOW HAZARD

Consett is 800ft above sea level, and the railway westwards to Stanhope reaches over 1,000ft before Burnhill and a summit of 1,445ft at Weatherhill. Another highly-elevated stretch was the whole of the Tow Law—Burnhill junction line, over 1,000ft high. Bad winter weather was therefore always likely. Consett is one of England's snowiest towns, while the Wear & Derwent line was certainly one of the most affected in England. Waskerley MPD always possessed a snowplough and others were stationed at Gateshead and other places not far away. Hardly a year passed without snow disrupting traffic, often for weeks, and there were especially bad years, as in 1886 and 1937. In February 1937 three locomotives and two ploughs came off the rails while clearing deep drifts at Weatherhill. Acworth in his *Railways of England* relates how a snowplough was sent to free the *Flying Scotsman* express in a drift north of Newcastle, the plough 'having been out all day clearing the roads around Consett'. In the very next week he mentions that 'on the moors near Consett with three engines we drove the plough through several hundred yards of snow nine feet deep'.

The Weardale Iron Co line from Parkhead to Rookhope reached a summit of 1,670ft above sea level, and it suffered from traffic disruption in almost every winter. *The Durham County Advertiser* of 11 May 1883 had a paragraph: 'The railway between Park Head and Bolts Law along which is carried the upper Weardale ironstone and limestone was blocked with snow on Wednesday forenoon so that the snowplough had to be brought into requisition. The snow in some of the cuttings was from three to six feet deep.' The month in question was May!

The weather affected the railway in its last years and at its closure. Snowdrifts in 1962-3 and 1965-6 both caused cessation of traffic west of Burnhill for several weeks. Fluorspar, ganister and sand traffic at Parkhead and Weatherhill was diverted to Eastgate station, about three to four miles away in the Wear valley, at such times. When the Burnhill ammunition depot closed on 12 March 1969, BR proposed closing the line from Consett. Inclement weather came to the line's rescue and closure could not be effected for several weeks, as the rolling stock could not be retrieved from the Burnhill siding.

OXHILL CROSSING

In 1899-1900 the local council requested the NER to replace the Oxhill level crossing on the S & T route between Annfield Plain and Stanley with a bridge. The crossing, on the main road linking Stanley with Consett and Annfield Plain, was frequently closed to road traffic because of the heavy coal traffic on the line. The NER estimated the cost of a road overbridge as £2,300. The council was somewhat impatient and decided to force the issue by indicting the NER at Durham Quarter Sessions, a fact noted by the NER on 1 March 1900. The railway company decided to discuss the matter with the council and negotiations were conducted. They were broken off on 5 July 1900. The NER then announced that it would apply to Parliament for an Act to enable it to replace the crossing with a bridge, and asked to council to suspend its indictment. But the council still indicted the company.

On 26 July 1900 the NER minutes record that the council's indictment was heard at Durham Assizes on 16-17 July and 'the jury returned a verdict in favour of the Company on all counts'. The NER was undoubtedly somewhat annoyed by this affair, and felt no obligation to spend money on a bridge at Oxhill, and the plan was therefore dropped.

The council, however, did not let the matter drop. It instituted proceedings in the Queen's Bench Division with a view to testing the validity of the verdict of 'not guilty' and on 16 April 1901 the Lord Chief Justice and Mr Justice Lawrence upheld the verdict. So the level crossing still remains, and with today's traffic it causes worse traffic hold-ups than ever before.

THE LINTZ GREEN MURDER

There can be few railways in the country which have close associations with murders, especially an unsolved murder with such mystery behind it as the episode on the NER Blaydon & Consett branch. The murder took place in peaceful countryside at the quiet station at Lintz Green on the night of 7 October 1911. The *Durham County Advertiser* of 13 October tells the story:

'A shooting tragedy was enacted late on Saturday night at Lintz Green station on the Derwent Valley branch of the North Eastern Railway, Durham. The passenger train from Newcastle to Blackhill arrived about 10.45, and after setting the train safely away, Mr George Wilson, stationmaster, travelled across the line to the down platform and walked outside the station to his house which adjoins the station and is a secluded one, standing amidst trees and shrubs. Mr Wilson had traversed his garden and almost reached the doorway when he was deliberately shot by an assailant, presumably in ambush. The bullet which must have been fired from a powerful weapon penetrated right through Mr Wilson's left breast and struck against the wall of his house being flattened out. A blank cartridge was subsequently found by the side of a footpath leading to Friarside and Burnopfield. Samuel Elliott, Robert Wailes and Thomas Middleton, miners, who, after leaving the train had proceeded along the footpath for a distance of about 200 yards on their way home heard the report and immediately after, Miss Wilson a young lady of about 24 years, gave a loud scream. They ran back and saw Miss Wilson and Fred White, booking clerk, standing in the open doorway. Mr Wilson was lying prostrate upon the ground, bleeding from a wound but was not dead. They assisted to carry him into the house and Middleton, being an ambulance man, unloosened his tie and collar and removed the front, afterwards giving Mr Wilson a drop of brandy. Mr Wilson was asked to speak, but although he tried, there was only a gurgling in his throat and in a few moments he expired.'

The police soon arrived and searched the area, hampered of course by the darkness. Nobody saw who fired the shot, nor was there discovered any trace of the assailant. The stationmaster was of a 'quiet inoffensive disposition', sixty years of age, and had formerly been a signalman at Blackhill. He had no known enemies. The police soon accepted robbery as the probable motive, as apparently sand had been thrown in Mr Wilson's eyes before he was shot, and a cloth gag was lying beside his body. In fact Mr Wilson had very little money on his person – just the coppers from the booking office sweetmeat machine and a little money of his own, but no railway takings.

Rumours and theories abounded. Disgruntled miners or railwaymen, and lunatics, were strongly canvassed as the likely villains. 'Perhaps', said the *Advertiser*, 'it was a miner, amongst whom there are many rough characters . . . one of these . . . perhaps had some petty grievance against the stationmaster.' Mr Wilson was buried at Burnopfield beside his wife, following an inquest on 9 October 1911. No one was ever charged with the crime and the deed has passed into local folklore.

Lintz Green station at that period regularly carried off a prize for its floral charms, it being the best kept and most beautiful station on the line. Now it is derelict, although its natural setting is still beautiful, but several of the station houses, including the stationmaster's, are still inhabited. A family named Donnelly who resided there in recent years declared the house to be haunted. On wild nights it is reported that the sound of a train passing can be heard at the station, as if the murder has condemned Lintz Green to spiritual unrest.

'WOR NANNY'S A MAZER'

The Derwent valley railway is also the scene of a local song, less famous than 'Blaydon Races' but well known in the region. 'Wor Nanny's a mazer' will need no translating for Geordies, and refers to a man and his wife who go to Rowlands Gill station to catch a train to Newcastle for a day's shopping, and find they have missed it. They have time on their hands before the next train and venture, after hesitation, into a nearby public house. The result is that Nanny becomes drunk and is soon feeling 'varry queer' and the landlord becomes so irate that Nanny is 'hoyed ootside o' the door', so inebriated that 'she cuddent sit up'.

The first verse runs:

> Wor Nanny an' me myed up wor minds te gan and catch the train,
> Te gan te the toon te buy some claes for wor little Billy an' Jane,
> But when we got te Rowlan's Gill the morning train was gyen,
> And thor wasn't another one gan' that way till seventeen minutes te one.
> So aa ses te wor Nan its a lang way te gan an aa saa biv hor feyce she was vext,
> But aa ses nivvor mind we hev plenty o' time we'll stop an' gan on wi' the next,
> She guv a bit smile wen aa spok up an ses, thor's a pibbilick hoose alang theor,
> We'll gan alang theor an get worsels warm an' a glass o' the best bittor beor.
> But Nan was se stoot aa knew she'd not waak, an' she didn't seem willing te try,
> Wen aa think o' the trubble aa'd wiv hor that day aa'd like te borst oot and cry.

Chorus:

> And ay wor Nanny's a mazer and a mazer she remains,
> And as lang as aa live aa winnet forgett the day we lost the trains.

(By permission of J. G. Windows Limited, Newcastle. For the full song, see *Portrait of County Durham* by P. A. White.)

Today that public house still flourishes near the derelict station and the frequent *Venture* bus service precludes anyone nowadays from having time enough to become inebriated while awaiting public transport to Newcastle!

Appendixes

APPENDIX I

CHRONOLOGY

	1710	Main Way wagonway (Pontop—Derwenthaugh) in use.
	1712	First section of Tanfield wagonway in use.
	1712	First section of Tanfield wagonway in use.
	1727	Tanfield—Dunston (Redheugh) in use.
	1768	Tanfield wagonway linked to Main Way at Tanfield Moor.
22 May	1829	Newcastle & Carlisle Railway Act of Incorporation.
15 May	1834	Stanhope & Tyne Railroad opened west of Annfield.
22 May	1834	Blaydon Gateshead & Hebburn Railway Act of Incorporation.
10 September	1834	S & T Annfield—South Shields opened.
26 November	1834	N & CR Blaydon—Hexham opened for goods traffic.
9 March	1835	Blaydon—Hexham opened for passenger traffic.
11 June	1836	N & CR Blaydon—Derwenthaugh opened.
1 March	1837	Derwenthaugh—Redheugh opened.
May	1837	Brandling Junction Railway begin relaying of Tanfield wagonway.
21 May	1839	N & CR Blaydon—Newcastle opened for goods traffic.
29 August	1839	Sacriston wagonway opened.
21 October	1839	Blaydon—Newcastle opened for passenger traffic.
11 November	1840	Tanfield wagonway relaid to Tanfield Moor.
13 May	1842	S & T company dissolved: Pontop & South Shields Railway formed.
14 May	1845	Weardale Extension Railway opened.
24 May	1847	N & CR Swalwell branch opened.
31 July	1854	NER formed.

213

APPENDIXES

20 September	1854	Marley Hill—Kibblesworth (Pontop & Jarrow Railway) opened.
April	1855	Burnopfield—Dipton opened.
14 July	1856	S & D and N & C Union Railway Act of Incorporation.
13 July	1857	NER Lanchester Valley Branch Act.
1 July	1858	Hownes Gill viaduct opened.
3 March	1859	Tyne Dock opened.
4 July	1859	Waskerley Deviation opened.
3 June	1862	S & D Crook—Tow Law deviation Act.
17 July	1862	NER—N & CR Amalgamation Act.
17 July	1862	NER Blaydon & Conside branch Act.
1 September	1862	Lanchester Valley Branch opened.
13 July	1863	NER—S & D Amalgamation Act.
10 April	1867	Crook—Tow Law deviation opened for goods traffic.
18 June	1867	Blaydon & Conside branch opened for goods traffic.
2 December	1867	Blaydon & Conside branch opened for passenger traffic.
2 March	1868	Crook—Tow Law deviation opened for passenger traffic.
5 June	1868	Hownes Gill—Consett North loop opened for goods traffic.
1 October	1868	Crook—Consett (Carr House) passenger trains diverted to Benfieldside (Blackhill).
10 November	1870	Scotswood Bridge (Blaydon) collision.
21 December	1874	Knitsley viaduct derailment.
November	1877	Baxter Wood spur lines opened.
1 July	1881	Tanfield branch-locomotives replace horses and some inclines.
May	1883	Aldin Grange station opened.
1 January	1886	Annfield Plain—East Castle deviation opened.
23 May	1887	South Pelaw—Annfield Plain deviation Act.
16 October	1893	Dunston Extension Railway and new Dunston staiths opened.
16 October	1893	South Pelaw—Ouston junction loop opened.
13 November	1893	South Pelaw—Annfield Plain deviation opened for goods traffic.
1 February	1894	South Pelaw—Annfield Plain deviation opened for passenger traffic.

APPENDIXES 215

1 May	1896	Final change of name to Blackhill, of Consett & Blackhill, formerly Benfieldside station.
17 August	1896	Annfield Plain—Consett—Blackhill passenger service begun.
April	1900	New Blaydon locomotive shed opened.
29 August	1904	Derwenthaugh branch opened (Norwood junction—Derwenthaugh junction).
1 March	1905	Dunston-on-Tyne goods station opened.
22 April	1907	Dunston—Gateshead loop opened (Redheugh incline subsequently closed).
5 January	1908	Blaydon & Consett branch widening completed.
1 January	1909	Newcastle—Dunston-on-Tyne passenger service begun.
1 July	1909	High Westwood station opened.
1 February	1916	Knitsley station closed to passengers.
1 May	1918	Dunston-on-Tyne station closed.
1 October	1919	Dunston re-opened.
30 March	1925	Knitsley re-opened to passengers.
23 May	1926	Dunston-on-Tyne station closed.
11 July	1927	Aldin Grange station renamed Bearpark.
1 February	1934	Shield Row station renamed West Stanley.
1 May	1939	Blackhill—Tow Law passenger service withdrawn.
1 May	1939	Lanchester Valley passenger service withdrawn.
9 September	1940	Waskerley and Annfield Plain locomotive sheds closed.
4 May	1942	High Westwood station closed.
	1946	Stanley—Pelton Level (inclines) closed.
28 April	1951	Weatherhill and Crawley inclines closed.
1 February	1954	Blaydon & Consett branch passenger service withdrawn.
5 July	1954	Ryton station closed
23 May	1955	Pontop branch (Newcastle—Annfield Plain Blackhill) passenger service withdrawn.
11 June	1956	Tow Law—Crook passenger service withdrawn.
24 August	1962	Most of Tanfield branch closed.
11 November	1963	Blaydon & Consett branch closed completely.

APPENDIXES

18 May	1964	Tanfield branch closed south of Redheugh Iron & Steelworks at Teams.
2 February	1965	West Auckland locomotive shed closed.
8 March	1965	Crook—Bishop Auckland passenger service withdrawn.
15 March	1965	Blaydon locomotive shed closed.
24 May	1965	Consett locomotive shed relegated to signing-on point.
5 July	1965	Wear Valley junction—Tow Law line closed.
2 August	1965	Waskerley and Parkhead (Blanchland) goods stations closed.
6 June	1966	Rowley goods station closed.
20 June	1966	Lanchester Valley branch closed.
29 April	1968	Burnhill junction—Weatherhill line closed.
11 April	1969	South Pelaw—Stella Gill—Pelton Level—Craghead line closed.
1 May	1969	Consett—Burnhill junction line closed.
	1969	Bowes Railway (Pontop & Jarrow) closed – Marley Hill—Burnopfield and Marley Hill—Kibblesworth, except at Marley Hill.
13 August	1970	Marley Hill sidings closed.

APPENDIX 2

MILEAGES

1 NEWCASTLE & CARLISLE RAILWAY. BLAYDON—WYLAM

	Miles	Chains
Scotswood Bridge Junction	0	0
Blaydon East Junction	0	48
Blaydon Station	0	53
Ryton	2	66
Wylam	5	4

2 BLAYDON—LOW FELL

	Miles	Chains
Blaydon East Junction	0	0
Consett Branch Junction	0	30
Blaydon Goods Junction	0	33
Blaydon Loop Junction	0	69
Blaydon Main Colliery Junction	0	72
Blaydon Curve Junction	1	5
Derwenthaugh Junction	1	31
Whickham Junction	2	16
Dunston Station	3	11
Norwood Junction	3	32
Dunston Staiths Junction	3	35
Dunston Extension Junction	3	37
Low Fell Junction	4	79

3 WHICKHAM JUNCTION—REDHEUGH

	Miles	Chains
Whickham Junction	0	0
Dunston West Junction	0	27
Dunston East Junction	0	64
Redheugh Bank Foot Junction	1	37
Redheugh Goods Yard	1	64

4 CONSETT BRANCH

	Miles	Chains
Scotswood Bridge Junction	0	0
Blaydon Loop West Junction	0	22
Blaydon Junction	0	28

APPENDIXES

	Miles	Chains
Swalwell Junction	0	52
Swalwell Station	1	21
Rowlands Gill	4	32
Lintz Green	5	76
High Westwood	8	24
Ebchester	9	29
Shotley Bridge	10	22
Blackhill	11	44
Consett North Junction	12	49
Consett South Junction	12	59
Knitsley	14	43
Lanchester	17	45
Witton Gilbert	21	30
Aldin Grange	23	45
Baxter Wood No. 1 Junction	24	25
Relly Mill Junction (Bishop Auckland Bch)	24	53
Relly Mill Junction (Main Line)	24	55
Durham	25	49

5 STANHOPE KILNS—BURNHILL JUNCTION

	Miles	Chains
Stanhope Kilns	0	0
Ashes Quarry Junction	0	25
Crawley Bank Top	0	42
Weatherhill Bank Top	1	55
Parkhead	2	22
Rookhope Branch Junction	2	32
Meeting Slacks Siding	4	51
Waskerley	5	74
Burnhill Junction	7	20

6 CONSETT—CROOK

	Miles	Chains
Consett South Junction	0	0
Hownes Gill Junction	0	30
Rowley	1	37
Burnhill	4	31
Burnhill Junction	4	56
High Stoop	8	34
Sunnyside Colliery Junction	9	61
Tow Law	9	69
West Durham Junction	13	14

	Miles	Chains
Crook Junction	14	17
Crook	14	23

7 HOWNES GILL—SOUTH PELAW/OUSTON JUNCTION

	Miles	Chains
Hownes Gill Junction	0	0
Consett East Junction	0	29
Consett Station	1	29
Bradley Crossing Junction (Medomsley Br)	2	13
Leadgate	2	45
South Medomsley Junction	3	13
Castles West Junction (East Castles)	3	75
Castles East Junction	4	6
Annfield Plain	5	55
Annfield Plain Junction	6	10
Annfield Plain East Junction	6	11
Shield Row	8	10
Beamish	9	64
Pelton	11	76
South Pelaw Junction	12	68
Ouston Junction	13	47

8 ANNFIELD PLAIN—SOUTH PELAW VIA INCLINES

	Miles	Chains
Annfield Plain East Junction	0	0
Stanley Siding	1	13
West Stanley Goods Depot	1	62
South Pelaw Junction	6	9

9 TANFIELD BRANCH

	Miles	Chains
Redheugh Bank Foot Junction	0	0
Marley Hill	3	66
East Tanfield	6	0
Margaret Pit	6	31
Tanfield Lea Pit	6	45
Tanfield Moor	7	61

10 LENGTHS OF MISCELLANEOUS NER BRANCHES & LOOPS

	Miles	Chains
Swalwell Colliery Branch	0	45
Dunston East Junction—Norwood Junction	0	54
Dunston Staiths Branch	0	77
Consett Branch Junction—Blaydon Junction	0	20

	Miles	Chains
Blaydon Loop	0	26
Swalwell Junction—Blaydon Curve Junction	0	42
Dunston Extension Junction—King Edward Bridge South Junction	1	23
Consett North—East Junction	0	35
Medomsley Branch	1	36
South Medomsley Colliery Branch	1	1
Annfield Plain Junction—East Pontop Colliery	1	9
Baxter Wood No 1—No 2 Junction	0	18
Baxter Wood No 2—Deerness Valley Junctn	0	24
Baxter Wood No 2—Bridge House Junction	0	37
Sunnyside Colliery Junction—Sunnyside	1	21
Hedleyhope Colliery Branch	0	40
Sunnyside Bank Foot Branch	0	45
Crook—Crook Goods Station	0	29

APPENDIX 3

RECEIPTS, EXPENSES AND TRAFFIC

TOTAL STATION RECEIPTS AND EXPENSES IN 1907

Station	Receipts (£)	Expenses (£)
Ryton	5,006	429
Blaydon	23,169	3,053
Derwenthaugh	9,148	224
Redheugh	5,386	392
Dunston-on-Tyne	28,935	823
Swalwell	3,622	522
Rowlands Gill	9,551	887
Lintz Green	2,626	482
Ebchester	3,736	682
Shotley Bridge	1,534	289
Blackhill	88,454	2,683
Knitsley	528	236
Lanchester	4,258	587
Witton Gilbert	4,308	596
Aldin Grange	890	361
Rowley	1,035	359
Burnhill	177	198
Tow Law	4,351	827
Crook	25,893	1,695
Consett	8,083	3,062
Leadgate	3,103	726
Annfield Plain	10,242	2,898
Shield Row	13,268	691
Beamish	3,197	392
Pelton	5,666	618
Parkhead	2,481	78
Stanhope Kilns and Waskerley	1,071	655

PASSENGERS AND RECEIPTS AT ALL STATIONS DURING 1890 AND 1930

Station	1890 Passengers	Receipts (£)	1930 Passengers	Receipts (£)
Ryton	74,158	2,482	10,497	335
Blaydon	218,679	5,341	77,460	3,224
Swalwell	68,792	1,616	12,372	455
Rowlands Gill	45,214	2,012	23,328	867
Lintz Green	46,902	2,800	5,192	182
High Westwood	–	–	9,979	680
Ebchester	48,368	1,799	7,804	188
Shotley Bridge	15,542	992	12,573	368
Blackhill	99,110	6,776	46,675	3,858
Knitsley	4,189	204	2,400	105
Lanchester	34,398	2,051	5,281	345
Witton Gilbert	34,673	1,337	18,161	579
Aldin Grange (Bearpark)	28,286	544	14,017	183
Rowley	6,567	240	2,655	90
Burnhill	4,392	189	5,220	188
Tow Law	32,551	2,044	24,060	1,243
Crook	86,624	3,448	26,985	3,309
Consett	–	–	14,973	2,219
Leadgate	–	–	9,383	638
Annfield Plain	–	–	29,206	2,491
Shield Row	–	–	21,906	2,191
Beamish	–	–	11,354	620
Pelton	–	–	9,755	529

PASSENGER, PARCELS & LIVESTOCK TRAFFIC AT ALL STATIONS IN 1913

Station	Passengers	Receipts (£)	Receipts (£)* Parcels	Heads of Livestock
Ryton	153,820	6,304	312	0
Blaydon	289,027	8,690	939	4,422
Dunston-on-Tyne	65,122	642	256	0
Swalwell	70,532	2,062	141	460
Rowlands Gill	131,285	6,525	493	1,553

* Including dogs, horses, carriages.

APPENDIXES 223

Station	Passengers	Receipts (£)	Receipts (£)* Parcels	Heads of Livestock
Lintz Green	33,132	1,810	53	0
High Westwood	98,916	5,282	202	0
Ebchester	36,818	1,026	151	1,802
Shotley Bridge	33,422	1,518	249	0
Blackhill	145,849	9,843	772	†
Knitsley	6,871	349	54	1,652
Lanchester	43,608	2,568	264	6,240
Witton Gilbert	81,311	3,153	264	2,993
Aldin Grange	47,150	980	62	0
Rowley	9,746	428	84	1,293
Burnhill	5,183	199	11	0
Tow Law	41,223	2,967	487	10,468
Crook	123,246	6,800	1,370	6,432
Consett	79,041	3,331	1,118	11,016
Leadgate	67,733	2,146	169	0
Annfield Plain	114,212	7,084	873	2,858
Shield Row	170,308	12,399	1,238	5,185
Beamish	66,524	2,398	157	692
Pelton	78,316	3,656	339	1,912

GOODS AND MINERAL TRAFFIC AT STATIONS IN 1897

Station	Goods Forwarded tons	Received tons	Minerals‡ tons	Goods Receipts (£)
Ryton	5	21	0	19
Blaydon	30,818	56,963	54,245	11,588
Derwenthaugh	32,453	38,969	68,047	4,578
Redheugh	82,278	93,675	943	20,112
Swalwell	20,837	6,032	78,829	2,078
Rowlands Gill	30,341	7,233	338	3,216
Lintz Green	10,343	1,145	124,523	724
Ebchester	3,540	8,244	181	878
Shotley Bridge	0	0	1,220	—
Blackhill	241,017	593,364	21,777	113,801
Knitsley	85	490	289	63
Lanchester	5,995	6,647	5,081	1,216

* Including dogs, horses, carriages.
† Included with Consett.
‡ Coal, coke, lime, limestone.

GOODS AND MINERAL TRAFFIC AT STATIONS IN 1897

Station	Goods Forwarded tons	Goods Received tons	Minerals* tons	Goods Receipts (£)
Witton Gilbert	4,017	24,844	51,641	1,961
Aldin Grange	0	0	0	–
Rowley	9,191	3,195	1,704	709
Burnhill	0	0	0	–
Tow Law	3,760	14,468	0	1,732
Crook	53,126	53,581	477†	12,252
Waskerley	1,837	7,888	1,742	699
Parkhead	9,131	858	576	556
Stanhope Kilns	9,808	168	3,620	934
Consett	1,330	21,741	128,357	3,746
Leadgate	7,130	4,906	539,406	1,238
Annfield Plain	9,009	42,206	2,046	3,509
Shield Row	266	17,777	79	1,467
Beamish	2,484	11,792	508	404
Pelton	5,512	40,122	0	1,683

LIME AND LIMESTONE FROM STANHOPE KILNS DISTRICT ON NER IN 1885

	tons	cwt	NER receipts £	s	d
Stanhope (Consett Iron Co) Limestone	79,043	3	6,586	18	7
Stanhope Burn Limestone	12,586	6	705	18	11
Rookhope Limestone	37,248	19	2,405	15	4
Stanhope Kilns Lime	10,629	11	1,957	4	9

GOODS AND MINERAL TRAFFIC AT BLACKHILL AND CROOK DURING 1901-6 PERIOD

BLACKHILL

	Goods Forwarded (tons)	Goods Received (tons)	Minerals (tons)
1901	230,736	115,270	24,273
1902	227,731	105,538	25,435

* Coal, coke, lime, limestone.
† Crook mineral station.

	Goods Forwarded (tons)	Goods Received (tons)	Minerals (tons)
1903	271,964	107,009	26,805
1904	265,643	148,775	27,181
1905	283,409	164,166	25,076
1906	282,270	165,288	16,558

CROOK

	Goods Forwarded (tons)	Goods Received (tons)	Minerals (tons)	Crook Mineral Station (tons)
1901	72,774	53,656	327	7,497
1902	80,707	62,898	952	8,508
1903	87,014	61,825	951	8,524
1904	83,514	60,349	493	7,546
1905	91,160	61,513	0	6,500
1906	84,400	73,529	422	7,813

APPENDIX 4

MISCELLANY

CROOK—DURHAM RAILWAY PROPOSALS

Although the Deerness Valley and S & D Stanley branch railways have not been dealt with in detail in this book, some mention should be made of several proposals to improve the route formed by these lines (which included two inclines) into a passenger railway to link Crook with Durham. To get to Durham people from Crook had to go to Bishop Auckland and change trains.

The NER received a 'memorial' from the inhabitants of Crook and district on 30 April 1886, requesting a passenger railway direct to Durham. It urged the NER to build a three mile line between Crook and Waterhouses (Deerness Valley branch) to afford the 24,000 people of the Crook area a convenient service to the county town. The memorial was the result of a public meeting at Crook on 18 January 1886, and was supported not only by Crook itself but by the Brandon & Byshottles local board, Auckland District Highway board and the Guardians of the Poor of the Auckland Union. On 3 June 1886 a deputation from the area, led by the Mayor of Durham, went to York to reinforce their views. The net result was that the NER stated that it was not prepared 'to undertake the works referred to'.

The matter lay dormant for some years until on 6 July 1897 the NER received a letter from Crook & Billy Row parish council urging reconsideration of the question 'since meanwhile the populations concerned have in every case increased'. The NER despatched W. J. Cudworth, its divisional chief engineer, to examine the possibilities. Mr Cudworth reported his findings and views on 30 September 1897. He mentioned that the existing line from Crook to Waterhouses with its 1 in 9 and 1 in 26 inclined planes, carried 126,000 tons of coal and coke yearly from Stanley and Wooley collieries. The Stanley branch crossed a 320ft high ridge, which a locomotive line could only surmount by 'heavy tunnelling'. He considered there were two possible routes to avoid the expense of much tunnelling. One of these routes curved round from Crook east of the Stanley branch, but still required heavy engineering crossing one very deep valley, and requiring a 25 chains tunnel. This line would be over five miles long and would have a 1 in 50 ruling gradient. It would cost over £82,000 and compared with the existing railway link 'it was doubtful whether much, if any saving on working costs could be effected'.

The second possibility looked more hopeful. This line ran up the Deerness valley from Waterhouses to Tow Law where the existing line to Crook could be utilised. This 3 mile 54 chain line could be constructed 'at reasonable cost' (£40,500 – £11,000 per mile), and earthworks and bridges would be moderate. A gradient of 1 in 39 would be necessary, very steep but 'not impracticable', and Cudworth cited a length of 1 in 39 on the Tow Law—Consett line. 'A station might be provided at Hamilton Row', near Waterhouses. The area was thinly populated so that the chief use of the line would be for through passenger traffic. It would provide a 9 mile 44 chain railway between Crook and Waterhouses, the latter being some six miles from Durham.

The NER did not pursue the matter, however, and the Stanley branch remained to link the Crook area with the Deerness valley for mineral traffic only. Passenger continued to go from Crook to Durham via Bishop Auckland. Stanley colliery had closed by 1920 and the incline into the Deerness valley was abandoned, severing the through route.

LETTERS FROM CHARLES ATTWOOD, WEARDALE IRON CO, TOW LAW

3 January 1849 To the Wear & Derwent Junction Railway Co:

'We are under the necessity of complaining most seriously of the utter want of such supply of trucks of the sort used between Stanhope and Newcastle as is inconvenient to the Company as of our needs and completion of our contracts.'

10 January 1849 To Hawks Crawshay & Sons (Gateshead iron foundry) re iron deliveries:

'The stoppage of the Stanhope & Tyne line has caused a delay in the delivery which we are sorry for.' (18 tons of Grey Forge Iron at 48s [£2.40] per ton)

16 January 1849 To Stockton & Darlington Railway Co:

'We forwarded from Stanhope on Thursday and Saturday last, 200 tons of pig iron addressed to Messrs Richardson & Co, Newcastle, for shipment to Boston, US by a vessel now waiting and we are much surprised to learn this morning that none of it had yesterday reached Redheugh. We believe unless it arrives this afternoon it will be too late and the consequence will not only be great disappointment but a heavy loss.

'It is most unpleasant to us to have so frequently to complain of such irregularities and as in this instance we had already apprized your company of the importance of punctuality, we cannot avoid expressing our excessive annoyance at the delay.'

17 January 1849 To the York Newcastle & Berwick Railway Co:

'We beg to call your attention to the balance of an order for railway chairs of which the last were supplied to you in June, viz: £202 12s 3d [£202.61] as specified.'

'NEWCASTLE DAILY JOURNAL' RAILWAY ADVERTISEMENTS IN 1883

Issue No 8469; 4 April 1883

'On Friday April 6th a late train will be run from Newcastle to Blaydon and Wylam at 10.45pm stopping at Scotswood and Ryton.'

Issue No 8477; 13 April 1883

'Afternoon excursion. On Saturday the 14th April an Excursion Train will leave Newcastle for Corbridge and Hexham at 1.50pm. Fare there and back 1s 0d [5p] Third Class. The return train will leave Hexham at 6.30pm and Corbridge at 6.38pm the same day.'

Issue No 8543; 29 June 1883

'Afternoon Excursion. On Saturday the 30th June an Afternoon Excursion Train will leave Newcastle at 2.15pm for Shotley Bridge. Fare there and back 1s 0d [5p] Third Class. The return train will leave Shotley Bridge at 7.50pm the same day. For further particulars see special bills.'

Issue No 8544; 30 June 1883

'Silloth Route. Daily communication with Liverpool and bi-weekly communication with Dublin, and all stations on the North British and North-Eastern Railways. For particulars see Monthly time bills; and for rates with Liverpool & Dublin and with railway stations to all parts of Scotland via Hexham and the Waverley route, apply to: G. S. Thomson, North British Railway offices, Forth Station, Newcastle-on-Tyne.'

APPENDIXES 229

RIDING MILL—LONGCLOSE WOOD (CONSETT BR) RAILWAY SCHEME

In the Consett Iron Co records held in the Durham county archives, there is a plan for a railway between Riding Mill (Newcastle & Carlisle branch) to Longclose wood, north east of Hamsterley (Blaydon & Consett branch). The plan is undated but must be of the 1865-70 period. The scheme is perhaps an echo of the Stocksfield—Rowley project described in Chapter 3.

The plan shows a $9\frac{1}{2}$ mile line named the 'Newcastle & Carlisle and Consett branch railway', running from a point one mile east of Riding Mill station and curving southwards on 1 in 53 and 60 gradients. The line passes one mile north of Whittonstall village and runs down the Milk Burn (now Milkwell Burn) valley, west of Chopwell, to cross the river Derwent to the west of Blackhall Mill. The line then climbs eastwards at 1 in 55/66 gradients to join the Consett branch in Longclose wood, east of Hamsterley, running just to the north of White Byerside Farm. The whole line has steep gradients, and several sharp curves of up to 20 chains radius.

The purpose of this line was probably the same as for the defunct Stocksfield—Rowley line to connect Consett with the Carlisle line at its narrowest point to enable West Cumberland haematite to reach Consett ironworks. The Longclose junction faced east – towards Lintz Green – because of the terrain.

I have found no other references to this project.

THE OPENING OF THE FIRST PART OF THE STANHOPE & TYNE RAILWAY
(from the *Newcastle Daily Journal* 17 May 1834)

'A party of gentlemen left Annfield at 8 o'clock in the morning by a railway waggon tastefully fitted up for the occasion, and arrived at the termination of the line about eleven, highly gratified with the whole line of road but especially with that part of it which crosses the precipitous ravine called the Hownes. At one o'clock the first four lime waggons were started from the spacious range of kilns belonging to the company and speedily ascended the steep inclined plane adjoining Stanhope amidst the cheers of an immense crowd of spectators who, notwithstanding the wetness of the early part of the morning had assembled from all parts of the adjacent country. A splendid dinner had been provided for 400 persons by the spirited proprietors of the railway, but the hilarity of the occasion was much damped by the occurrence of a serious and fatal accident.'

NEWCASTLE DERWENT & WEARDALE RAILWAY PARLIAMENTARY DEPOSITED PLANS (BOOK OF REFERENCE) 10 NOVEMBER 1860

'Railways from Newcastle-upon-Tyne and Gateshead to the South Durham & Lancashire Union Railway, and also other railways in connection therewith; Powers to Lancaster & Carlisle, London & North Western and North British Railway Companies to run over, work, and use the intended Railways and other Railways . . . Running Powers over and Station and other Accommodation on South Durham & Lancashire Union and Eden Valley Railways.'

List of lines intended

First: 'A railway commencing on a piece of waste ground in the borough of Gateshead . . . and thence passing from, in, through or into the several parishes, townships, chapelries and extra-parochial or other places following or some of them (that is to say) Gateshead, Whickham, Ryton, Winlaton, Tanfield, Chester-le-Street, Ebchester, Medomsley, Lanchester, Wolsingham, Brancepeth, St Andrew Auckland, Muggleswick, Whitworth, Lamesley, Swalwell, Low Hand or Low Side, Fell Side, Ryton Woodside, Stella, Chopwell, Burnopfield, Lintz Green, Benfieldside, Conside & Knitsley, Billingside, Collierley, Iveston, Greencroft, Kyo, Satley, Butsfield, Lanchester & Hamlets, Esh, Healeyfield, Rowley and Roughside, Holmside, Burnop & Hamsteels, Langley, Hedley Hope, Crook & Billy Row, Binchester, Cornsay, Willington, Stockley, Brandon & Byshottles, Escomb, Helmington Row, Thornley, Newton Cap, Hunwick & Helmington, Newfield, Byers Green, Pollards Lands, Evenwood & Barony, Old Park, Bondgate in Auckland, St Helens Auckland, West Auckland . . . terminating by a junction with the authorised railway of the South Durham & Lancashire Union Railway at a point at or near the intended point of junction of that railway with the Stockton & Darlington Railway in the township of West Auckland.' (In a field known as Sugar Hill Fields.)

Second: In a field owned by the Lord Bishop of Durham in Gateshead, from a junction with No 1 Railway, through Gateshead to NER Gateshead & Redheugh branch at the top of Gateshead incline.

Third: From No 1 railway at Redheugh, to a Tyne bridge, across the bridge to join the Newcastle & Carlisle main line 'at a point 124 yards or thereabouts to the east of a bridge whereby the said

APPENDIXES 231

main line of the Newcastle-upon-Tyne and Carlisle Railway is carried over a lane called the Shot Factory Lane'.

Fourth: From No 3, entirely within Elswick township-short branch line.

Fifth: From No 1 in township of Swalwell and 'terminating by a junction with the rails of the Redheugh Branch of the Newcastle & Carlisle Railway . . . at or near a point 175 yards or thereabouts east of the bridge by which the said Redheugh Branch Railway is carried over the River Derwent'.

Sixth: From at or near the Golden Lion public house in the hamlet of Winlaton Mill 'terminating in the township of Whickham Fellside . . . by a junction with the railway firstly described'.

Seventh: From No 1 in Benfieldside township 'at or about 150 yards from the south end of a plantation called or known by the name of Bell's Wood . . . terminating in the same township or parish at or near the south west corner of Shotley Grove Low Mill belonging to and in the occupation of Messrs Annandale & Company'.

Eighth: From No 1 'in or near a wood in the township of Conside & Knitsley commonly called Consett High Wood, and at or near a point 480 yards or there abouts north of the south-east end of the Hown's Gill viaduct of the Stockton & Darlington Railway . . . terminating in the same township and parish at a point 35 yards or thereabouts west from the north west corner of a building belonging to the Derwent & Consett Iron Co (Ltd) known by the name of the No 4 and 5 Plate and Slitting Mill'.

Ninth: From No 1 at Consett High Wood 480 yards north of the southeast end of Hownes Gill viaduct 'terminating by a junction with the authorised branch line of the NER company, called the Lanchester Valley Railway' (476 yards east of Hown's Farm).

Tenth: From No 1 'at or near the second arch numbering from the southeast end of the said Hown's Gill Viaduct' passing through the parishes of Conside & Knitsley, Mugglewick, Roughside & Rowley, and 'terminating in the last named parochial chapelry and township by a junction with the S & DR at or near a point 517 yards or thereabouts east of the Cold Rowley station of the S & DR'.

Eleventh: From No 1 in Hedleyhope township 'terminating at a point about 30 yards west from the pattern shops of the Tow Law Iron Works'.

Twelfth: From No 1 in Brancepeth township to the 'old pit shaft of Oakenshaw Colliery' in Stockley township.

Thirteenth: From No 1, 180 yards from Newton Cap Colliery, via Willington, Byers Green, Hunwick, to the Byers Green branch of the West Hartlepool Harbour & Railway Co in Whitworth parish.

Fourteenth: From No 1 entirely within Bishop Auckland township, to a junction with the S & DR.
'And it is intended by the said Bill to empower the Lancaster & Carlisle Railway Co and the London & North Western Railway Co and the North British Railway or any of them, to subscribe towards the construction of the said intended railway and works, and towards the expenses of carrying into execution all or any of the powers to be conferred by the said Bill, and to accept, take and hold shares in the capital to be authorised by the said Bill, and to apply their corporate or other funds, and to raise new capital by new shares or stock.'
In the event of the SD & LU or Eden Valley companies amalgamating with any other company 'the provisions and powers of the present Bill will pass to the Amalgamated Company'.

Joseph Watson (Newcastle)
Bowser & Ward (Solicitors,
Bishop Auckland)
J. Newall (Parliamentary Agent,
London)
10 November 1860

Bill to be deposited in the Private Bill Office of the House of Commons on or before 22 December next.

HOUSE OF COMMONS COMMITTEE – FURTHER
EXAMPLES OF EVIDENCE, JUNE 1861

Mr Ralph Ward Jackson, Chairman, West Hartlepool Railway Co, examined by Mr Cripps, 'wished to get an alternative and independent outlet for his system, hemmed in as it was by the S & D. This was rendered the more necessary by the close alliance of the S & D with the North Eastern. He had grievances, for example, coal from Brancepeth colliery on the West Durham line to Ferryhill,

APPENDIXES 233

instead of going by the Byers Green branch was sent round by Leamside, near Durham, thus travelling 18 miles instead of 6 miles. The new NDW line would facilitate the conveyance of coal from Tow Law and Crook to West Hartlepool for shipment.'

Mr John Irving, Vice-Chairman, Carlisle & Silloth Bay Railway, examined by Mr Calvert, 'spoke of the injury which had been inflicted on his line by the diversion of traffic in consequence of the arrangement between the N & CR and NER. The N & CR directors had encouraged the formation of the line, but after it was made the N & CR refused to take traffic in consequence of the agreement he had mentioned.'

Mr William Cawkwell, Gen Manager LNWR, examined by Mr Cripps, 'stated that there was a very large traffic between Liverpool and Hartlepool which would be increased by the improved facilities for transit offered by the new line. The route from Liverpool to Newcastle via Carlisle was not a bad route. Practically there was no route by Carlisle as the N & CR was bound by agreement with the NER to refuse through rates. At present the shortest route between Liverpool and Newcastle was by the North Western to Leeds and by the NER thence to Newcastle. They had however to send traffic by Normanton, which gave the NER a longer mileage and involved another change of system, as it had to go over a part of the Lancashire & Yorkshire. If the South Durham & Lancashire Union were not amalgamated with the NER it would be in the interest of the former to develop through traffic by Tebay. Such amalgamation would however reverse their policy.'

Mr Thomas Bouch, NDW engineer, examined by Mr Burke, said: 'His object in laying the line out was to serve the large population and rich minerals of the district and to open up a good through route between Liverpool and Newcastle. He had selected the best line the country could afford for that object. The main line was 38m 6ch in length, with a 966ft summit a mile east of Tow Law. Maximum gradient on the main line – 1 in 70 (steeper on some of the branches). He proposed to have stations at Dunston, Swalwell, Winlaton, near to Burnopfield, Ebchester – which would also serve Medomsley, Shotley Bridge, Black Hill, Satley, Tow Law, Job's Hill (near Crook), and Bishop Auckland. Earthworks on the line – 44,000 cubic yards per mile, against 77,000 cubic yards per mile on the proposed NER line. Grand total of costs – £425,000 (£450,000 to be sought in capital). Cost of land – £74,861; main line works – £189,713; branches – £102,232; stations and junctions – £33,000; he had 50 bridges on the main line at a cost of £16,500. He had laid a junction with the Lanchester Valley line of the NER by which

P

traffic could be sent to Durham – he did not however think there would be very great interchange of traffic between the Derwent and Lanchester lines. From Hounsgill [sic] to Tow Law the district was not very populous. There were one or two villages. It was a wooded country.' Mr Merewether interjected: 'When I was there the trees must have been out on a visit' (laughter).

Bouch continued, examined by Mr Locke and Mr Cripps: 'His bridge across the Tyne was somewhat higher than the High Level bridge. This line would not do any injury to the N & CR by the proposed junction with it. He would have a station of his own at Newcastle under any circumstances, but he could make only a cheap station for cattle etc, if an arrangement were come to with the N & CR for access to the Central station.

'The North Eastern only wanted to get hold of the Blaydon & Conside branch to use as a block line. That was the only outlet from Newcastle which was not in the hands of the NER and if it were made over to them also, Newcastle would be completely at their mercy.'

Mr Thomas MacNay, S & D secretary, 'said that the SD & LU line could be open in about a fortnight, and the Eden Valley which was connected with it in the autumn of the present year. The proposed line (the NDW) would be a directly competing one with the S & D.

'He replied to allegations made by Messrs Attwood and Dyson (Weardale Iron Co); when they spoke of a week's detention in the traffic they must be under a mistake. The detention must take place at the sidings at the two ends – the place of export and Tudhoe. Mr Attwood's memory was treacherous when he said that the company's rates had not been reduced in his case. They had been reduced from 1s 8d [8p] to 1s 2d [6p]. Since 1858 there had been no complaint on the part of Mr Attwood as to the working of the traffic and he was quite sure that if in the opinion of Parliament the Sunnyside line ought to be improved by being made a locomotive line, the directors of the S & D would be most willing to carry out any such improvement'.

Mr T. E. Harrison, NER engineer said: 'The North Eastern had no objection to giving the North Western a through route and through booking via Bishop Auckland and the SD & LU line to any station on their system, and to introduce a clause in their (NER) Bill to that effect.' Mr J. Swift of the LNWR, commenting on the future of the South Durham & Lancashire Union Railway to Mr Rodwell (cross-examining on behalf of the S & D), said that 'to all intents and purposes the amalgamation of the South Durham with the S & D was practically an amalgamation with the North Eastern, although it might not be brought formally before Parliament for some time.

APPENDIX 5

RECENT TIMES

MOLTEN METAL TRAINS TO CONSETT

On 4 August 1969 began a daily transfer of molten metal from Teesside to Consett, when three specially designed wagons bearing the metal (temperature 1,600° C) left Cargo Fleet works, Middlesbrough. This was the first time that molten metal had been carried for any appreciable distance by BR. The project had been planned by the British Steel Corporation and BR to provide Consett with the iron needed to maintain production while blast furnaces were being rebuilt.

Each train is hauled by two English Electric Type 3 locomotives, and the three 'torpedo' cars each can carry a maximum of 300 tons of hot metal, with three spacer wagons between cars to distribute the load over bridges. The weight of a fully laden car is on average about 242 tons, and the overall length nearly 85ft. Each vessel is sealed with a special lid that has a 15in insulation layer. The trains have a maximum speed of 20 mph, and take a route via Stockton, Ferryhill, Leamside, Pelaw, Gateshead and Beamish.

Two trains daily are eventually planned by in late 1970-1.

THE RAILWAYS IN APRIL 1970

The Newcastle & Carlisle line has changed quite a lot within ten years, and colour light signals occur at Blaydon, while semaphores remain on the Redheugh branch. A gantry of NER lower-quadrants at the east end of Blaydon station disappeared in 1967. The motive power depot has almost vanished save for a derelict brick office, and all the sidings here and those nearby for goods, have gone. The Blaydon—Dunston—Low Fell lines retain their NER character, and colour lights only intrude east of Norwood junction signal box, where the Tyne Yard signal box takes over. At Dunston West there is a siding where a notice states that only Class J71, J72 and J77 engines are to be used, while a very nice North Eastern Railway notice near Dunston East box states clearly that 'Engine drivers are requested not to pass this board with their engines, by order' – presumably into a siding.

The Tanfield branch has all but disappeared, and a road is being built on its formation at Teams on the Dunston—Gateshead boundary. The Blaydon & Consett and Lanchester Valley lines are returning to nature, but a new future now awaits the former. In 1971 the whole line from Swalwell station to Blackhill is to become a grass bridle path – the County Council's 'Derwent Walk'. Some £34,000 is to be spent on it, mainly on repairing bridges and removing others that are unnecessary and dangerous. The remaining stations, such as Lintz Green and Ebchester, are to be restored to 'return them to some of their former glory.' And will serve as rest or picnic places and points of exit or access to the walk. It will be interesting to see if Lintz Green, which for years was awarded a prize by the railway authorities for its beauty and tidiness, will be restored from its present dilapidation. A nature walk will perhaps be the best use of the former railway considering its scenic attractiveness.

At Blackhill, the line remains in use to Consett North, where many sidings are used by Consett Iron Co traffic, and goods trains leave and arrive regularly from Tyne Yard. The line to Waskerley and Weatherhill was removed in the autumn of 1969 and the spring of 1970, and the derelict Consett South signal box awaits demolition. The hulks of Burnhill junction and Rowley signal boxes were still present recently.

On the Lanchester Valley branch, the formation is remarkably intact, and some of the stations have so far survived vandalism quite well. At Lanchester there is only a single platform, which may confuse future historians. The large water tank, dating from 1862, still remains there. At the southern end of the line, even the Relly Mill—Bishop Auckland branch has now been closed and removed, but Relly Mill signal box is a last reminder of the NER era, although it, too, is bound to disappear.

In the Crook—Tow Law district, not a rail remains. At Tow Law it is becoming difficult to believe there ever was a railway, as new development is taking place. At Crook, where just five years ago a regular diesel multiple unit service shuttled down to Darlington, rails, signals (including fine NER semaphores) signal boxes and lineside architecture have gone, while the ruined station and platform stands stark and dreary, a forlorn NER notice warning trespassers not to go where only rubble now remains.

So the Consett—South Pelaw line provides a reminder of better days. The occasional branch and siding remains, together with a siding or two at Annfield Plain, and the old Stanhope & Tyne line at Oxhill. At South Pelaw, the once busy lines to Stella Gill and beyond await their removal. Stella Gill Flatts signal box and the railway offices at Stella Gill and the foot of the Waldridge incline are all derelict. The National Coal Board dismantled the line at Pelton Level in late 1969. However South Pelaw signal box still controls a fine collection of semaphores, and whether the Tyne colour light signals will be extended to replace this box is, as yet, unknown.

The 1960s finally saw the end of a long and grand railway era in north-west Durham, and enthusiasts will contemplate the many classes of steam locomotive with their heavy traffic, especially of minerals.

Bibliography

Minute Books, Traffic Books, Maps and Plans, Timetables and miscellaneous material of the NER, LNER, S & D etc.
Railway Acts and Parliamentary plans.

Tomlinson, W. W. *The North Eastern Railway – Its rise and development* 1914
Hoole, K. *A Regional History of the Railways of Great Britain* Vol IV 1965
Rounthwaite, T. E. *The Railways of Weardale* 1965
Maclean, J. S. *The Newcastle & Carlisle Railway* 1948
Lee, C. E. *The wagonways of Tyneside* 1951
Allen, C. J. *The North Eastern Railway* 1964
Maclean, J. S. *Locomotives of the North Eastern Railway* 1906
Mountford, C. E. *The History of John Bowes and Partners up to 1914* (MA Thesis, Durham University 1967)
Ahrons, E. L. *Locomotive and Train working in the latter part of the Nineteenth Century* 1962
Acworth, W. *The Railways of England* 1889
Ransome Wallis, P. *On engines in Britain and France* 1957
Hoole, K. *North Eastern Railway locomotive stock as at 31.12.20* 1969
Casserley, H. C. & Johnston, S. W. *Locomotives at the Grouping* 1966
Consett Lions Club *The Consett story* 1963
Bourn, W. *History of the parish of Ryton, etc* 1896

Newspapers and periodicals:
Durham County Advertiser, Newcastle Journal, Consett Guardian, Consett Chronicle, Newcastle Courant, Evening Chronicle, Stanley News, Durham Chronicle, Railway Magazine, NER Magazine, LNER Magazine, Railway World, Railway Observer, Railway Gazette, Railway News, Locomotive Magazine, North Eastern Railway Association Express, Stephenson Locomotive Society Journal.

Acknowledgements

I should like to acknowledge the assistance of a number of people and organisations in the preparation of this book, especially Mr W. MacDonald, British Transport Historical Records Archivist at York and his assistants, and I must thank British Railways for other assistance. Messrs J. Dolan, W. Fawcett, G. C. Holden, K. Hoole, T. E. Rounthwaite, B. Thompson, and P. R. Walker gave valuable assistance with various aspects, and Messrs Palmer of Blaydon kindly helped with photographic work.

I owe a debt to the *Durham County Advertiser* for permission to consult their files, to the National Coal Board, to the county archivists of Durham and Northumberland, and to various libraries, particularly the Newcastle and Durham city libraries and Consett and Annfield Plain county libraries. I am obliged to all those who have supplied photographic material.

Dr R. A. Muse, of Altrincham, Cheshire, read the text and suggested various alterations and improvements which have been incorporated.

Index

Illustrations are in italic type

Accidents, Beamish, 202; Blaydon (1870), 203-4; (1878), 204-5; Hell Hole Wood, 201-2; Knitsley, 205; Knitsley viaduct, 199-200; Ouston junction, 200-1; South Pelaw, 201; Twizell incline, 206; Weatherhill, 205-6
Acts of Parliament: Annfield hill deviation, 119-20, 123; Annfield Plain & Team Valley, 126; Blaydon & Conside, 99; Blaydon Gateshead & Hebburn, 39; Derwenthaugh branch, 146; Lanchester Valley, 73; Newcastle & Carlisle, 38, 39, 41; N & CR–NER amalgamation, 45, 99; Pontop & South Shields, 29; Stockton & Darlington & Newcastle & Carlisle Union Railway, 60; Sunnyside deviation, 61
Addison, 49, 153, 172-3
Admiralty, 101
Ahrons, E. L., 180
Aldin Grange, 80, 82-3, 85, 89, 159, 214-15, 218, 221-4
Allendale, 41
Alston, 41
Amalgamations: Newcastle & Carlisle–NER, 45, 99; Stockton & Darlington–NER, 180; Wear Valley Railway, 57
Anderson, John, 58-9
Annfield—East Castle deviation, 123-4
Annfield lime kilns, 23, 26, 142-3
Annfield Plain, 16, 22-3, 89, 118-20, 126, 130, 131-8, 141-3, 167-70, 183, 202, 214-15, 219-24, 229, 237
Annfield Plain MPD, 124, 136, 186, 189
Annfield—South Pelaw line, 126-33
Annfield—West Stanley widening, 118

Ashes quarry, 67-8, 198
Atlas curve, *145*, 150
Attwood, Charles, 55-6, 58, 227-8, 234
Axwell Park, 110-12, 166

Barnard Castle, 98, 107, *165*
Baxter Wood junctions, 81, *90*, 160, 214, 218, 220
Beamish, 32, 123, 126-7, 130-1, 137, 141-2, 167-70, *176*, 201-2, 219, 221-4
Beamish wagonway, 14, 18, 128, 169
Bearpark, 80, 82-3, 86, 156, 159, 215, 222
Beechburn valley, 53
Beeching, Dr, 159, 177
Belmont, 29
Benfieldside, *see* Blackhill
Bensham, 130, 146
Bensham curve, 151
Birtley, 120, 123-4, 126, 130-1
Bishop Auckland, 11, 53, 72-3, 89, 96, 107, 161, *165*, 226-7, 232-4, 237
Bishop Auckland & Weardale Railway, 53, 57
Bishopley, 71
Blackfield, 161
Blackhill, 27, 64-5, 72, 78, 84-6 *88*, 90, 92, 100, 102-9, 111-14, *115*, 120, 134-8, 143, 156, 159-60, 163-71, *175*, 182-4, 186, 188, 191, 199, 206, 209, 214-15, 218, 221-5, 237
Blackhill MPD, 90, 119, *133*, 186, 189, 192-3, 195
Blackmore, John, 39, 41
Blackpool, 168
Blanchland, 20, 161, 216
Blaydon, *34*, 37-44, 46, 49, 97, 101, 104, 110, 113, 117, 146, 149-53, *154*, *157-8*, 166, 171-4, 185-90, 192-6, 203-4, 210, 213-15, 217, 220-3, 228, 236

241

INDEX

Blaydon & Consett branch, 78, 84, 98-117, 150, 153, 162-6, 173, 214-15, 229, 234, 237
Blaydon Burn, 49, 111, 172
Blaydon, Gateshead & Hebburn Railway, 39-41
Blaydon Loop, 113, 149-51, 166
Blaydon Main colliery, 49, 104, 116, 150
Blaydon MPD, 42, 117, 153-4, *158*, 173, 185, 187-90, 192-5, 215
Blenkinsopp colliery, 42
Boldon, 16, 170, 196
Border Counties Railway, 45
Borough Gardens MPD, 184-5, 187, 190, 192
Bouch, Thomas, 58, 92, 94, 97, 233-4
Bouch, William, 21, 58, 180
Bowes Bridge, 46-7, 183-4, 190, 194
Brancepeth, 73
Brandling Junction Railway, 26, 28-9, 41, 46-7
Brandon & Byshottles, 226
Bray, J., 54
Bridge House junction, 81
Brockley Whins, 28-30, 204
Burnhill, 59, 64, *65*, 71-2, *140*, 160-2, 182, 207-8, 218, 221-4, 237
Burnhope, 23, 80, 169
Burnopfield, 47, 101, 210, 230
Bus services, 89-90, 109, 148, 156, 163-4, 172-3
Byermoor, 48, 177
Byers Green, 54, 95, 232-3

Caledonian Railway, 44, 46
Carlisle, 42-4, 46, 110, 152, 172-3, 181, 187, 191, 194, 204, **233**
Carr House, 21, 27-8, *52*, 56, 59, 63-5, 78, 103, 118-19, 170
Carr House inclines, 21, 59
Causey, 13, 46
Cawkwell, W., **233**
Charlton, E., 78, 104
Chester-le-Street, 11, 22-3, 32, 120, 123, 136, 156, 171
Chopwell, 50, *87*, 109, 172, 229
Clara Vale, 153, 173
Cleveland iron ore, 60, 73, 79
Cleveland Bridge & Engineering Co, 81
Closures of lines: Blaydon & Conset,
166, 215; Burnhill jcn—Tow Law, 160; Burnhill jcn—Weatherhill, 162, 216; Consett—Burnhill jcn, 162, 216; Lanchester Valley, 160, 216; Pontop & Jarrow, 177, 216; Rookhope branch, 160; Stanhope —Weatherhill, 161, 215; Stanley—Pelton Level, 168, 215; Stella Gill line, 168, 216; Tanfield branch, 174, 215-16; various wagonways, 169, 172-3; Washington—Boldon colliery, 170, 196; Wear Valley jcn—Tow Law, 162, 216

Cold Rowley, *see* Rowley
Collieries: Addison, 49, 153; Axwell Park, 110-11, 166; Beamish, 169; Bearpark, 80, 83; Blackhill, 111; Black Prince, 66; Blaydon Burn, 49, 111, 172; Blaydon Main, 49, 150; Burnhope, 23; Burnopfield, 47-8, 177; Byermoor, 48, 177; Clara Vale, 153, 173; Chopwell, 50, 172; Craghead, 23, 168; Derwent, 35; Dipton, 48; East Castle, 123; East Pontop, 220; East Tanfield, 174; Eden, 141; Garesfield, 14, 49, 107, 172; Greenside, 153, 173; Handen Hold, 168; Hedleyhope, 66, 220; Inkerman, 66, 161; Lanchester, 80; Langley Park, 80, 83; Lilley drift, 111-12, 166; Lintz, 48, 110; Louisa, 118, 168; Malton, 80, 83-4; Marley Hill, 14, 46-8, 177, 216; Medomsley, 18, 35, 111, 119, 141, 169; Morrison Busty, 170, 197; Peases West (Roddymoor), 63, 66; Pelton, 118; Pontop, 14, 48; Sacriston, 23, 32, 169; South Garesfield, 107, 110; South Medomsley, 119, 141, 169, 220; South Pelaw, 138; South Pontop, 124; Stargate, 49, 153, 172; Tanfield Lea, 13, 46, 174; Tanfield Moor, 13-14, 18, 26, 174; Towneley (Emma), 49, 153, 173; Victoria Garesfield, 110, 166; Waldridge, 18, 32, 35, 169; Washington, 18; Watergate, 47, 174; West Pelton, 169; West Shield Row, 128; West Stanley, 141; West Thornley, 66; Westwood, 110; Wooley, 57, 66, 226

INDEX

Consett, 11-12, 21, 56, 60, 65, 73-9, 85, 93-4, 96-7, 99-101, 104, 112, 118, 120, 124, 132, *133*, 134, *135*, 136-8, 141-2, 156, 159-62, *165*, 166-71, *175*, 186, 202, 207-8, 214-16, 218-19, 221-4, 231, 236-7
Consett—East Castle widening, 127, 133-4
Consett Iron Company, 68, 80, 99, 104, 108, 110, 115, 118-19, 127, 132-3, 138, 149, 197-8, 229, 237
Consett North—East loop line, 132, *133*, 220
Contractors: Anderson, J., 58-9; Atkinson, W. C., 82; Bray, J., 54; Cooke, A. J., 134; Forster, G. & Lawton, W., 31; Forster, G. E., 118; Kell & Groves, 136; Lawton, B. C., 75, 78; Lawton, J., 111; Morkill & Prudham, 99, 102, 104, 106; Nowell, H. M., 112-13; Nowell, J. D., 134; Ridley J. & T., 59; Ridley, T. D., 132; Scott, W., 81; Shanks, D., 89; Tench, A., 110; Tone, J. C., 80; Whitaker Bros, 127, 132
Corbridge, 152
Court of Chancery, 74
Coxhoe, 159, 161
Craghead, 23, 32, 168, 181, 216
Crawley, 11, 17-18, 21, 56, 67, 68, 71, 161, 205, 215, 218
Crook, 11, 53-4, 57-66, *69*, 71-3, 95, 97, 160-2, 184, 186, 188-9, 195, 214, 216, 218-27, 230, 233, 237
Crook—Tow Law deviation, 60-3, *64*
Crook—Waterhouses proposed line, 226-7
Cudworth, W. J., 226-7
Cumberland iron ore, 60, 73, 99, 104, 112

Darlington, 63, 72, 81, 160-1, 185, 188-9, 191-2, 194-5
Dean & Chapter of Durham, 16
Deerness Valley Railway, 57, 81-2
Derwenthaugh, 11, 13-15, 41-4, 50, 113, 146, 148-50, *157*, 174, 178, 213, 217, 221, 223
Derwenthaugh branch, 146-7, 150
Derwent Iron Co, 27-30, 53-4, 60, 73, 118

Dipton, 13, 48
Dunn, W., 96-7
Dunston, 11, 13, 41, 46-7, 125-8, 144, 146-52, 174, 178, 187, 189, 197, 200, 215, 217, 219, 221-2, 236
Dunston Extension Railway, 144, 146, 151, 214, 217
Dunston—Gateshead loop line, 146-7, 151, 215, 220
Durham, 11, 28-9, 73, 77, 79-82, 84-6, 89, 104-7, 156, 159, 199, 218, 226-7, 234
Durham Junction Railway, 28-9
Durham MPD, 79, 186, 191, 193-4

East Castle, 21, 120, 123, 127, *133*, 142-3, 219
Eastgate, 208
Ebchester, 60, *87*, 102-3, 107-9 111, *114*, 163-4, 218, 221-3, 230, 237
Eden Hill incline, 22
Eden Valley Railway, 96, 230, 234
Edinburgh, 46, 98, 190, 203-4
Edmondsley, 80
Excursion trains, 105, *114*, 159, 164, 167-8, 182, 228
Explosives, 161

Fatfield, 14, 22, 31
Ferryhill, 81, 159, 236
Fletcher, Edward, 180-3, 204
Fluorspar, 161, 208
Fogoes viaduct, 102, *121*
Friarside, 110, 209
Frosterley, 63, 161
Fugar incline, 46, *51*

Galashiels, 46 152
Ganister, 71, 208
Garesfield wagonway, 14, 49-50, 104, 172, 178, 197
Gateshead, 11, 28-9, 31, 41, 124, 130, *140*, 146-8, 150-1, 174, 178, 180-2, 184-5, 187-96, 207, 215, 220, 227, 230, 236-7
Gateshead MPD, 146, 184-5, 187-95
Gibside, 101, 104
Giles, F., 37-9
Gilesgate, 29, 82
Gradient profile, *100*
Granville, Rev A. W. B., 82
Greencroft, 86

INDEX

Greenside, 153, 172-3
Gresley, H. N., 190

Haltwhistle, 37, 171
Hamilton Row, 227
Hamsterley, 107, 110, 166
Harrison, C. A., 128
Harrison, Thomas E., 15-16, 28, 78, 99, 102, 143, 206, 234
Harrison, W., 14-15
Hartlepool Railway, 28
Hawick, 46, 98, 190, 193
Haydon Bridge, 41-3
Healeyfield, 17, 20-1, 59, 66
Hedleyhope, 66, 220, 230, 232
Hexham, 37-8, 40-2, 44-6, 59, 96, 99, 151-2, 171-3, 186, 190-1, 193-4, 213, 228
High Spen, 14, 49-50, 172
High Westwood, *87-8*, 109-10, 163-4, 215, 218, 222-3
Hog Hill tunnel, 17
Holmside, 23, 80
Hoole, K., 142
Hownes Gill, 17, 20-1, 58, 63-5, 76, 92, 97, *121*, 218-19, 229
Hownes Gill loop line, 65, 214, 218
Hownes Gill viaduct, 58-9, *121*, 162, 214, 231
Hudson, George, 29-30, 44
Hutchinson, Colonel, 61-2

Inclines: Addison, 49, 173; Annfield, 22, 118-20, 123-4; Carr House, 17, 21, 59; Causey, 46; Crawley, 17-18, 71, 161; Eden Hill, 22; Fugar, 46-7, *51*; Hedleyhope, 66; Hobson, 47, 49; Hownes Gill, 21, 59; Kibblesworth, 177; Lobley Hill, 46; Meeting Slacks, 20, 57; Nanny Mayors, 20-1, 54, 56-7, 59, 65; Redheugh, 44-5, 181, 187, 215; Rookhope, 55; Stanley, 22, 118, 168; Stanley (Crook), 57, 226-7; Sunnyside, 54, 56-8, 60-3, 65; Tanfield Moor, 46, 174; Twizell, 22, 206; Vigo, 22, 31; Waldridge, 22-3, 33, 168-9, 238; Weatherhill, 17, 20, 72, 161, 218
Iron ore, 27, 55, 60-1, 66, 73-4, 79, 99, 104, 112, *122*, 127, 136-7, 170, *176*, 185-6, 193, 196, 206-7
Irving, J., 233

Jackson, Ralph W., 232
Jarrow, 48
Jenkins W., 127

Kibblesworth, 48, 177, 214, 216
King Edward bridge, 147, 150-1
Knitsley, 70, 73, 76-7, 81-5, *85*, 86, 89, 159-60, 215, 218, 221-3, 230
Knitsley viaduct, 75-7, 82, 90-1, 199-200
Kyo, 120, 123

Lamesley, 50, 124, 130, 160, 170
Lancashire & Yorkshire Railway, 95, 233
Lancaster & Carlisle Railway, 96, 230, 232
Lanchester, 70, 73, 75-83, *84*, 85-6, 89, 104, 112, 156, 159-60, 199, 214-16, 218, 221-3, 230
Lanchester Highway Board, 116
Lanchester Valley Extension, 78-9, 100, 103, 170
Lanehead quarry, 68
Langley Park, 80, 83, 89
Leadgate, 119-20, 133-4, 137, 141-2, 168-9, 219, 221-4
Lead traffic, 14, 23, 41, 55-6, 65, 68, 148
Leamside, 73, 79, 201, 233
Lemington, 37
Lime kilns, 18, 23, 26, 55, 71, 142-3, 224
Lime traffic, 23, 68, 161, 224
Lintzford, 111
Lintz Green, 101-4, 107-11, 116, 120, *121*, 163-6, 209-10, 218, 221-3, 230, 237
Lintz wagonway, 48
Liverpool, 93, 95, 97, 164, 233
Livestock traffic, 71, 83, 112, 141, 163, 222-3
Lockhaugh, 101-2, 112-13, 166
Locomotives: BR diesels, *176*, 196; BR steam types, *122*, *139*, 192-3, 195-6; GNR 'D2', 188; Industrial types, 197-8; LMS Ivatt '4MT', 162, 192, 195; '4MT' 2-6-4T, 162, 192, 195; '8F', 190; LNER Classes, Pacifics, 150, 189, 191; 'A5', *69*, 191, 194; 'B1', 191-2, 195-6; 'D49', 189-91, 193-4; 'J39', *175*, 189-91, 194, 201;

INDEX 245

'J94', 192-4; 'K1', 70, *139*, *175*, 192-3, 195; 'K3', 189-90, 194; 'L1', 192; 'O1', *122*, 193; 'V1/V3', *87*, 169, 189-91, 193-4; 'V2', 191, 194; 'WD', 192, 195; 'Y3', 189; NBR, Atlantics, 191; 'D30', 171, 190; 'D32', 190; NCB types, 177, 181, 197; N & CR engines, 180-1; NER Classes, Atlantics, 184, 187; Class '38', 182; '59', 182, 186; '398', 180, 186-7; '476', 181, 187; '675', 181; '686', 181; '708', 181; '901', 181; '1001', 180, 186; '1440', 181; 'A', 182, 186-8; 'B', *158*, 182-3, 186, 188; 'BTP', *88*, 181, 183, 186-7; 'C', 182-4, 186-8, 190-2, 194; 'D', 187-9; 'E/E1', 183, 193; 'F', 183, 187; 'L', 183, 190; 'M', 183, 187; 'N', 183, 186, 190-1; 'O', *34*, *87*, 109, 130, 151, 167, 183, 186-94; 'P/P1/P2/P3', *157*, 184, 188-9, 191, 194-6; 'Q', *34*, 183, 187-8; 'R', 184, 188-90, 193; 'S/S3', 184, 189; 'T/T1', 184-6, 188-90, 192; 'T2', *33*, 117, *139*-*40*, *158*, 162, 185, 189, 192-6, 201; 'T3', *122*, 137, 185-6, 190, 193-4; 'U', *51*, 183-4, 187, 190, 194; S & D engines, 180; S & T engines, 22, 179-80
London, 14, 29-30
London & North Eastern Railway, 138, 164, 171, 188-91
London & North Western Railway, 92, 94-8, 230, 232-4
Longclose wood, 229
Low Fell, 128, 130, 144, 146, 151, 160, 217, 236

McDonnell, A., 182, 186
Maclean, J. S., 150
MacNay, T., 61-2, 234
Main Way wagonway, 13, 49, 178
Medomsley, 14-18, 35, 101, 111, 119, 169, 230
Medomsley branch, 16, 21, 23, 28, 35, 119, 141, 169, 219-20
'Memorials' to NER, 82, 120
Mileages, 217-20
Milk traffic, 111-12, 164
Middlesbrough, 132, 236
Molten metal traffic, 236

Morrison Busty colliery, 170, 197, 200
Muggleswick Common, 15, 54

Nanny Mayors incline, 20-1, 54, 56-7, 59, 65
National Coal Board, 50, 169, 177, 181, 197, 238
Nature trail, 166, 237
Newburn, 37, 173
Newcastle, 11, 36-9, 41-6, 72, 79, 84, 86, 92-9, 103-9, 111-12, 123-4, 126, 130, 134-8, 142, 146-53, 156, 164, *165*, 166-9, 171-3, 181, 183-4, 186, 189-91, 199, 202-4, 206, 209-11, 213, 215, 227-8, 230, 232-4
Newcastle & Carlisle Railway, 16, 36 *et seq*, 60, 63, 92-9, 104, 146-54, 171-3, 177, 179-83, 186-7, 189-91, 194, 213-14, 217, 230-1, 233-4, 236
Newcastle & Darlington Junction Railway, 29
Newcastle & Derwent Valley Railway, 92-4, 97
Newcastle Central station, 43-4, 46, 92-3, 104, 124, 126
Newcastle Derwent & Weardale Railway, 94-8, 107, 230-5
Newcastle Forth station, 43-4, 96, 150, 153
Newcastle Shotley & Weardale Jcn Rly, 92
Newcastle Shot Tower station, 39, 42
Newcastle 'The Close' station, 41-2
North British Railway, 45-6, 92-3, 96-9, 152, 171-2, 186, 190-1, 193, 203-4, 228, 230
NER bus services, 89, 156, 207
Northumberland & Durham District Bank, 60, 74
Norwood cokeworks, 146, 197
Norwood junction, 146, *147*

Ord & Maddison, 68, 71
Ouston junction, 128, *129*, *131*, 170, 200-1, 214, 219
Oxhill, 170, *176*, 208-9, 237

Parkhead, 20, 55, 68, 71, 160-2, 218, 221, 224

Peases West colliery, 63, 66
Pelaw Main wagonway, 50
Pelaw—Washington line, 30
Pelton, 14, 18, 22, 30-2, 118, 120, 123-8, 130, 137, 141-2, 144, 167, 201, 219, 221-4
Pelton Level, 23, 136, 168-9, 190, 194, 206, 238
Penrith, 96, 107
Peth lane, 174
Pickering Nook, 48
Plawsworth, 80
Pont Burn viaduct, 102
Pontop, 13-15, 48, 119, 130, 136
Pontop & Jarrow Railway, 47-9, 110, 177, 214, 216
Pontop & South Shields Railway, 27-30
Prudhoe colliery, 42

Quarries, 66, 68, 71, 161

Railway 'mania', 92
Rainton, 28-9
Ransome & Marles works, 170
Raven, Sir Vincent, 117, 184, 187
Redcar, 178
Redheugh, 39, 41-5, 47, 96, 99, 144, 148-50, 181, 187, 213, 216-17, 219, 221, 223, 228, 230-1, 236
Relly Mill junction, 73, 80-2, *90*, 218, 237
Relly Mill viaduct, 73, 89
Riccarton Junction, 45, 152, 172
Rich, Colonel, 61-2
Richardson, J., 27
Riding Mill, 36, 40, 63, 229
Riding Mill—Longclose Wood line, 229
Rippon, C., 14
Rippon, Mrs V., 68
Rolling stock, 187-8
Rookhope, 14, 55-6, 66, 68, 160, 198, 207, 224
Rounthwaite, T. E., 188
Rowlands Gill, 13-14, 92, 101-3, 105, *106*, 107-12, 120, 163-6, 210-11, 218, 221-3
Rowley, 59-60, 63-6, 71-2, 124, 160-2, 216, 218, 221-4, 229-31, 237
Ryton, *34*, 37, 39-40, 46, 49, 151-3, *155*, 171-4, 215, 217, 221-3, 230

Sacriston, 23, 32, 80, 89, 213
Sacriston & South Shields Railway, 32, 35, 124
Sacriston wagonway, 23, 32, 169, 213
Saltburn, *114*
Scotswood, 37-9, 43, 173
Scotswood bridge, 36-8, 41-5, 149, 154, 203
Scotswood bridge junction, 92, 94, 97, 100-1, 104, 166, 217
Scotswood Newburn & Wylam Railway, 153, 173
Sentinel steam railcars, 105, 191
Shield Row, 123, 126, 130, 137-8, 141-2, *143*, 167-8, 215, 219, 221-4
Shildon, 189
Shotley Bridge, 11, 101, 103, 105, 107-9, 111, 163-4, 218, 221-3, 228, 233
Shotley Bridge Iron Co, 27, 78
Signal boxes, 49, *52*, 81-2, 84, *88*, 105-6, 115, 128, 132, *157*, 162, 170, 174, *176*, 202, 236-8
Signals, 65, 76, 174, 236-8
Snow, 20, *52*, *121*, 207-8
Snow's Green, 103, 106
South Durham & Lancashire Union Rly, 66, 93-8, 107, 230, 232-4
South Garesfield colliery, 48, 107, 110-11
South Medomsley branch, 119, 141, 169, 220
South Moor, 89, 118
South Pelaw junction, *122*, 125-8, *129*, 130, 136-8, *139*, 142, 168, 170, 178, 201, 214, 216, 219, 237-8
South Shields, 15-18, 21-3, 26, 29-32, 35, 81, 213
Stainmore, 68, 192
Stanhope, 11, 14-15, 17-18, 20, 23, 27, 55-6, 59, 63-4, 66, *67*, 68, 71, 161, 218, 221, 224, 227, 229
Stanhope & Tyne Railway, 14 *et seq*, *33*, 35, 53, 76, 92, 118, 143, 162, 179-80, 213, 218, 227, 229
Stanley, 12, 89, 108, 120, 124, 126-7, 142, 167, 201-2, 208
Stanley branch (S & D), 57, 226-7
Stargate, 49, 153, 172

INDEX

Steam autocars, *88*, 109, 138, 147, 183
Steam wagons, 142
Stella, 37, 49, 153, 173, 195-7
Stella Gill, 22, 31-2, 118, 124, 126, 128, *129*, 136, *139*, 142, 168-9, 200, 216, 237-8
Stephenson, Robert, 16-17
Stocksfield, 39-40, 60, 74, 229
Stockton & Darlington Rly, 53 *et seq*, 73-4, 76, 79, 92-9, 118, 180, 214, 226-7, 231-2, 234-5
Stockton & Darlington & Newcastle & Carlisle Union Railway, 60, 214, 229
Stranraer, 172
Sunderland, 11, 79, 136, 147, 195
Sunnyside colliery, 66, 161, 220
Sunnyside deviation, 60-3
Sunnyside incline, 54, 56-8, 60-3, 65
Swalwell, 36, 38, 41, 43-4, 96, 101, 103, 106-11, *112*, 113, 115, 163-6, 197, 218, 221-3, 230-1
Swalwell branch, 43-4, 197, 213
Swalwell—Rowlands Gill widening, 112-13

Tanfield branch, 13-14, 26, 29, 46-7, 49, *51*, 146, 174, 177, 183, 187, 190, 194, 206, 213 215-16, 219, 236-7
Tanfield East, 46, *51*, 174
Tanfield Lea, 13, 26, 46-7, 174
Tanfield Moor, 13-14, 18, 26, 46, 48, 174, 213
Tanfield Moor—Annfield line, 16, 18, 22, 26, 29-30, 46
Tanfield Moor—Lintz line, 46, 48, 110
Teams, 146, 174, 177, 237
Team Valley line, *32*, *50*, *80*, 123-4, 128, 130, 135, 144, 151, 200
Team wagonway, 50, 197
Tebay, 66, 93-8, 107, 233
Teesside, 159-60, 178
Timetables, 43-4, 63, 72, 79, 86, 106, 108, 137-8, 151-2, 156, 159, 161, 164, *165*, 167, 172
Token working, 76, 82, 112
Tomlinson, W. W., 21, 65, 76
Tow Law, 11, 56-7, 61, *62*, 63, 66, 69, 71-2, *139*, 160-2, 188-9, 207, 215-16, 218, 221-4, 227, 232-3, 237
Tow Law ironworks, 56, 58, 61, 66, 71, 95, 232
Traffic receipts, 40, 48, 55, 66, 72, 83, 85, 89-90, 108-10, 137-8, 141, 148-9, 152-3, 159-60, 163-4, 167, 171, 221-4
Tudhoe, 61, 66
Tursdale jcn—Relly Mill line, 81, 159
Tyne Dock, 26, 30-2, 35, 124-5, 127, 136-7, 170, 178, 184, 193, 214
Tyne Dock company, 26
Tyne Dock MPD, 31, 136, 184-5, 187, 190, 192-3, 195-6, 201
Tyne Improvement Commission, 45
Tyne marshalling yard, 160, 170, 173, 196, 236

Usworth, 35

Viaducts: Derwent (Swalwell), 101, 112-13; Fogoes, 102, *121*; Hownes Gill, 58-9, *121*, 162, 214, 231; Knitsley, 75-7, 82, 90-1, 199-200; Lockhaugh, 101-2, 112-13, 166; Pont Burn, 102; Relly Mill, 89; Rowlands Gill, 101-2, 106
Victoria Garesfield, 110, 166
Vigo, 22, 31

Waldridge colliery, 18, 23, 32, 35, 169
Waldridge incline, 22, *33*, 136, 168, 238
Wallis, W., 14
Washington, 16, 18, 28, 30-2, 35, 136, 170, 201
Washington—Pelton service, 31-2
Waskerley, 15, 20, 54, 56-7, 59, 63-5, 161-2, 218, 221, 224, 237
Waskerley deviation, 59
Waskerley MPD, 57, 90, *158*, 160-1, 182, 186, 188-9, 207, 215
Waterhouses, 226-7
Wayleaves, 15-16, 26, 29, 53
Wear & Derwent Junction Rly, 54-7, 60, 65, 207, 227
Weardale Extension Railway, 54-5, 57, *64*, *69*, 213, 218-19

INDEX

Weardale Iron Co, 55-6, 66, 160, 198, 207, 227-8, 234
Wear Valley Railway, 57, 63, 71, 161, 208
Weatherhill, 17, 20, *33*, 56, 72, 162, 205, 207-8, 215, 218
West Auckland, 93-4, 96-7, 186, 189-92, 195, 230
West Dunston staiths, 146, 149
West Durham & Tyne Railway, 124-5
West Durham Railway, 54, 61, 66, 95-6
West Hartlepool, 95-6, 195, 232-3
West Hartlepool Railway, 95-6, 232
Westoe, 14, 16
West Pelton, 168-9
West Stanley, *122*, 128, 130, 141, 167-9, 201-2, 215, 219
West Thornley colliery, 66

Westwood colliery, 110, 164
Wetheral, 38
Whickham junction, 150, 217
Whitehall, 66, 71
Whitley Bay, 164, 167
Wilson, G., 209-10
Winlaton Mill, 14, 48-50, 197, 231
Witton Gilbert, 76, 79-80, *81*, 83, 85-6, 89-90, 156, 159, 218, 221-4
Wolsingham, 53
Worsdell, T. W., 151, 182-3, 188
Worsdell, Wilson, 109, 130, 151, 182-4, 192
Wylam, 37, 39, 153, 174, 217, 228

Yolland, Colonel, 45, 204
York, 133, 196
York Newcastle & Berwick Rly, 30, 44, 206